Production House Cinema

In *Production House Cinema: Starting and Running Your Own Cinematic Storytelling Business*, renowned video storyteller Kurt Lancaster offers both students and professionals a practical guide to starting their own video production company and creating cinematic, client-based video content. Utilizing practical know-how along with in-depth analysis and interviews with successful independent production houses like Stillmotion and Zandrak, Lancaster follows the logistics and inspiration for creating production house cinema, from the initial client pitch all the way through financing and distribution. The book includes:

- an examination of the cinematic and narrative style and how to create it;
- a discussion of the legal procedures and documents necessary for starting and operating a production house;
- advice on crafting a portfolio, reel, and website that both demonstrate your unique style and vision and attract clients;
- a guide to the financial business of running an independent production house, including invoicing, accounting, and taxes—and how much you should charge clients;
- tips for how to better communicate with clients, and how to develop and shape a client's story;
- a breakdown of how to select the right gear and equipment for a shoot, on budget;
- cinematic case studies that offer detailed coverage of several short films made for clients.

Kurt Lancaster teaches digital filmmaking at Northern Arizona University. His students have created their own video production houses, worked as producers and cinematographers, and created national and regional award-winning films and promotional videos. Kurt is also the author of *DSLR Cinema*, *Cinema Raw*, and *Video Journalism for the Web*. His client list includes the Grand Canyon and the Timpanogos Caves National Monument for the National Park Service; the American Community School in Amman, Jordan; Ha:san Preparatory and Leadership School in Tucson, Arizona for the National Institute of Health; Pedras Mesa Demonstration Ranch in Arizona; Altez Ecofarm at Hasta Gard in Stockholm, Sweden; the *Law of the Desert Born* graphic novel promo for Louis L'Amour Enterprises, Inc.; and the Institute of Tribal Environmental Professionals at Northern Arizona University, among others. He earned his PhD from NYU.

Production House Cinema

Starting and Running Your Own Cinematic Storytelling Business

Kurt Lancaster

Focal Press
Taylor & Francis Group

NEW YORK AND LONDON

First published 2016
by Focal Press
711 Third Ave, New York, NY, 10017

and by Focal Press
2 Park Square, Milton Park, Abingdon, Oxon OX14 4RN

Focal Press is an imprint of the Taylor & Francis Group, an informa business

Library of Congress Cataloging in Publication Data
CIP data has been requested for this title.

ISBN: 978-1-138-63806-8 (hbk)
ISBN: 978-0-415-81619-9 (pbk)
ISBN: 978-0-203-78349-8 (ebk)

Typeset in Giovanni and Franklin Gothic
by Florence Production Ltd, Stoodleigh, Devon, UK

Printed and bound in India by Replika Press Pvt. Ltd.

This book is dedicated to my four bros:

Tal, Scott, Jason, and Joseph

Contents

About the Author

Kurt Lancaster teaches digital filmmaking at Northern Arizona University. His students have created their own video production houses, worked as producers and cinematographers, as well as making national and regional award-winning films and promotional videos. Kurt is also the author of *DSLR Cinema*, *Cinema Raw*, and *Video Journalism for the Web*. His client list includes the Grand Canyon and the Timpanogos Caves National Monument for the National Park Service; the American Community School in Amman, Jordan; Ha:san Preparatory and Leadership School in Tucson, Arizona; the National Institute of Health; Pedras Mesa Demonstration Ranch in Arizona; Altez Ecofarm at Hasta Gard in Stockholm, Sweden; the *Law of the Desert Born* graphic novel promo for Louis L'Amour Enterprises, Inc.; and the Institute of Tribal Environmental Professionals at Northern Arizona University, among others. He earned his PhD from NYU.

Photo by Kathryn Moller.

Acknowledgments

Many thanks to my editors at Focal Press. Emily McCloskey was open to revising a previous contract, so I could write something that was close to my heart and on the cutting-edge. Elliana Arons, the editorial assistant for this book, helped get the book through the various stages. Simon Jacobs would later take over the project and carry it through completion.

I want to especially thank Wes Pope for his valuable suggestions for this book. It would not have been the same without his insights and suggestions (he gave me sixteen pages of notes, single spaced). His energy and talent make him a valuable asset for his Master's-level multimedia journalism students at the University of Oregon.

I could not have written this book if it wasn't for the time and patience of those I interviewed.

- At Zandrak in Boston in July 2014: Andrew Hutchisen, Charles Frank, David Brickel, and Kyle Harper. Andrew and Charles had many things to say about their new business; I learned much from them and their energy is infectious.
- Amina Moreau at Stillmotion, who endured an audio recorder stuck in front of her face as I tried to get a clean recording in a noisy coffee shop in Portland in December 2014. Her insights on how Stillmotion began its approach to clients provides the heart to this book.
- Patrick Moreau, busy with multiple projects, answered my questions about how Stillmotion is run and how *My Utopia*, a beautiful short film profiled in this book, was conceived.
- Justin DeMers at Story & Heart discussed the importance of licensing footage as a potential income stream for filmmakers.
- Brody Lowe talked to me about the art direction of *My Utopia*. His insights on how they used keywords to make decisions on the film was helpful.
- Alexandria Bombach, a former student of mine, made a feature-length documentary about Afghan photographers. Her insights on the Kickstarter campaign were helpful and it allowed her to make the film she wanted.

- David Eckenrode talked about how he gets freelance work for Agence France-Presse and the BBC while living in a small town in Durango, Colorado.
- Léo Hamelin explained how she went from working full time at a French television news network to doing freelance multimedia journalism in New York.
- Don Pickard of Tom C. Pickard & Co, gave me some great points about the importance of getting insurance for production houses.
- Emily Best, who founded the crowd-funding Seed&Spark, shows her passion and desire for independent filmmakers to make a living from their work. We need more people like her championing the cause!
- Kevin Ketchner is an inspiring instructor at NAU—he knows his stuff and he's dynamic. Thanks for being a good sport for the Honor's video.
- Wolf Gunnerman, director of the Honors Program at Northern Arizona University.
- Tyler Stableford does some cool stuff with a camera—his work is always inspiring.
- My good friend, Beau L'Amour, gave me thoughtful advice about both the psychology of camera motion and the lenses chart I created for this book.
- Sandra Kowalski hired me to help make cinematic promotional videos at NAU's University Marketing. She gave me the space to experiment with new ways to tell stories and she supported me in putting together the student team that grew out of the university's Creative Media and Film department. Many of these students would go on to get jobs in the industry. They include Javeon, Jenna, Conner, Paisley, Michael, Mariah, Marteen, Mari, and Reed.
- My students in the Creative Media and Film program at NAU. And my wife Stephanie and stepson Morgan, who are always there for me.

All of these people are special in my heart, since they shared something of themselves and made this book that much stronger. And if I missed anyone, my apologies. It wasn't intentional.

I want to give special thanks to the members of the Scholarship and Creative Arts Activity grants committee for awarding me a summer grant that gave me time to complete this manuscript.

Foreword

Here's one HUGE truth I've learned in just over a decade in this industry. Being a storyteller is one kick-ass profession. It may just be one of the most rewarding jobs out there. As storytellers we get to meet, and learn from, a collection of folks who introduce us to more experiences and perspectives than many get the privilege of enjoying in a lifetime.

More than that though, as storytellers we get a skeleton key of sorts that unlocks nearly every door around if used properly. We can get access to amazing venues, time with remarkable people, and even have the opportunity to go deep and ask things that normally take years of friendship to be able to discuss.

Just this past year I had the opportunity to tell three stories of absolutely remarkable people. The first was a man who, at nineteen, became quadriplegic when his motorbike flew off the road. With only 6 percent of his body function he went on to get an engineering degree, modify an airplane, and fly solo across Australia. The second was a lady who was raised with an elephant as a sister from the time she was six. She became so close to elephants that she opened a sanctuary and is treated as if she is one of the herd. And the third was the great-great-grandson of Charles Darwin, a very eccentric man who produced many PR stunts such as hosting a dinner party on top of the highest mountain in Peru. He's now on a mission to fulfill Charles Darwin's single biggest regret of not being able to do more for his fellow species. Chris is on a mission to prevent the mass extinction of species and his journey thus far is completely fascinating.

Here's the point though—more than the stories themselves, just the act of spending time with these people changes the way you see the world. And the experiences you have with them stay with you forever. We really do become the stories that we choose to tell. Then we get to take these stories and share them with the world. We can take a story like that of Dave Jacka, the quadriplegic pilot, and spread it across the globe so that his story helps others realize that we are far more capable than we ever imagined.

And this is where it gets *really* exciting. Never before has the barrier of entry been so incredibly low for somebody to get into filmmaking, create strong stories, and distribute them globally. As a comparison, one of my first paid gigs was for a news shooter whose camera cost him a mortgage on his mother's house (no joke) and was something he'd pay off over decades. Today, with nothing more than the cellphone in our pocket, we can film, edit, and deliver a story.

With the barrier being so low, it's no longer a question of who can get access to the tools, and it's so much more about who can create content that will attract the eyeballs. That's why this book is so incredibly important. Kurt's *Production House Cinema* will help you understand the industry today. It offers you a real-deal portrait of everything you need to do to set up a business, pitch to clients, and set yourself apart.

Our storytelling studio, Stillmotion, started in a university dorm room. We started our own business and as our stories became stronger, they started to get noticed, and we got some amazing calls from people like AT&T, Apple, the NFL, CBS, and more. Not one of those clients asked if we had a formal film degree. They looked at our stories and asked if we could create something like that for them.

Remember, your perspective is the strongest lens you'll ever attach to a camera. Develop your thinking on what story truly is, on how the industry works today, and dive right in.

The future is yours for the taking like never before.

Patrick Moreau
Co-founder of Stillmotion

Introduction

The Business of Cinematic Storytelling in a Video Production House

Growing up watching reruns of *Star Trek* in the 1970s and television throughout the 1980s, I would mute commercials as a habit. They grated against my senses and I felt less intelligent by being exposed to such work. In fact, when I started directing theater, making short documentaries and short fiction work, and teaching filmmaking, I never wanted anything to do with commercials, or promotional films—nothing to do with business or work for clients. I didn't even want to teach it to my students.

There's a certain style to a lot of commercial work that's far from cinematic. Messages hitting you over the head with a buy, buy, buy mentality that's as far from cinema and art as anything I've ever experienced. Occasionally, there are exceptions, of course. One of the most famous cinematic commercials aired during the 1984 Super Bowl—filmmaker Ridley Scott's Apple Macintosh ad (see https://www.youtube.com/watch?v=8UZV7PDt8Lw).

FIGURE 0.1
Apple's 1984 Super Bowl commercial became a benchmark for cinematic—style commercial work. Directed by Ridley Scott. (Courtesy of Scott Free Films.)

This is a commercial for a product, but was created in a cinematically powerful way. Scott and his team consciously constructed a commercial on a grand scale and it was designed to pull you in through a mini-story using the elements of visual shots, sound design, and editing rhythm—and it defined the Apple brand in the process. It doesn't hit you over the head with a message to sell you something—the stuff that drove me to mute commercials as a kid. Indeed, in a *Forbes* interview, William Gelner, executive creative director at the advertising agency 180 LA, says that the 1984 Apple ad created more buzz than any other commercial in the history of the medium. "What I personally love most, though, is that it did all this without relying on kids, talking animals, a kick in the balls or any of the other conventions we've come to expect from this genre."[1]

Obviously, Super Bowl commercials have big budgets, so production companies can spend the time needed to make large-scale, Hollywood-style projects. Even though such examples were interesting, it wasn't enough to get me to teach or produce such work. In the back of my mind, I wished that all commercials were as cool as Ridley Scott's. I would continue to avoid watching or muting local commercials from car dealers, drug companies, and grocery stores, believing that the producers of such stuff continued to do their thing in a certain way, because either they never believed in the Ridley Scott cinematic vision or they didn't have the budget to make it happen.

But then two things happened over a period of several years while teaching at my current school, Northern Arizona University:

1. I was blown away by a promotional piece about a café for troubled youth in San Francisco by a Canadian production company called Stillmotion. I read their blogs, screened some of their videos and tutorials to my students—and started applying their techniques to short documentary work.

2. One of my students, Jay Butler, recommended that I direct a promotional video for University Marketing at NAU. But there was only one way I would do it. Sandra Kowolski, the director of the department, wanted an approach to the creation of videos that was "different" from what she was used to getting (what might be called a staid corporate video style). I had just written *DSLR Cinema* and told her my desire to apply cinematic storytelling techniques to promotional videos may just be the look she wanted. She agreed, and some of the work would go on to win awards.

These two moments coalesced and I started teaching and accepting client-based work using cinematic techniques combined with storytelling.

I had originally conceived of writing a sequel to *DSLR Cinema*, but after talking with my publisher, I pitched them a different book. Our video/film program at NAU, Creative Media and Film, had recently gone through a curriculum re-envisioning.[2] We shaped the major to not only include filmmaking, documentary, and media studies, but also a client-based class, where students learn how to not only shoot in a cinematic way, but also how to write pitches, proposals, budgets, treatments, and work directly with local clients. Realizing that this style can be taught, there was room in the market for a book that focused on the cinematic style applied to client-based work. I wanted to write a book that would explore the entire process of creating and running a production house business (one of our capstone classes is called Production House Experience) in order to give students and would-be professionals who are just beginning their career a source for knowledge and inspiration about how to start their own production house company.

But this book is not really a how-to manual. It pulls together the experiences of a couple of successful start-ups and explores how they created their businesses and approach their work. This book is about the process by which a production house gets made—from the initial vision, to the legal paperwork, to the ways you get and interact with clients, including the preproduction and production planning and processes that create the final short client-based films.

On another note, some may be disappointed that I haven't included other cinematic-style production houses. There are hundreds. I could have made the choice to provide an overview of a dozen of these different companies or go deeply into one or two. I chose to go deep rather than broad, in order to provide more detail to the reader. I feel that in the details is where deep learning begins.

Having interviewed members of the Stillmotion team, who are now based in Portland, Oregon, as well as using some of their tutorials and storytelling models in the classroom over the past several years, I feel they're a good choice for this book. They started their company shooting weddings while at university, and due to their application and development of their cinematic style and storytelling methods, they went from a simple event filmmaking company (like many others) to catching the attention of the NFL in one of their wedding videos. They would go on to earn multiple Emmy Awards for their endeavors. Not bad for never studying filmmaking at university! For that reason alone, I was intrigued by their process. At the same time, they consciously shared their approach to other filmmakers (I still use their tutorial on shooting with a monopod), giving back to their community of students and filmmakers trying to discover their visual style and storytelling magic. They're one of the key players in understanding the cinematic process in video production houses.

I also include Zandrak Productions, a production house in Boston, because it's a fresh startup, with its members just a couple years out of university.[3] On the surface, that doesn't sound like anything special and I wouldn't be convinced necessarily, since there are so many more established production houses doing cinematic work. Why focus on a few guys from Boston? I'd never even heard of them, until I read an interview with Charles Frank on the community section of filmandmusic.com, one of the best locations for finding inspiring stories about up-and-coming as well as established indie filmmakers (https://film andmusic.com/).[4] The interview with this nineteen-year-old was insightful and I read how he works for a company called Zandrak. I went to their site and saw a project they did for Hasbro, which told the story of a father writing a letter to his son as he is about to go off to college. It touches on the themes of birth, growth, connection, and family as it shows visuals of the son playing Hasbro games as a child, interacting with his sister and family, and growing up (see https://vimeo.com/79679870).

This commercial was made on a shoe-string budget in the apartment of Zandrak's founder, and the baby was brought in from a friend of a friend. It was directed by Charles Frank who turned down an acceptance to NYU's film school in order to work for Zandrak. The founder of Zandrak, Andrew Hutcheson, is just a couple of years out of film school at Emerson College. These guys didn't apprentice with commercial producers. They know film and apply those techniques to commercial work. Their Hasbro commercial is selling a product, of course, but it doesn't *tell* you to buy the product. It pulls you in emotionally through the characters and the universal themes revolving around life experiences. Hasbro loved it and had the commercial broadcast nationally. It's a commercial that I would never mute. (See Figure 0.2.)

I went to their offices in Boston and talked to them, and became convinced that not only do they have the talent to make strong client-based work, but what they have to share is invaluable to those thinking about starting their own video production business. They, like Stillmotion, belong in this book.

At the same time, the cinematic style used by Stillmotion and Zandrak can be easily taught and the ideas are easily accessible. Taking the universal tools of cinema, students—as well as professionals who are used to doing client-based work in a corporate video way—can take ideas and inspiration from Stillmotion's

FIGURE 0.2
A scene from Zandrak's Hasbro commercial. (Courtesy of Zandrak.)

MUSE storytelling process, as well as from Zandrak (among others) and begin to create strong work that expresses depth and meaning. For example, a team from my senior capstone class created a promotional film for a local nonprofit, the Hozhoni Foundation, a place where people with developmental disabilities can create art and find respect (see https://vimeo.com/109904066). These students have studied filmmaking and video production over the course of nearly four years and they're presumably on the verge of graduating and entering the professional world, at least at an entry level. For that class project, this team was inspired by some of the work done by Zandrak and Stillmotion. They created a short film that engaged a cinematic style and told a story about dignity (see Figure 0.3). Is it perfect? No, but it's got more heart than much of the stuff I've muted on television for years—certainly stronger than most of the local productions I've seen in the preshow advertising at Flagstaff's Harkin's Theaters. The students (Justin Castaneda, Lori James, and Chris Navarro) earned an award at the Broadcast Education Association's Festival of Media Arts (2015) in Las Vegas.

The filmmakers I interviewed at Stillmotion and Zandrak provide inspiration. They express a vision and energy that I like. Much of the approach to this book is through storytelling, using interviews from Patrick and Amina Moreau of Stillmotion and from Andrew Hutcheson and Charles Frank of Zandrak, among others. By using their stories, I hope to move beyond the cut-and-dry style of some texts that provide just the nuts and bolts of running a business or shooting a scene in a certain way. Focusing on their stories, their particular projects stemming from startup case-studies, I hope that readers will use them as learning tools in order to find new ways to tell stronger, more compelling client-based stories in a cinematic style.

FIGURE 0.3
A student at the Hozhoni Foundation presents his work of art. (Courtesy of Castaneda, James, and Navarro.)

Fundamentally, I want readers to learn how to make emotional connections to clients so that they tell stories rather than simply sell products, services, or provide messages. I want the production house filmmaker to uncover ways to conduct compelling interviews, to discover how to put together a visual treatment that makes clients take notice, to stage scenes and shoot them in a way where every shot, every cut, and the sound design makes the difference between a client receiving a project that's like everything else out there or getting a project that's so unique an audience leans forward, emotionally connecting with the piece.

CHAPTER OUTLINE

The first part of the book, Creating Your Own Independent Video Production House Business, comprises the first four chapters in which I examine the process of setting a vision, going into the legal paperwork, and envisioning a website and portfolio sample.

In Chapter 1, Telling versus Showing: The Tools of Cinema in Client-based Storytelling, I examine in detail some of the key techniques of the cinematic style and how they can be applied to a variety of work. I examine how to use the tools of cinema to create compelling edits for pacing and rhythm by looking at a promotional film for Canon by Tyler Stableford. This cinematic style is contrasted with a narration style to storytelling used in broadcast news.

In Chapter 2, Creating a Vision: The Cinematic-Style Video Production House, I examine how Stillmotion began as a startup wedding business while Patrick and Amina were at university studying psychology. Through them, I explore what it means to create a vision and mission statement for your business.

Chapter 3, Making it Legal: Filing an LLC, Writing Contracts, Music Rights, and Getting Insurance, is perhaps one of the most important chapters of this book, providing the tools needed to make your business legal and to protect it. It lays out the steps to creating a limited liability company, provides sample contracts from Zandrak, explains how to create an invoice through online applications, get an insurance quote online, and how to write off business expenses so you'll pay less taxes.

Chapter 4, Creating Presence: The Portfolio Reel and Website that Reflects Your Style and Vision, examines in-depth the website of Stillmotion, while also looking at sample portfolio films from both Stillmotion and Zandrak. By using these examples, you can generate ideas in how you might approach your website and portfolio work. It doesn't tell you how to design a website or portfolio film, but it discusses why these particular websites and portfolio pieces are so compelling so you can use them as role models.

In the second part of the book (Chapters 5–7) we cover the different tools for Running an Independent Production House Business, which covers the ideas of working with clients and developing pitches and proposals. In addition, I examine some of the gear needed and what you should be looking for when buying or renting gear.

Chapter 5, Making Money: The Cost of Doing Business, Generating Income Streams, Setting Up Invoices, and Planning Your Taxes, includes a process by which you can figure out how much you need to make in order to run your business successfully. It also includes an overview of how to work out your personal as well as your business budget. This chapter also considers different ways to generate income, submitting invoices, and planning for your taxes—some of the bigger-picture things that revolve around the daily operations of your business.

Chapter 6, Developing a Client's Story: Making a Connection, Finding the Story, and Writing a Pitch, Proposal, and Budget, examines Stillmotion's approach to treating clients and making a connection with them. This is one of the key elements of this book, since if you can't do this you won't be in business long. It also provides a detailed example of a visual pitch proposal for Zandrak's Moodsnap.

In Chapter 7, Cinematic Gear on a Budget: What You Need and What it Does, I look at the some of the equipment you need to start shooting at a professional level utilizing cameras under $5,000, wireless lav mics, shotgun mics, monopods, tripods, sliders, and jibs, among other useful equipment. But the majority of the chapter is dedicated to understanding what you're looking for in a computer, camera, and other types of gear. If your camera records in 8-bit H.264 codec (nearly every DSLR and lower-end cameras do), then you should know why this is not a good thing and how to overcome that limitation. It explores such concepts as: What is the difference between rolling shutter and global shutter? What's the deal, 4K or raw? What's the difference between shutter speed and shutter angle and what does it do? These types of questions will be explored as we delve into the guts of cameras and audio gear so you will understand what you should look for, rather than just shooting with something because it's popular. The knowledge from this chapter can be applied to nearly any camera you get, so even if a camera isn't mentioned or listed, you'll be able to read the specs to see if it is something you will want to use.

In the final section of the book, Crafting the Cinematic Style, I go into details with case studies of cinematic-style client-based projects from Stillmotion and Zandrak. Lastly, I examine the process in crowd-funding your own personal projects, using Alexandria Bombach's successful campaign for her documentary, *Frame by Frame*.

In Chapter 8, A Book Promotion Case Study: From Keywords to Storyboards in Stillmotion's "My Utopia," I explore Stillmotion's creative process in developing keywords and applying them to a production based on Stephanie Henry's nonfiction book about her past abuse. Rather than following conventional documentary style, Stillmotion created a narrative short based on Stephanie's high-school essay about how she faced abuse. The chapter includes their notes on character, keywords, and some of the storyboards developed for the opening sequence of their film.

In Chapter 9, An App Promotion Case Study: Directing with Spontaneity in Zandrak's "Our Songs," I include extensive interviews with Charles Frank, the director of the Moodsnap app, exploring how he made creative decisions in shaping the narrative thrust of this short.

Chapter 10, A Crowdfunding Case Study: Financing *Frame by Frame*, explores crowdfunding techniques and the unique ways a couple of different companies situate themselves, including Seed&Spark and Kickstarter. I provide a case study of Alexandria Bombach, a young woman who graduated from college in 2008— at the birth of the great recession—and sold everything she had to start making films and working with clients. It explores how she used Kickstarter to fund a feature documentary about four Afghan photojournalists working in the post-Taliban reconstruction. It is now on the festival circuit and received a glowing review from *The Hollywood Reporter*. She raised $70,000 from Kickstarter, which funded the project. It examines the campaign in detail, providing pointers on how you can use crowdfunding to fund your personal projects.

PURPOSE OF THIS BOOK

Ultimately, I want to show that when the tools of cinema are used properly, they help create something magical. Even as I write this in July 2015 while visiting relatives in Wolfeborrow, New Hampshire I see a story on *CNN* break to commercial—my automatic reflex is to mute it, but it's too compelling as I watch beautiful shots unfold, taking me on a journey about a man and his dog—it's a Subaru commercial told in a cinematic style.[5] The next commercial blares out in a standard "smack you in the face" style, attempting to convince me that they're a great insurance company and I'm groping for the mute button. The differences are stark. The Subaru commercial is simply more powerful and a pleasure to watch; the other one not so much.

There are plenty of cinematic-style commercials being made—more so than at any other time. For example, The Herd Films in Vancouver reveal their storytelling filmmaking talent in their 2014 commercial for Chevrolet, "Maddie." It tells the story of a woman and her elderly dog. As the commercial progresses, we see the woman and the dog in key moments from their lives going back in time linearly—to the point where the woman as a girl picks out Maddie, her dog, from a litter of puppies.[6] The commercial spot, directed by The Herd Films' Lloyd Lee Choi, tells a story with emotional depth in 70 seconds. It doesn't feel like a commercial. It feels magical. Cinema should be magical and when filmmakers apply techniques of cinema to commercials and promotional projects—you get what I call production house cinema, creating moments of cinematic magic through visuals shaped by strong cinematography, every shot beautifully lit, with a sound design that's compelling, and an editing flow with rhythm.

FIGURE 0.4
Maddie looks at her owner in the Chevrolet commercial, "Maddie," about the life process of aging and living moments. Directed by Lloyd Lee Choi from The Herd Films of Vancouver, Canada. (Courtesy of The Herd Films.)

The intent of this book is to convince client-based producers to use different facets of the cinematic style so that we get more commercials and promotional projects that feel and look like small pieces of cinema. It is my hope that this book will inspire a new generation of film students and filmmakers who want to work with clients to create compelling story-based commercials, promotional films, and multimedia journalism, among other types of cinema-based projects.

In many ways, I want filmmakers creating client-based work to think about what Ursula K. Le Guin says about the nature of aging and the memories of youth as she writes about her mother's passing:

> I see a little red-haired child in the mountains of Colorado, a sad-faced, delicate college girl, a kind, smiling young mother, a brilliantly intellectual woman, a peerless flirt, a serious artist, a splendid cook—I see her rocking, weeding, writing, laughing—I see the turquoise bracelets on her delicate, freckled arm—I see, for a moment, all that at once, I glimpse what no mirror can reflect, the spirit flashing out across the years, beautiful.
>
> That must be what the great artists see and paint. That must be why the tired, aged faces in Rembrandt's portraits give us such delight: They show us beauty not skin-deep but life-deep.[7]

If anything, the best of cinema tries to capture people's life-deep moments. It takes a conscious use of cinematography, storytelling, and an understanding of humanity to capture such fleeting essences, and if you can begin to capture such moments through your personal work and for your clients, then you've done your job—you've created something authentic that will likely move an audience.

PART I
Creating Your Own Independent Production House Business

CHAPTER 1
Telling versus Showing
The Tools of Cinema in Client-Based Storytelling

What specifically is the cinematic style? How is it different from some mainstream commercial work? I start here since the premise of the book hinges on an understanding and definition of the cinematic style, what it means, and how you can apply it to client-based work. I start by examining a couple of moments from a *60 Minutes* piece and a promotional work in order to show the difference in style when a work is created from narration and a work created cinematically (using shots, voice, sound design, and editing for rhythm). In addition, I look at Stillmotion's concept of the psychology of the lens—the importance of choosing the right lens for a shot, as well as charts defining and showing how different types of camera movement, shot sizes, angles, and lenses impact how audiences perceive the psychology of a scene. This is followed by a description of Stillmotion's MUSE storytelling process. In short, I examine some of the tools of filmmakers in order to drive home the understanding needed to create cinematic-style client-based stories.

THE NARRATION STYLE

Commercial narration and news narration are similar—they share a broadcast style that grew out of radio news broadcasts where words told stories through descriptions of action. News reels—some heavy with propaganda—during World War II perfected this style. Education films from the 1950s to the 1970s brought this style to film in public schools. Images were mainly used to illustrate what the narration—the omniscient "voice of God" style—told the viewer.[1] Words told the story. Images illustrated the story like decorative wallpaper. Most commercials and television news follow this narration-driven style.[2] In cinema, visuals (along with a compelling audio design) tell the story and words are frosting on the cake—take them away and you can still follow the emotional structure of the story through the shots and soundscape. Words, narration, and dialogue—when used cinematically—sweeten that visual and sonic structure.

To illustrate this style, I'll look at a couple of moments from Lara Logan's "The ascent of Alex Honnold"[3] from CBS's *60 Minutes*. It tells the story of Alex's insane free solo climbs that, in Logan's words, sets the tone: "He scales walls higher than the Empire State building, and he does it without any ropes or protection" (Logan and Newton, 2011). I compare this work of journalism with a staged promotional film by Tyler Stableford, "Shattered,"[4] which tells the story of another climber, Steve House, who looks like he is climbing ice without rope. Both of these projects offer compelling stories told in two different ways.

Perhaps comparing the two isn't necessarily fair.[5] This book isn't really about journalism, but what I find interesting is how commercials and promotional shorts sometimes mimic the narration-based style of broadcast journalism (from shorts produced on *The Weather Channel* to *60 Minutes*). Since Stableford's brilliant promotional short is a great example of cinematic client-based work, I really like how it contrasts with the real news story. So why compare the two? Because the style of the broadcast news piece—heavy with narration that tells us what's going on—is a stylistic choice, not a hard and fast rule in nonfiction work. And since it's a choice in style, the audience will perceive the story differently than in a film produced in a cinematic style. The comparison and contrast works, because I'm focusing on how the respective *stylistic choices* between the two impact an audience differently.[6]

The key point I want to make is how different techniques work and impact audiences so that we can avoid what doesn't work and apply what does work in order to improve our own projects and learn how to use the best tools to capture an audience's attention. As Wes Pope, who teaches Multimedia Journalism at the University of Oregon, notes, different storytellers blend different approaches. He describes at least five styles of documentary storytelling alone: "journalistic, interview driven, cinema vérité, reenactment, and reflexive." Production house producers should be aware of different styles (whether it's from news, documentary, or fiction) and apply elements from these different styles in order to best shape the stories they need to tell for their clients. For example, both Stillmotion and Zandrak produced work that utilize fiction and documentary techniques, the former in a book promotion, the latter for an app commercial (both covered as case studies in Chapters 8 and 9). *60 Minutes* could have chosen to emphasize more cinematic techniques and focus less on the omniscient narration style—but that's what they do. In the process they lose some of the potential cinematic magic (and perhaps maintain journalistic integrity—but that stylistic argument is open to debate).

CINEMATIC TECHNIQUES

These are four major tools filmmakers use to help create cinematic experiences:

1. *Shots*—the visuals—are designed to tell the story. There are a wide variety of shot sizes and camera angles used to create stories—from extreme wide shots to extreme close-ups. Many filmmakers provide coverage (shooting

a range of shot sizes and camera angles in order to give the editor more choices in editing)—and make sure everything gets covered. Specific shots capture specific emotional moments, providing a visual storytelling palate for the editor. (If visuals don't carry the story emotionally, then you get the wallpaper effect—shots used to decorate the words of a narrator, thus nearly any type of shot would do.) This also includes camera movement. (See the latter part of this chapter for a detailed examination of the psychological effects of camera angles, camera movement, and lenses.)

2. *Voices of characters*. Characters are the ones who speak—not an omniscient "voice of God" narrator.

3. *Sound design*. Ambient audio collected in the field or used from sound libraries—as well as using the right piece of music at the right time (the proper emotional shift occurring in a story)—helps immerse the audience into the world of the story. If there is little to no forethought or design of the sonic landscape of the film, then you've thrown away half of the resources of a filmmaker and lost one of the most powerful tools a filmmaker can use. (Check out Michael Ondaatje's *The Conversations: Walter Murch and the Art of Editing Film*, Knopf, 2002 and the transom.org interview with Murch at: http://transom.org/2005/walter-murch/.) Studying both of these will prove a treasure-trove for those wanting to dig deeper into cinematic storytelling.

4. *Editing for pacing and rhythm*. The editor's job, says Karen Pearlman in her work *Cutting Rhythms* (Focal Press, 2009: 58), is to shape moments of tension and release in the audience by crafting "the rise and fall over time of intensity of energy." There are many good books on editing, but this kernel of wisdom continues to echo as a universal principle for nearly all editing projects. This includes the shaping of audio and visuals in such a way that the audience is pulled into the world of the film and taken for a ride. Both visuals and the sonic landscape must be treated equally in the edit in order to pull off an effective experience for an audience.

NARRATION AND DECORATIVE SHOTS

If narration is used improperly—when it tells the story rather than helps enlighten the story—we begin to lose the power of cinematic techniques and we may fail to pull the audience into the story. An example of this occurs at 2:25–2:53, at the climax of Alex's ascent in the *60 Minutes* work, "The Ascent of Alex Honnold." We hear Logan's words as we see five shots, her voice is in italics (see Figures 1.1–1.5):

This is Alex in the film, Alone on the Wall. *He's done more than a thousand free-solo climbs, but none were tougher than this one.* [This narration provides context and is ok.]

FIGURE 1.1
Courtesy of *60 Minutes*.

Here he is, just a speck on the northwest face of Half Dome: [We see this in the shot, so we don't need someone to tell us about it.]

FIGURE 1.2
Courtesy of *60 Minutes*.

You can barely make out the Yosemite Valley Floor below, as he pauses to rest: [Again, the visuals—along with a strong sonic landscape—pull us into a story, while narration that tells us what we're seeing and hearing pushes us out of a story.]

FIGURE 1.3
Courtesy of *60 Minutes*.

He's the only person known to have free-soloed the northwest face of Half Dome. [Pan and tilt up for next two images]: [This narration provides context, so it is ok.]

FIGURE 1.4
Courtesy of *60 Minutes*.

FIGURE 1.5
Courtesy of *60 Minutes*.

Overall, these shots are good—some are even strong—but their impact is lost in the narration.

In another segment, where Honnold is hanging on another cliff face, we hear this from Logan (see Figure 1.6): "Alex moves seamlessly across a section of flaky, unstable rock, pausing to dry a sweaty hand in his bag of chalk. There's nothing but him, the wall, and the wind." But all of this can be seen and heard, while the narration gets in the way of the cinematic possibilities of this moment. We hear breathing and some ambient wind but the audio mix doesn't make it stand out, because it is lost in the voiceover. In addition, the cinematographer could have zoomed in to a close-up so we could see Honnold's expression, visually driving home the moment. But the narration does it for us.

The cinematic impact of a close-up and a sound design has no priority. Instead, the producers chose to allow a narration to tell this part of the story. This is a stylistic choice and for those who want to engage in cinematic-style stories in production house work, it's the wrong choice. The right choice would stem from this key question: *What does it feel like to hang on the face of a cliff thousands of feet off the ground?*

A cinematic approach would have forced the thinking about what kinds of visuals and audio are needed to answer this question. Perhaps this moment could have been told by the subject (through Honnold's voice, rather than a narrator).

Notice that with this narration, it doesn't matter what type of shot we see of Honnold. Any shot of him on the wall reaching into the chalk bag fulfills the requirement of decorating the narration—thus it's called wallpaper.

FIGURE 1.6
Logan's voice in "The Ascent of Alex Honnold" tells us what Alex does in a play-by-play style. (Courtesy of *60 Minutes*.)

By making the choice to engage in a voiceover narration style instead of a cinematic style, the emotional power of this scene fizzles. This same kind of mistake[7] is made countless times in commercials and promotional shorts as well. For example, in a local 30-second commercial for Central Fresh Market we see in the second shot a woman holding a basket and an orange pepper as she looks at the camera and smiles, stating, "I shop here because the fresh meats, fruits, and vegetables make meal planning a breeze" (see https://youtu.be/n0uyaAgl-Hk and Figure 1.7). This is narration masquerading as dialogue and I include it as a warning. You may have characters speak with no narration, but if they're selling a product in the dialogue—then it fails the cinematic test (and becomes the kind of stuff I muted out as a child and still avoid watching, today). We know when the cinematic style is working because shots and sounds, when rendered effectively, are designed to emotionally engage an audience and pull us into the universe of the film.

FIGURE 1.7
A commercial for Central Fresh Market engages in the broadcast style to sell its products. (Courtesy of Central Fresh Market.)

Is there a correct way to do narration? In Zandrak's Hasbro commercial, "Growing in Pieces" (see http://www.zandrak.com/hasbro), mentioned in the Introduction, the voice of the father provides an authentic voice through the device of writing a letter to his son who is about to go off to college (see Figure 1.8). Yes, this is staged and a work of fiction, but the technique used here is one we can learn from.

FIGURES 1.8
The father writes a letter to his son in Zandrak's Hasbro commercial, "Growing in Pieces," providing us with an authentic voice that pulls us into the story. (Courtesy of Zandrak.)

I always say that narration should be used if it helps provide context for a story so the audience doesn't get lost. Indeed, Werner Herzog, in Paul Cronin's book, *Werner Herzog: A Guide for the Perplexed* (Faber & Faber, 2014: 117), describes how he uses narration in his documentaries: "I have the feeling my presence can give a film a certain authenticity, something you don't necessarily get from listening to a well-trained actor with a polished voice. I realized there was value in me being the chronicler of events and presenting my own viewpoint on things." Herzog's documentary films tend to engage in multiple styles of storytelling, including a "mix of reflexive, cinema vérité, and interview styles," says Wes Pope of the University of Oregon.

CREATING SONIC LANDSCAPES

Walter Murch, the only person to have earned an Academy Award for film editing and sound mixing, discusses a discovery he made while mixing audio for Francis Ford Coppola's *The Rain People* (1969). He describes how a scene from the film takes place in a telephone booth near a highway. But when he added street noise to the scene, the voice of the actress (Shirley Knight) was lost when he brought the levels up to a volume where he could hear the traffic. He says, in Ondaatje's *The Conversations: Walter Murch and the Art of Editing Film* (Knopf, 2002: 244):

> I discovered that if I used what you might call a *precipitant* sound, something we associate with a specific environment but that is itself distinct, then the other sounds come along automatically. What I did was record somebody dropping a wrench fifty feet away—as if fifty feet away from the booth, in the garage of the service station where the woman in the movie is stopped. It was important that it was far away, and that it was a certain kind of wrench dropping on a certain kind of polished concrete. If you've ever been in such an environment, you know what that sounds like and you know that such sounds are commonplace in service stops near big highways.

> That little sound was able to bring along with it, imaginatively, all the traffic. But the traffic exists in your mind. I spent a lot of time trying to discover those key sounds that bring universes along with them.

He continues:

> This metaphoric use of sound is one of the most flexible and productive means of opening up a conceptual gap into which the fertile imagination of the audience will reflexively rush, eager (even if unconsciously so) to complete circles that are only suggested, to

answer questions that are only half-posed. What each person perceives on screen, then, will have entangled within it fragments of their own personal history, creating that paradoxical state of mass intimacy where—though the audience is being addressed as a whole—each individual feels the film is addressing things known only to him or her.

The first minute of Tyler Stableford's "Shattered" expresses several shots of early dawn landscapes, a close-up of Steve House's face—breath visible in the chilly air as he pauses and looks up at the early dawn sky. As he walks, we hear his boots crunching and squeaking against the crystalized snow.

When we hear House's boots crunching on snow, it is a type of snow that is crystallized at a cold temperature (usually the single digits or teens on a Fahrenheit scale)—it is the type of snow I remember hearing in the cold winter growing up in Maine. And there's really no reason why this type of sound design cannot be used in the narration-centered or omniscient-style work. It really requires less talking onscreen.

House's breathing and the crystal crunch of snow becomes Murch's falling wrench onto a polished concrete floor—the precipitant sound—that brings along with it the feeling of the cold, wind, and icy snow of House's journey and it activates my imagination (my memories), helping to further authenticate and bring immediacy to House's journey.

If sound design is lacking in your project, you've lost half of your film. Take the time to be as creative with your sound design as you are with shooting your images. As Pope notes, "Visuals and sound work together 50/50 to create scenes. Visuals stop being b-roll and start to carry the narrative." If you want strong visuals, create a strong sound design. Conversely, if you create a weak sound design (or none at all), then your film will tend to express weak visuals (even when they look good). One of the failures of the *60 Minutes* piece is the lack of a strong ambient sound design that would enhance the feeling of Honnold's climb.

EDITING FOR RHYTHM THROUGH SOUND AND PICTURE

Along with Stableford's compelling shots and sound design, the rhythmic edit brings together these elements. In Stableford's work, we see how his editor, Dave Wruck, takes the director's shots and creates an emotional and physical rhythm around energetic cuts at the climax, while the opening scenes of the film provide long duration shots that allow us to enter House's world slowly, through visuals and sound design. Let's break the climax down (4:21–5:59) and see how Wruck crafts this moment. House's monologue (in italics) is cut as I depict it here (Figures 1.9–19):[8]

Shot 1 [4:21–4:28]

I've shared rope with 19 people who are now dead. Killed by . . .

FIGURE 1.9
Image courtesy of Stableford Studios.

Shot 2 [4:29–4:32]

. . . mountains. Most were simply in the wrong place . . .

FIGURE 1.10
Image courtesy of Stableford Studios.

Shot 3 [4:33–4:35]

. . . at the wrong moment.

FIGURE 1.11
Image courtesy of Stableford Studios.

Shot 4 [4:36–40]

The wrong place . . .

FIGURE 1.12
Image courtesy of Stableford Studios.

Shots 5–7 [4:41–4:42]

FIGURE 1.13
Image courtesy of Stableford Studios.

Shot 8 [4:43–4:45]

Is it here?

FIGURE 1.14
Image courtesy of Stableford
Studios.

Shots 9–12 [4:46–4:47]

FIGURE 1.15
Image courtesy of Stableford
Studios.

Shot 13 [4:48–4:49]

The wrong moment.

FIGURE 1.16
Image courtesy of Stableford Studios.

Shot 14 [4:50–4:51]

Is it now?

FIGURE 1.17
Image courtesy of Stableford Studios.

Shots 15–18 [4:52–4:53]

Shot 19 [4:54–4:59]

Will I know? [Eyes close. Sound of exhaling breath.]

In 38 seconds we get nineteen cuts with a variety of shots ranging from wide to extreme close-ups, the shots clearly telling the story with intentional and emotional impact. The lens in some shots is so close we can feel the intimacy of House's struggle. But at the same time, note how Wruck shapes the sound design with as much care as the visual edit. This cannot be understated. The more you are aware of how to mix images (shot sizes, shot angles, shot duration) with sound (ambient, sound effects, and music), the stronger your film. Use Stableford's film as a model for editing excellence.

One last note about cinematic storytelling, think about shots and the lenses you use in a psychological way, says Patrick Moreau from Stillmotion. His background in psychology gives us a way to think about how to use lenses and shot sizes, and it will also help with understanding how to shoot the story and how the editing can help tell the story when there is intention with the shot sizes and lens choices. We clearly see this intention of lens choices and shot sizes in Stableford's promo, for example.

THE PSYCHOLOGY OF THE LENS[9]

One of the strengths of Stillmotion is how their projects engage in such strong intimate images. This is why they moved from shooting weddings to shooting for the NFL ("The Season: Super Bowl XLV") and why Callaway hired them to create intimate profiles of Callaway golfers. They not only understand story, they understand how to use lenses in a psychological way.

FIGURE 1.20
A fleeting, but intimate moment of an NFL player's worried, furrowed brow captured in Stillmotion's NFL video, "The Season: Super Bowl XLV." The long lens and shallow focal depth isolate the player and shape the psychology of the drama Moreau helped craft through lens choices. (Image courtesy of Stillmotion.)

With a university degree in psychology, Moreau engages "psychology to tell stories" in his documentary work and now in his commercial work. He explains to me that psychology "helps us really understand the people we are working with as well as the stories we are trying to tell and how we can use our equipment to tell those stories better or in a more relevant way." It's not a set formula, but rather, it's being present and making conscious decisions when it comes to camera and lens selection.

A wider lens and deep focus allows Moreau to capture his subject in a space that reveals the character's emotions in an intimate way. Moreau explains how the psychological filmmaking process "forces us to question everything we are doing and it makes us really think about why this lens or why this camera tool" when shooting a scene.

Like all stories, it begins with character and not technology. "A big part of all of the filmmaking we do is really getting to know the people we are working with," Moreau says. In many ways, this is the next step, the application of their MUSE story process, in production (described below). Then they can begin to "think about how we can interpret the story through our gear." Lens selection is a big part of that gear choice. "A lot of people don't really realize that when you change a lens you change a lot more than depth of field or field of view," Moreau feels.

Within Moreau's psychology of the lens, it's a lot more than just framing the field of view. "People think you go to a wide lens because I want more in my frame or I go to a tight lens because I want less in my frame. Right?" But, he explains, you can easily change your field of view with a single lens by walking closer or farther away from a subject. "So if we can shoot somebody really close with say a 24mm lens or really far away with a 135mm lens what is the difference?" Moreau asks, but the bigger question is deciding "where we should be with which lens." The answer is tied to not just how the shot should be framed, visually, but the psychological frame: "We always try to think of who our subjects are and how we can use our lenses to best communicate them."

An example of using a wide lens occurs, Moreau says, when "you have somebody that is a little bit sillier or more comedic." The Stillmotion team would move in close with the wide lens because it will "stretch and exaggerate people and really play off the energy, and you are going to feel their movement and the life in them a lot more."

On the other hand, Moreau might use a long lens for a character "who is a little more dramatic." Perhaps you want to accent this type of character by making him or her "a little more disconnected and looking outside in." The long lens, Moreau adds, "is going to compress things, bring the features in, and that really shallow depth of field has you focus specifically on what we want you to focus on—but it also makes you feel that you are watching" the character from a distance, "rather than as an actual participant that a wider lens set closer will do."

FIGURE 1.21
Moreau's Stillmotion team captures an intimate moment in the wedding story, Winnie + Jerry.
(Image courtesy of Stillmotion.)

This kind of psychological and intimate lens work isn't just about setting up a shot, however. Rather, Moreau's background as a wedding cinematographer prepared him and his team to be ready to shoot "things as they happen." By getting to know our couples, we are then able to predict things in a participatory manner. This cinéma vérité approach to filmmaking allows him to craft commercials that are "real" in the way of all cinéma vérité documentaries: "We don't ask them to do something again." Life happens in the moment, and to capture that moment is the artistry of Patrick Moreau's psychological style of documentary filmmaking (and Stillmotion will weave this approach, along with interviews, into many of their projects). If a subject/performer is asked to stop and do an action over—especially when there are large crews—you may "lose that same honesty in what they are doing," Moreau says.

For example, Moreau's Stillmotion produced a series of intimate portraits of the Callaway golfers. In some cases, the series required his team to go into golfers' homes. A large film crew and large cameras would have negatively impacted the intimacy Moreau was looking for. "We would shoot Trevor with his child in his backyard playing basketball or in his living room playing ping pong with his trainer," Moreau says, "and being able to have small cameras, small gear we can get in there really quickly but still have that high production value." (See Figure 1.22.)

Without such "small setups" with a "really small" crew, Moreau contends, it would have been difficult to get the shots he wanted. He feels subjects want to know that you're going to tell their story properly and show them in the way they want to be shown. They're "very vulnerable letting you into their

FIGURE 1.22
Patrick Moreau's Stillmotion produced a series of intimate portraits of Callaway golfers. Here, Trevor's child in the foreground plays with his father, soft focus in the background. The small size of the DSLR, along with a small crew, fostered his team's ability to get such intimate shots. They use a Canon C100, now, with the top handle off to get the same intimacy (since the C100 is just a bit bigger than a 5D). (Image courtesy of Stillmotion.)

house," Moreau adds, but "by being very low impact and being a step ahead of them and letting them be themselves you get a very intimate reflection of who these people really are." This is a key point in production house projects. Don't take advantage of people and their spaces.

These intimate moments in the Callaway shots, Moreau believes, stem from the fact that "these moments are exactly like the way they would have happened whether we were there or not and to me this is the power of small cameras, such as DSLR and the C100. They allow you to capture real things." And they expressed the production values of broadcast TV. He feels "the power is in the size," providing the intimacy of realistic human portraits that "almost have an event edge to it, whether or not it is a natural event or it is just working with somebody who doesn't have acting experience."

PSYCHOLOGICAL IMPACT OF CAMERA ANGLES, CAMERA MOVEMENT, AND LENSES

Below are several charts summarizing some of the psychological effects of camera angles, camera movement, and camera lenses. These don't offer a formula or a hard and fast rule. In many ways, the impact of how the lens is used or how a camera moves or is angled is really dependent on the style of the story you're telling. It is your responsibility as the filmmaker to set the rules of consistency in how a certain type of lens, camera movement, and camera angle is used in shaping different psychological situations. Also note that depending on the camera you're using, you may have a different angle of coverage based on the sensor size. A 50mm lens on a C100 is different than one placed on a Digital Bolex, for example. All the focal lengths I'm providing will be based on the standard 35mm cinema scale—what we see in the Canon C100 and 70D DSLR, for example (the APS sensor is close to 35mm scale)—see Chapter 7 on cinematic gear for further discussion about this.

Types of Shots

The following terminology will help stage the descriptions in the charts that follow.

- *Normal lens*: The point of view of a single eye (not two).

- *Objective shot*: Omniscient viewpoint.

- *Subjective shot*: Subjective point of view. We're conscious a camera is being used, whether it's from a security camera or a news camera, for example.

- *Emotional distance and intimacy in shot sizes*:
   - Wide: Captures and sets the characters' locations in a scene. Psychologically, it offers the least intimacy. It's similar to having a conversation between two people standing against opposite walls in a room.

   - Medium: Normal conversational distance between people. Psychologically equivalent to people having a conversation at a comfortable distance without invading personal space.

   - Close-up: Distance of intimacy. We're now in someone's personal and emotional space. Psychologically we see this in emotional extremes of fights and sexual tension, as well as baring the emotional self, such as in a confession. This is why many people fall in love with movie stars—the close-up makes us feel we're intimate with them, emotionally. As Patrick notes above, when composing a close-up with a long telephoto lens, it "makes you feel that you are watching" the character from a distance, "rather than as an actual participant that a wider lens set closer will do."

- *Depth of field shot*: Use focus to frame a shot (foreground and background). Depth of field changes with aperture and with types of lenses—a wide angle will tend to provide deep focus, while a telephoto or long lens will provide a shallow depth of field, where you can choose whether the background, middle ground, or foreground is in focus, allowing the filmmaker a different type of framing. A *rack* focus occurs when changing focus within the same shot (going from foreground in focus to background in focus with the foreground falling out of focus, for example).

Camera Angle

The height of the camera and camera angle in relationship to the subject also determines the psychological nature of a scene:

- *High angle shot*: The camera's point of view is from on high looking down onto the subject, causing the subject to look up at the camera, resulting in a sense of subservience and weakness. There is no intimacy in this type of shot, due to the balance of power being off.

- *Low angle shot*: The camera's point of view is looking up at the subject, so the subject must look down at the camera, giving them dominance, authority, superiority, and strength. There is no intimacy in this type of shot, due to the balance of power being off.

- *Level shot*: Camera's lens is at eye level to the subject. It provides a sense of evenness of power since no one is looking down or up at someone. Use a level shot with a normal lens and it will provide intimacy in a close-up, due to an equal power relationship.

- *Dutch angle shot*: Camera tilted unevenly from the horizon line. Tends to induce a sense of disarrangement or confusion on the part of the subject.

- *Front shot*: When on axis and level, provides the strongest intimacy since the full face is exposed.

- *Side or profile shot*: Seeing action from the side, it pulls us away from intimacy since we're not seeing the full face where emotion is most fully expressed.

- *Rear shot*: The strongest emotional distance from a character, since we do not see their face. Because of this, we also feel tension because we don't know what the character is feeling, doing, or looking at.

Camera Movement

In addition, camera movement is another level of influencing the emotions of a scene and what it reveals. Some filmmakers add motion for the sake of visual stimulation—and in some cases that technique works. But when used consciously, camera movement can be used to reveal information and emotion, and even a passage of time, cinematically. Vincent Laforet, in an interview, discusses how many amateurs move the camera for the sake of moving the camera, resulting in unmotivated camera movement:

> The reality is that they're breaking one of the cardinal rules, which is every camera move should be motivated to do something either by the action in front of it or the director's will to reveal or conceal something, to walk you through a space, or to make you feel a certain emotion.[10]

Some terms dealing with camera movement:

- *Shaky cam shot*: The handheld look. Use a wide lens to minimize extreme motion. The longer the lens, the more obvious and extreme the shake. The camera calls attention to itself, providing a newsreel or raw documentary feeling as if the action is occurring unstaged in the moment.
- *Absolute motion*: When the camera moves, but stays in one place on its axis (such as on a tripod), the foreground and background move at the same rate of speed onscreen. Found in pan, tilt, and zoom shots. Not naturally occurring with our eyes.
- *Relative motion*: When the camera moves *through* space, the foreground moves more quickly relative to the background. Naturally occurring when we pan or tilt our head. Found in push-in, pull-out, jib, and tracking shots.

TABLE 1.1

Psychological Impact of Camera Movement

Type of camera movement	Tool	Motion type	Uses and psychological impact
Pan	Tripod	Absolute	Covers space from left of screen to right and vice versa on a static axis (tripod). • Use to cover subject movement, moving from one subject to another to show the relationship between them in space. • Use to cover someone's reaction. Following the eyes, the energy of one person looking at another, we pan to see what the looking character sees. • Use to cover a person drawing attention to an object and following it, used in some ways as the continuation of a physical action. • Psychologically, an audience wants to see what another character is looking at, so the pan releases this tension as we follow the gaze.
Tilt	Tripod	Absolute	Covers space from bottom to top of screen and vice versa on a static axis. Similar to the pan, but looking vertically up and down rather than horizontally left and right, revealing what is on the bottom of the screen to the top and vice versa. • Use to cover someone's reaction. Following the eyes, the energy of one person looking up or down at another, we tilt to see what the looking character sees. • Use to cover a person drawing attention to an object and following it up or down, used in some ways as the continuation of a physical action. • Potential to reveal importance of grandeur of an object or subject, by tilting up to reveal a towering

continued . . .

TABLE 1.1

Continued

Type of camera movement	Tool	Motion type	Uses and psychological impact
			figure, perhaps menacing to the subject if shot from a low angle. • Changes the power relationship in a scene when height of the angle is changed from low to high and high to low.
Zoom	Lens	Absolute	Change focal length within a shot (quick zooms are referred to as snap zooms). • We're conscious that a camera is being used (to create the effect of newsreel footage, like a live event—someone with a camera covering an event, providing a subjective look). • Use to move closer or farther away from the subject while maintaining absolute motion, so only use if the subjective view is needed. • Effective as a snap zoom to push the audience quickly into an emotional moment abruptly, causing them to feel off balance (such as in battle scenes or some other intense physical activity), providing the subjective sense that the action is unfolding by the moment and the camera is there subjectively to cover it as it happens.
Push in (dolly)	Track, slider, Steadicam, gimbal, jib	Relative	Camera physically moves closer to the subject or object. • Use to intensify or heighten emotion in a scene as the audience feels like they're entering the intimate space of a subject. • Move slowly to make the shift in emotion subtle. • Move quickly for obvious impact.
Pull out (dolly)	Track, slider, Steadicam, gimbal, jib	Relative	Camera physically moves away from the subject or object. • Use to diminish emotion in a scene as the audience feels like they're moving out of the intimate space of a subject. • Move slowly to make the shift in emotion subtle. • Move quickly for obvious impact.
Parallel (or lateral) tracking	Track, slider, Steadicam, gimbal	Relative	Camera physically follows the action of a character in parallel to the subject's movement. Or it reveals different action in a shot, even passing time. • Tracking away from a character creates distance from the subject and may reveal loneliness or disconnectedness from the world.

continued . . .

TABLE 1.1

Continued

Type of camera movement	Tool	Motion type	Uses and psychological impact
			• Tracking towards a character allows us to enter the emotion of a character from a distance, suggesting a connection. • Profile shots are far less intimate than a frontal shot.
Jib (crane)	Jib, gimbal	Relative	Camera physically can move up and down in space, as well as allowing it to push in and/or pull out of space within the same shot. (The up or down and push or pull may be done simultaneously.) • Use to reach deep into space (or a set) where it may be difficult to get a shot otherwise (such as with tracks). • Use to pull back and leave a scene, departing from a character and leaving them in a landscape—good way to exit a specific type of scene, causing a de-establishing shot. • Use to swoop into a scene and feel around the space that could not be shot with another type of move. • When starting low and moving up, reveals an expanse of scenery and distances us from the emotional point of view of characters. • Looking down from above provides an omniscient view of landscape and action. • When starting high and moving low, provides a shift from omniscient point of view to a personal intimacy as we enter the emotional space of the characters.
Handheld	Hands, gimbal, Steadicam	Relative	The handheld look, when done smoothly, offers a way for the visual movement to float through space. • Use to provide a sense of floating and peace.

Additional resources on camera movement:

- Steven D. Katz's *Film Directing: Cinematic Motion* (Michael Wiese Productions, 2004).
- Vincent Laforet's *Directing Motion* (see http://directingmotion.mzed.com/).

Lenses

Note: The more extreme the lens, the more it calls attention to itself, causing a subjective viewpoint, while normal lenses tend to be objective in their viewpoint.

TABLE 1.2

Psychological Impact of Lens Size

Lens size	Depth of Field	Shot type	Psychological impact
Fisheye or convex lens 6–12mm	Deep focus	Super wide GoPro cameras utilize equivalent wide-angle lenses.	The image curves along the edge of the shot and causes the image to be distorted. • Provides a sense of expansiveness in wide shots • May be for comedic effect or where distortion and confusion is needed when brought close to a subject. • Could be used to show that it's a subjective view, such as a security camera.
12–18mm	Deep focus	Super wide	Provides expansive clarity, a view showing details from foreground to background. Places character(s) within a heightened sense of space. A tight close-up on subjects may lead to visual distortion. (You can place the lens close to a subject in the foreground and have the background fall off in focus.) • Use to provide a large sense of grounding a character in space and location in wider shots. • Use to provide an expansive view of a scene. • Use for a sense of instability or zaniness in tight shots.
18–34mm	Deep focus Open aperture to get shallow depth of field	Normal wide	A step below a "normal" field of view, the standard wide-angle view provides a sense of space, because it not only picks up details from foreground to background through deep focus (under normal aperture), but it also covers the area around the edge of the subject when doing a wide shot. A tight close-up on subjects may lead to visual distortion in lower focal lengths. • Provides a grounded sense of space and setting. Places character(s) within a heightened sense of space. (You can place the lens close to a subject in the foreground and have the background fall off in focus.) • Use to provide a sense of grounding in space and location in wider shots. • Offers a bit of instability or zaniness in tight shots when brought close to the subject. • Makes you feel like you're participating in the action.

continued . . .

TABLE 1.2

Continued

Lens size	Depth of Field	Shot type	Psychological impact
35–55mm	Deep focus at high aperture Shallow focus at low aperture	Normal view	Psychologically for viewers, this is the normal field of view for the human eye (one eye)—lenses don't capture peripheral vision. There's no distortion on the edge of the frame. • Use when offering a sense of "normality" to a scene and equal balance of power. • Normal lenses offer intimacy when the camera is level.
60–100mm	Image begins to get compressed, providing a shallow depth of field	Fairly tight	Depending on the tightness of a shot, can provide a decent reach to get a character in a tight close-up with a shallow depth of field—image starts getting compressed and shallow in narrow fields of view as the lenses get longer. • Use to provide focus on a single character or cutaway shot. • Use to provide a sense of distance in an intimate scene.
100–400mm (or longer)	Compressed shot with shallow depth of field at normal aperture	Tight	For reaching close when a bit farther away from a subject—really compresses the background and foreground. • Use when you need to get close to a subject when the camera is farther away. • Provides a subjective view tied to a distancing of intimacy in a scene.
Tilt shift lens (variety of focal lengths)	Shallow to deep depending on the focal length and aperture of the lens	Dependent on the focal length of the lens	Allows you to adjust focus within a specific field of view within the shot, providing a highly stylized shot. • Can provide a sense of miniaturization to a scene. • Use to stylize the subject or scene, such as in a dream state or drug-induced altered viewpoint.

MUSE—A STORYTELLING TOOL FROM STILLMOTION

At the risk of sounding like I'm plugging Stillmotion's course, they do offer MUSE, a process and toolkit for learning how to tell "moving" stories with intention. They offer a course on their storytelling method—more info at: http://Learnstory.org.[11] In their course, they give production house storytellers and filmmakers the tools to develop character-centered stories. They include methods for developing the story—not techniques of production. This is a well-intended goal and a missing piece for many who lack such skills. Many people understand the filmmaking process, especially those who have gone to film school, but it seems that few know how to find and create a strong story. If anything, if you apply the cinematic techniques discussed in this chapter to a strong story, you'll likely make a strong film.

Stillmotion's vision for MUSE is:

> We see a world where storytellers of all varieties—filmmakers, bloggers, marketers, agencies, non-profits—are more intentional in the stories they craft, and that their stories truly do change the world. We see a world where filmmakers are no longer tripods—they have the confidence in what they are trying to say with a story, and the incredible clarity to bring it to life in a way that moves their audience, thrills their clients, and fully realizes the vision they have in their mind's eye. Where non-profits are using MUSE to connect people to their cause, raise more money, and create more impact. Where marketers and agencies use MUSE to be more conscious storytellers that use story to create results around things that matter. (MUSE Storytelling Tools, p. 5).

If you need to up your game on storytelling—and most of us do—MUSE is an online class with several learning modules, and directly reflects the ten years of learning and experience Stillmotion has applied to its Emmy-Award-winning work. The first half of the course (steps 1–4) is the process by which you listen to a client and the potential characters of a story with intention. It includes:

1. **People** are the characters in our story who give our audience someone to relate to. People connect with people, therefore we can use the notion of empathy to help move our audience.

2. **Place** is where your story happens. It grounds the story in reality. Place is more than just a backdrop—it's a way to let your story speak for itself, display your character's authenticity, and foster trust with the audience.

   It includes the environments, objects, situations, and time for your characters in the story.

3. Purpose is what your story says to the audience. It's what you want your viewer to take away from the story. By having a well-defined purpose, you take on one clear vision that resonates throughout your team. (This includes the development of keywords to guide the production.)

4. **Plot** is the structure of your story. It allows you to maximize the impact of your story by creating an emotional arc and organizing elements into the beginning, middle, and ending. This includes the development of conflict, questions that lead to answers, and a resolution.

The Stillmotion team feels that these "4 Pillars" help create a sense of "connection, authenticity, meaning, and engagement."

In short, the MUSE course provides a methodology to help find characters that speak to the heart, create stories that engage in meaning, and help shape a plot that stems from their uniqueness and passions, all of which revolve around an unanswered question that helps drive the story. Ultimately, it puts Stillmotion's ten years of award-winning production house work into a course that others can apply to their own work. See Chapter 8 on how Stillmotion applied some of the MUSE steps to the book promotional film, *My Utopia*.

Storytelling and Filmmaking Tools

Stillmotion's MUSE isn't the only way to develop stories and characters, of course. These resources will help you up your game in storytelling—some of which influenced Stillmotion's approach:

- Aristotle's *Poetics*. Read it here: http://classics.mit.edu/Aristotle/poetics.mb.txt

- Christopher Booker's *The Seven Basic Plots*. See a summary here: https://en.wikipedia.org/wiki/The_Seven_Basic_Plots

- Stillmotion's *MUSE*: http://Learnstory.org

- Alex Buono's *The Art of Visual Storytelling* bundle (Visual Style Workshop, Visual Subtext Seminar, Cinematography Workshop): http://vs2.mzed.com/download

- Vincent Laforet's *Directing Motion*: http://directingmotion.mzed.com/streaming

- Shane's *Inner Circle*: https://www.hurlbutvisuals.com/blog/shanesinnercircle

Worksheet: Shooting in the Cinematic Style

1. Identify the 4 Ps from Stillmotion's MUSE process:

   a. People

   b. Place

   c. Purpose

   d. Plot

   e. If you take the MUSE course, go through the steps for each client-based story you work on.

2. Write a descriptive shot list.

3. Choose the type of lens for each shot and/or scene in order to express the right psychological impact in a story (and this may involve changing the camera angle).

4. How do the shots show the story unfolding, visually? If shots are simply illustrating or decorating the dialogue or narration—and any shot would do the job— then revise it so that every shot counts, propelling the story forward visually.

5. Describe the soundscape for each scene—be sure that every piece of audio is consciously designed to enhance the mood of the story.

   a. Natural sound elements.

   b. Music (each scene does not need music; use music for emotional transition points); justify why you need music in a particular scene or at a particular moment.

   c. Voice

      i. Who speaks and why do they speak?

      ii. Does the voice tell the audience how to think and feel or does it share an emotional experience?

      iii. If there's too much talking without space in between dialogue or narration, then the ambient soundscape will get lost.

6. Identify the moments of tension and release in the film.

   a. Describe how audio is used to help shape the rhythm and pacing.

   b. Describe how voices help shape the rhythm and pacing.

   c. Describe how music helps shape the rhythm and pacing.

CHAPTER 2
Creating a Vision
The Cinematic-Style Video Production House

Now that we've defined and explored the tools of cinema that can be used in production house projects, let's examine how to discover and shape the vision of your potential company. We begin with Stillmotion, which began as a university student startup in Toronto, Canada with a focus on shooting weddings, and eventually evolved into an Emmy Award-winning production house in Portland, Oregon. At the heart of their business model is the production of cinematic-style client-based projects along with an education division for filmmakers who want to learn their approach to storytelling.

WHY SHOULD YOU START A PRODUCTION HOUSE BUSINESS?

Before the five different Emmy Awards came in, Amina Moreau tells me that Stillmotion—an internationally recognized cutting-edge production house[1]— "started with a boy wanting to impress a girl" while they were at university outside of Toronto. She smiles as she sits relaxed in a wooden chair of a coffee shop a few blocks from the Stillmotion "hangar," a large building that houses Story & Heart and Marmoset, a boutique music agency for motion images.[2]

The love story began in the realm of photography. And if Stillmotion has a style that's distinct from other production houses it stems from the fact that it didn't grow from a traditional film education background. Amina had a teenager's love of photography "infected" within her by her parents. By the time she got to university, she was studying psychology. "Patrick and I were hanging out and he thought photography was interesting mostly because he thought I was interesting," she laughs.

Their first business venture began with Amina and Patrick selling prints of her photography at a flea market. They discussed how they really wanted to make a documentary on the exploitation "of women, of children, of animals, and of the environment," conceived as four chapters with trips to sweatshops in Asia, factory farms, and deforestation of the rainforest. They wanted "to travel the world to do this documentary," she explains. But as students they had no money, no "video experience," and they lacked "life experiences," she adds. Patrick notes how he had never touched a camera before then: "I was not a photographer, I was not a filmmaker, I didn't dabble in it. I didn't do anything with film. I didn't look at it online, it wasn't a hobby, it wasn't even on my radar," he explains in a separate interview.

Yes, Patrick became interested in her, as Amina notes, but as he says, he was also "captivated by the way she was able to take something that I was seeing and turn it into something so much more magical. And it captivated me because I was all into psychology because of the power of perspective, how you can see something, how you can see the exact same thing in a completely different way. And that's what I had seen through her—her power of perspective to see the world in another way."

For Patrick, "that's what film allowed me to do and to explore." So despite the fact that he had no interest in film, he says when a 77-year-old Buddhist monk visited a philosophy class he was taking, it challenged his point of view in life. He discovered that "we could say something through film." Film would become "just a tool or vehicle to talk about these issues, these stories," he adds.

But like many things in life, they needed to realize that their dream would develop by taking a different route, and in some ways the least logical route. It didn't come through film school or a film major; they both majored in psychology. And when Patrick's roommate's boss was getting married, and the assigned photographer got sick, they needed someone fast to cover the wedding. Amina took the photo job and Patrick came along to shoot video for $350.

Although Amina's father wanted her to become a doctor, lawyer, or engineer, this first wedding job became the genesis of Stillmotion and would derail their planned career paths as psychologists. They wanted to shoot a documentary, but they took on more wedding jobs in order to fund the documentary, while at the same time gaining more shooting experience. "And then before we knew it we had a wedding business," Amina smiles. "And it's not something that we at the beginning really tried for, it just happened, we were doing something we loved." Their career plan to go on and get advanced degrees in psychology and start their own practice faded, although they jokingly said that they could make a two-sided business card: one for wedding photos and videos and the other for marriage counseling. In either case, it would take them nine years to make a documentary on exploitation.

Patrick mentions how he earned an award for his thesis and his professor didn't understand why he was pursuing a career shooting weddings. But this professor was at the wedding that he and Amina shot—and Patrick, being a motivated filmmaker, edited a two- to three-minute video of the ceremony that was screened at the reception. "He's in attendance," Patrick says about his professor, "and he gets to see this same-day edit that we produced for a classmate and I can remember him walking up to me after that and basically just shaking his head and said, 'I get it.'" By "seeing the emotional power, the impact on the room, how a story could effect people," Patrick felt a sense of "validation" from his mentor. It gave him courage to move forward with filmmaking, turning his back on his original career goal.

Patrick funded gear through student loans. He read about cameras on forums and other websites, teaching himself how to use them. He bought a Canon GL2 with a 35mm lens adapter.

Patrick and Amina eventually moved to Toronto and shot over a hundred weddings. But weddings are not that exciting—especially, as Amina points out—when "the plot is the same in every single wedding, so how do you make that interesting?" That's important for two people who don't like doing the same thing twice. And like the rest of the most of us, "at the beginning we made it interesting geeking out with new gear." The cinema hardware was just a "vehicle to talk about these exploitation stories and so we started making maps and plans for our original documentary."

They were one of the first companies to use the Steadicam in a wedding context and many "thought we were crazy for doing it, and all of a sudden everyone's using Steadicams at weddings so it took off." However, using slick moves isn't really filmmaking, Amina explains: "We made these technical decisions not

"Excitement is Contagious"

Rule 1 for starting a production house business: Everyone says, "Do what you love," Amina Moreau notes. And it's an important cliché. But even more important, the thing that will make a difference in why you would ever want to start a business and win over clients—it revolves around everything you will ever do: "Excitement is contagious," Amina says.

If you think that by doing the warm and fuzzy, people will flock to you—that doesn't happen. It doesn't. If you engage in something you truly believe in—but don't just believe in it, but live and breathe it because you love it and you're excited by it—that's what makes the difference. Any time you talk about it, whether it's to a potential client, a potential partner, a potential investor, anyone, if you're excited about it, they're going to be excited about it.

And if you get people excited about something you love, they're going to somehow invest in it whether it's emotionally, mentally, financially, even temporally—it's much easier to find opportunities when you're passionate.

People want to work with people that are doing something they're excited about. I think that's gotten us our clients, it's gotten us enough, but then use the rest of the excitement to go over and above their expectations. To not just do the bare minimum, to not just do an above average job, but do it the very first day. For example, "we're out filming with the marines for *A Game of Honor*, the very first day of shooting in the freezing cold, in an obstacle course for sixteen hours, and what do we do when we get back at two in the morning? We edited. We weren't asked to, but we did a rough cut of our footage and we handed it over to CBS, and we said look what we've done.

So not only did they see the absolute best shots (we still delivered all the footage), but what did they see first through the edit? They saw the absolute best stuff of ours, and they also saw that we're willing to go above and then some. And we showed them our editing capabilities. Then eight months later when it came down to edit, we played a big part in that edit. We took the initiative. Why? Because we were excited! So excitement is my best recommendation."

because it served the story better, but because it made it less boring." As Patrick puts it, the cinematic style "created a movie experience for those that knew the couple." It made their work stand out because of it. However, when a bride asked why they did a shot a certain way, it was a new beginning that changed everything. Amina explains, "She sat in our studio and the client explained how she loved a ring shot we did. Normally they might ask how it was done, but the client asked, 'Why did you do it that way?'" This got them thinking about story more than technique.

They eventually started slowly moving away from the traditional wedding style—incorporating their cinematic style of shooting and applying it to the psychology or motivation behind the characters in weddings. For example, Amina and Patrick would begin to shy away from the traditional content of shooting weddings, such as the cake cutting. "Why are you doing a cake cutting?" Amina asks hypothetically. "Well, because our parents did and our grandparents did and that's what they want." If she asked a client, "Why are you doing a cake cutting?" and then got an answer, "We're not, we have caramels," Amina immediately likes this type of client. And if they have a really great story about why they have caramels, then they would feature the caramels because "there's a story that says something about who they are as people. It's a representation of something deeper than just sugar on a plate," she continues. The character motivations—the story behind their fresh approach to a wedding—is what would motivate them to continue with weddings. She explains that if you want to do those types of weddings, as opposed to the traditional style, then place examples on your website—your portfolio pieces—that express the approach and style you want to do. "If you're not showing what you love," Amina explains, "you're going to be attracting more of what you don't love. I'd rather be showing one stellar piece a year and have it be the right one than twenty of other work you don't love." Patrick adds how this approach evolved to a "much more intentional and thoughtful way of doing projects leading to something that's a lot deeper." This something deeper was story. Patrick explains:

> What happened through that process of introspection was realizing that there was no story there and we were making up for the lack of affect with effect. What we started doing is analyzing. What is the story and how do you go deeper? How do we know we don't need that action or shot? That's when we started getting to know the clients and what made them different and highlighting those little nuances and creating character story arcs, resulting in questions in the viewer, which would later lead to the whole model that we now call MUSE. It started when we started asking those questions of why are we doing this and why doesn't this work and this feels so artificial on a surface level. There's got to be something else.

That something else would become the "JC plus Esther" wedding video (see Figure 2.1 and https://vimeo.com/6496808). It was Stillmotion's first project where they incorporated this new approach. And it must be noted that they were shooting live, documentary style, with no staging. Amina explains: "We made a strong commitment to never ask people to stop, slow down or re-do anything for us or any kind of acting." In addition, by shooting with DSLRs, they were also able to gain a sense of camera intimacy, and have the ability to change lenses. Add that to their approach to a wedding that is based on story and uniqueness of characters (rather than the generic conventional styles of wedding shoots where everyone performs the same role on their wedding day), and it would eventually change everything for Stillmotion.

"A few hundred thousand views later," Amina says about their new story-based wedding video, "we're living in Toronto, we're at the studio, and we get a phone call. It's a producer form the NFL network." Patrick had answered the phone and tells the caller, "Just hang on a second, please," and he turns to Amina and says, "Holy crap it's the NFL." The producer tells them that he saw this wedding video on Vimeo and ended up crying: "I don't know why, because I don't know these people." Amina explains that the NFL producer was so impressed that they could "create something so moving for a stranger about a wedding" that he wanted to "see what we can do in the football world."

Despite the fact that they were from Canada and really weren't into American football—in the end, the intimacy of their shooting style, their focus on characters, and the ability to capture and shape story through the lens made Stillmotion stand out and got them jobs. They would end up winning five national Emmys and additional jobs, including a documentary for the Army–Navy game, among other network live events, including shooting a brief interview with President Obama at one of the games.

FIGURE 2.1
The wedding film that would change everything for Stillmotion: "JC plus Esther." See: https://vimeo.com/6496808 (Image courtesy of Stillmotion.)

By following their passions for story, they were able to set the vision for Stillmotion, eventually moving from Toronto to San Francisco, then finally choosing Portland, Oregon as their home base. The vision stemmed from their experiences and approach to working with clients, finding the story, and not creating a production house where they become a "tripod." "You need to let the story move you before you try to move the story," Patrick tells me at a small homey coffee shop in a hip neighborhood of Portland's east side. He recommended the donuts that taste best when served hot.

The danger is getting stuck in the "pattern of habits" that lead you to "end up shooting you as if you are anybody else, and you just become replaceable," Patrick says:

> Because as filmmakers, storytellers, bloggers, as whatever our medium is, we often show up with a preconceived notion of who you are, what the story is and how you're going to approach it, and I even know what my favorite lens is and I know where I like to stand and I know how I like to use the light in this way.

The result? "You become a tripod, and I became a tripod, and you become replaceable and we both devalue each other," he adds. This was his initial approach to doing weddings. But to make Stillmotion stand out, they had to take a different approach. "When I start to see you as unique and different, and explore that and then allow that to inspire and move me, it's different every time. It's more work, but it's also more fun. It's actually challenging, but an audience connects with that approach." This revelation, which took several years to evolve, became the mission statement—the vision—for Stillmotion.

CREATING A BUSINESS MODEL THAT REFLECTS YOUR VISION AND MISSION

Without a unique vision that taps into who you are and the passions that drive you, then you're in danger of creating a company full of tripods, as Patrick Moreau would say. You should have your own story as to why you want to start a cinematic-style production house, which shows that you've thought deeply about it. If that's the case, then you really need to determine the vision for the company, its mission, and this really involves creating a plan. A plan that involves discovering who your competition is and what makes your approach unique.

Andrew Hutcheson of Zandrak recommends that you need to have a sense of vision for you company (even if it's a one person setup)—"establish who you are, what you're doing or want to do, where you're going to do it, how you're approaching it (is it going to be with a team or is it going to be you and you're going to hire directors, are you a one-man band, do you want to expand?)"

In many ways, Andrew adds, "You're figuring out what you're going to specialize in, who you can target that to. What's your client audience, that demographic? Is it insurance companies that specialize in life insurance policies? Are you really good at doing car commercials? Are you really good at doing these things?" It's not just the passion that's needed—but you really need to be good at it. And from there, branch out to similar areas to market your skills and passions.

"Find that and then you'll discover how to look at it like spheres of influence," Andrew explains. "You have your main circle. If you throw a rock into a pond, it creates a main ripple—those are your key clients. It might be weddings. What's a wedding like? It's kind of like a bar mitzvah—boom—that's one degree of separation away from weddings that you can branch out into. A wedding's kind of also like a graduation, or a commencement, or any sort of big event. You could document that. So now you've found not just weddings you specialize in, but you specialize in event videography. That's a broader umbrella. You can now branch out from working with your base pool of weddings to see what are the things related to that. What are the type of clients you could work for?"

This is the type of thinking you need to do before you jump into business. It's great to get excited about it, but Andrew feels that "the most important thing you can do for yourself is to take the time to write a business plan before you start. Too often people will say, 'I'm going to go into business and I'm going to start doing video production, and I'm just going to target clients that need music videos.' Great, but what's your plan?"

Andrew says to ask the hard questions: "What is different about you than anyone else? You can have it in your head, but the actual act of writing it down, anywhere from a one-pager to an actual business plan that defines who your audience is, how you plan to be profitable, what you project you're going to have to spend . . . the more you can write that down, the better sense it'll give you for what you're doing." This plan becomes the road map for your present and future course. So the first steps involve your vision and mission.

Vision and Mission Statement

A *vision* statement, Jennell Evans, President and CEO of Strategic Interactions, Inc., tells us in *Psychology Today*, revolves around the need to communicate what your company or organization hopes to achieve, while a *mission* statement is about why a company or organization exists, including "what it does, who it does it for, and how it does what it does."[3]

What this reasoning misses is the "why" question. Leadership expert Simon Sinek, says that companies—or the means by which many communicate—will lead to failure if they start with what they do and how they do it—that's the easy part. We know what they do. We usually know how they do it. But those who understand *why* they do what they do end up delivering from a strong sense of their purpose and belief—the emotional center of why a company exists. For example, in the case of Apple, Sinek says their belief and values—the why question—is this: "In everything we do we believe in challenging the status quo. We believe in thinking differently." (This would be their vision statement.) By starting with the emotional need they inspire people, which leads to the how: "The way we challenge the status quo is by making our products beautifully designed, simple to use, and user friendly." And the what: "We just happen to make great computers. Want to buy one?"[4]

By expressing the emotional needs of a company—by answering the why question—the purpose of a company can be defined and communicated. Start here when creating your vision and mission statement, since it's your opportunity to examine why you want to do this company, how you want to do it, and what you want to do with it.

Video production houses are numerous, and some might argue there's too many and too much competition to even bother creating a new one. But the premise of this book revolves around the growing need not just for more videos, but to tell stories cinematically—visually and with a conscious sound design tied to compelling storytelling.[5] This will set your work apart from the conventional-style production houses and those who work as tripods (just doing a job without any creativity). We've all seen bad commercials—projects that hit you over the head with jingles about how you must buy this product—the ones I turn off. Within the cinematic mode of shooting and telling stories, you'll want to define a style that represents who you are and your view of the world (the why question)—then explore how and in what ways your work, your company, will differ from Stillmotion in Portland, Oregon and Zandrak in Boston, or the companies you'll end up competing against in your city. Let's take a look at how these companies define themselves on the web.

Mission and Vision Statement Case Study: Stillmotion (http://stillmotion.ca)

Stillmotion's vision and mission statement is the means by which clients can read about what the company feels is important to it. The statement is short, quickly showing examples, but the primary material is in the two sentences: "Our approach is rooted in what social science has shown to be the foundation of emotional connection. We guide the heart to move the mind. It's educating the client about what story means to Stillmotion—it's not facts. It's people being impacted by events that change them. So if a client wants a story that is character centered and will potentially move and change their audience, then Stillmotion is one of the best in the business."

My sense of Stillmotion's mission statement rests in this last sentence: "We guide the heart to move the mind."

This is their vision. If we look at Stillmotion's portfolio examples, we can see how each one stems from this vision and mission—which revolves around the heart of the company.

Stillmotion is about creating moving stories cinematically in order to help their clients make social and personal changes in the world. Their aesthetic and their philosophy reflects a sensibility that "emotion is what people are looking for these days," Amina explains. Although they may have to take on projects that don't necessarily reflect their passion and vision in order to meet the bills, Amina is adamant that as creatives they cannot be just a "human tripod" (as explained earlier by Patrick)—just stand here and shoot. They're interested in developing stories. She feels that companies—clients—are looking for "emotional connection and human interest." "It's not just about the product anymore, it's not about the service, it's not about the facts," she adds. And when companies hire tripods, then those projects are "the boring commercials that are soon forgotten."

At Stillmotion, they don't want their clients' stories forgotten. They want their stories to reach to the heart of their clients' audiences and enact change. Therefore, Amina says, the projects they do tend to express "an emotional quality that is remembered and shared, and if you have a million views on YouTube for a commercial, you know that company is getting a lot of exposure." And with exposure comes the audience that connects to these stories with "a human interest, emotional aspect—whether sentimental or happy or angry"— the emotion gets the attention of an audience. Their aesthetics and their philosophy—their style of shooting isn't about telling, but showing, engaging an audience through the emotional connection they make through the psychology of the lens of their camera (see Chapter 1).

FIGURE 2.2
Vivian from *Stand With Me* works on a poster for her lemonade stand—an intimate story about a girl who wants to help end childhood slavery. Rather than focus on facts, Stillmotion wants to grab your attention through emotion in a story, in order to effect social change. (Image courtesy of Stillmotion.)

Vision and Mission Statement Case Study: Zandrak

While Stillmotion is most famous for telling stories through honest and emotional interviews in a documentary style, Zandrak's approach to story is a bit different. They do documentary-style work, but they also create stories through a narrative approach found in fiction filmmaking. It fills a niche, Andrew Hutcheson, who founded Zandrak, explains to me in their office across the street from Fenway Park in Boston. From their homepage (http://zandrak. com):

> We work with agencies, companies, brands, and independent creators to tell their story when it's not enough to just showcase a production. We cultivate whole experiences that invite people to engage rather than tune out. We don't make commercials: we tell branded stories.

Their mission statement is: "We work with agencies and brands to create experiences that present their identity in an engaging way."

- What do we do? Tell branded stories.
- For who? Agencies, companies, brands, and independent creators.
- How do we do it? By cultivating whole experiences that invite people to engage

Andrew, who also serves as the producer and colorist, says that their aesthetic comes from minimalism and narrative storytelling. The cursive Z became their logo to represent their style. This helped define the business. Previously, Andrew explains, when they were asked what they did, they used to say, "Well, we are an independent film company that does feature films and commercials and music videos and all this stuff." It was too generic. It didn't differentiate the company from others. Their team came from filmmaking and with a love for filmmaking, and were inspired by Spike Jonze and Wes Anderson, who make "really awesome films."

One day Andrew realized, "That's really the way to work with commercials." He asked himself, "How can you tell the best narrative of this company, how can you tell their story, their brand story?" By offering "a narrative approach and taking those sensibilities as narrative filmmakers to our commercial broadcast work" would be what separated them from the competition. Once they had defined their aesthetic, Andrew says, they told people that they "do branded storytelling." And they discovered that over the past few years, "branded content short films really took a big rise."

This became the answer to the why question. They lay it out on their homepage beneath the word WHY: "Films are how we speak. Collaboration is how we find words. Zandrak is how we have a voice." Why does Zandrak exist? "To apply the inspiration of filmmaking and the sensibilities of narrative filmmakers to commercial broadcast work in a collaborative way."

But this approach required building the right team. It was not a solo venture. Charles Frank, the director and editor at Zandrak, says that by shifting the company to a branded storytelling house, it was "such a natural transition for all of us, because we had all come from narrative storytelling." Each person at Zandrak came from a narrative sensibility. Charles says, "We dedicated our lives to building our narrative sensibilities. We found a solution for all of us to apply it to—branded storytelling—that was actually profitable and could help other people." This became the business model for their company. "That was just the most mind-blowing find that we could all imagine," Charles says.

Teamwork became the pieces "that when put together and rearranged, turned into something that we never would have found without each other." Going it alone might not have worked necessarily, because despite the fact that they had the gear, space, and philosophy, Andrew says,

> without the team we wouldn't have anything and that is what is so, so important. I feel like the tendency is to work with the people you have always worked with, or work with the person who you know has the most connections. Or work with the person who has the most toys or the most money. But really it was just that we all have a similar and shared vision and out of that philosophy it just gelled.

Finding the right person doesn't evolve from those who win Emmys or those who went to film school; it's about the philosophy, a shared aesthetic, then "we know that's the person for the job," Andrew explains. They are looking for the right attitude and a willingness to collaborate. Even though you may do projects solo—and there are small projects and multimedia journalists who do a lot of solo work (and it may be how you start out your company), ultimately, getting a good team together will take you to an entire new level of work.

Why do they have this company? As stated on their welcome page:

We love storytelling

It's how we understand the world around us and how we find out place in it. We believe that there is a meaningful way to tell every story, in any circumstance. Films are how we speak. Collaboration is how we find words. Zandrak is how we have a voice.

Come share a story with us.

In order to test their mission and vision for the company—to share a company's story where they would apply narrative style to commercial work—Andrew entered a contest for a Hasbro commercial. A lower-end marketing executive wanted to change how commercials were done at Hasbro, Andrew explains:

> For thirty years, Hasbro has been making thirty-second and fifteen-second commercials with the same production company. The same company. They literally have to have a thousand people within the Hasbro company to approve a concept before they move forward. It takes a huge level of approval for them to pass something through. And it's something they call the red tape syndrome. There are constraints, and it has to be this way, has to be cookie cutter.

According to Andrew, this executive went to legal and asked "if he was going to get in trouble for this and they said it might not be a good idea, but there is nothing they can do. This is your budget and you can do what you want with it." He took his small pool of money, and without consulting with anyone else—circumventing the red tape syndrome—he put his budget into Tongal.com, a site matching creatives with businesses whereby a community of creatives pitch ideas and the winning idea is chosen by a company. In essence it was a competition. He wanted something fresh and new for Hasbro.

Charles found the competition by coming across Tongal, a company that becomes a "catalyst to help independent filmmakers get in touch with big brands," on the web. Charles interacted with the client.

FIGURE 2.3
The Hasbro commercial placed Zandrak on the map and defined their narrative-based cinematic style for branding companies. (Image courtesy of Zandrak.)

This executive felt that "people don't often know what they want until they have it or see it." Andrew explains that it was "something fresh." After Zandrak made the 60-second commercial, the executive went to his bosses and asked for forgiveness: "I went behind your backs and made this 60-second commercial but I think it is really powerful." The higher-level executives loved it so much that they "decided to invest in broadcasting it and it was their best 60-second commercial of all time," Andrew says. Zandrak earned an award for their commercial and cemented their style.

Andrew Hutcheson, Zandrak Productions

A lot of people think there is this door that you are supposed to stick your foot in, and once you get your foot in the door everything works out. I don't know of any person that has had a bio written on them who have stuck their foot in the door and opened it slowly. You read the bio of people who kicked the door in, who came in guns blazing and that's the way to stand out in this industry. What can you do that is going to blow everyone out of the water?

"What I have learned from the Hasbro commercial," Andrew tells me, "is that there are huge companies that are entrenched in their views, but there has got to be at least somebody that believes in a new movement. And if you can convince one person, you can convince many." That's the Zandrak mission—to help change the face of advertising through narrative-based stories. "We took this cinematic commercial from Hasbro, and applied it to other clients. It established our brand," Andrew states. A case study of their Moodsnap app commercial comes later in the book—from pitch (in Chapter 6) to production (in Chapter 9).

In fact, Andrew explains, his primary goal is "to build a relationship and build a connection." In the example of Moodsnap, he sent the client work samples, "so he saw what we had been up too. It is always better to take the approach of letting what you do speak for you and not having to explain what you think are your best qualities." He met up with the client for pizza the following day. "Super casual. We went out and we started chatting and I don't even know if it was really us talking about business as much as we were just talking about, 'Wow, you get it.' We started talking about if we can find clients who are willing to buy into this new methodology, this narrative approach to advertising." Ultimately, Zandrak wants to start to "build a revolution that will help change the way people see advertisements, and it became a bigger conversation about advertising in general," Andrew says. He brought it home when he told the client, "I think we have a great opportunity to exercise what we are talking about. With our companies together. And immediately, it clicked and it made sense to him. And we both understood each other's philosophies and that translated well into actually doing work together." By finding the right client—with shared values—Zandrak was able to produce a project based on the vision of their company.

Although not every project reflects this narrative style, it is the mission, the vision that sustains their creativity. They may have to take on other projects, such as editing films for HBO, but they keep their eye on their unique creative approach.

Once you have your mission, the vision for your company set—the desire to do the company and the talent to support the vision—you need to turn that idea into a legal entity, produce contracts for projects, think about music rights, and purchase insurance, which is covered in the next chapter.

Worksheet: Starting Your Business

1. Why do you want to start this business?

   What motivates you to do this kind of work? This is where you need to be honest with yourself and discover if this is something you want to do more than anything else.

2. What is your niche?

   What makes your video production house different from others? What will be your approach? Research other types of production houses in your city. Determine how you can make a difference. You need to make sure there's a market for competition.

3. What is your vision?

   If you're not sure what you're really about, then think hard about how your style and your type of storytelling is different from anyone else's. See what kinds of styles and approaches the competition does and describe how your approach is different.

4. What is your mission statement?

   Similar to the vision statement, this is the public description of what you're really about.

5. Who is your audience—the potential clients?

6. What are you planned expenditures? (See Chapter 5.)

7. How will you become profitable? (See Chapter 5.)

CHAPTER 3
Making it Legal
Filing an LLC, Writing Contracts, Music Rights, and Getting Insurance

With an understanding of the process used to apply the cinematic style to client-based work, including ways to develop a story (Chapter 1) and the foundation for the vision of your company laid out (Chapter 2), the company's legalities must be discussed. Before getting clients, developing a project, and going into production, you need to actually form your company as a legal entity. In this way, the company (and you) are protected. This includes issuing contracts, getting insurance, discovering resources for music rights, and paying taxes. Without legal standing and the knowledge of your rights and the rights of others, your business will not last. This chapter will go over the process of:

- Creating a limited liability company (or corporation) (LLC).
- Using contracts (work with clients, locations, talent, music rights, etc.), including model contracts from Zandrak.
- Thinking about music rights.
- Getting insurance—what you need to cover your gear.

TURNING ZANDRAK INTO AN LLC

Andrew Hutcheson founded Zandrak while studying film at Emerson College in Boston. He ended up editing field documentary footage for an anthropology professor, and she wanted him to travel to India to help do the work and to pay him for the gig. He had run his own business in high school, where he filmed sports videos, creating admissions tapes for high-school athletes applying to different universities. So Andrew created an LLC to make his job official and to protect his assets since it was his first big job. He researched how to set up a limited liability company (LLC) on the web, and established Zandrak.

Andrew was inspired by his father who runs his own business doing color management for print and photo industries. He talked to his father about how he set up his business. "I was reading about how you incorporate, and things that were way above my head. I didn't need a pension and health plan. I'm one guy. But then through searching around I found out about an LLC." Andrew's search began with watching *500 Days of Summer*. "I noticed there was a company listed in the end credits called 500DS Films, Inc. as a production company." Curious, he looked up that company and discovered it was "just the entity that was made for the film." He realized there was a legal entity just for the one film, he explains, "and that every time you make a film, you make an LLC or an S-Corp." There are different benefits depending on the nature of the film and how you plan on structuring your legal entity, Andrew explains. "And the executive producers, the directors, and the head people are part of it."

Andrew dug deeper into the process on how to create an LLC and found that he could file it online. This was in 2010. He was nineteen at the time. He started Zandrak in New Jersey, where his parents live, as it was cheaper with a filing fee of $150. In Massachusetts he would have had to pay $500. Once he set up Zandrak as an LLC, "I used that as the vehicle for me to be able to go over to India and get paid on my first official gig through my company. I was over there for a month shooting and editing three different ethnographic documentaries."

His father had instilled within Andrew the importance of getting paid for work. "'If you aren't getting paid, it's a hobby not a career,'" he told me. "That stayed with me for a while because it's not necessarily something that I essentially agree with." There are filmmakers who do work for free, but they "find a way to make a career out of it! But what my father told me definitely stuck with me—I have to make money." When he was doing the high-school sports videos, his father told him that if he wanted to get more tapes to shoot footage, then he wasn't going to pay for additional tapes. Andrew had to find a way to make money in order to get the supplies he needed, so he became entrepreneurial and charged enough money to make a profit and use some of the money to buy the tapes.

CREATING AN LLC

You may think that since you're not setting up a business with a formal office, administrative assistant, and other employees that you can just work out of your home and not worry about all the legal paperwork. This is called a DBA (doing business as . . . company name). But in this situation, you're personally liable for everything, including your personal assets. If you file as an LLC, and then go bankrupt or are sued, only the company's assets are liable. Your personal property is protected from any damage.

To form an LLC, look up the rules in the state government for your particular state. Each one is different and priced differently. Do a web search and find the .gov website as it relates to LLC. There are businesses that will charge you a fee to file for you, but you don't need to pay someone, since you can do the work yourself and it's not complex. Here's part of the process I went through in the state of Arizona.

1. Determine the relative merits of where you incorporate. In terms of getting sued and tax breaks, this could make a big difference to where you run your business.

2. Do a web search and find the corporation division of the state government. The one you want is the .gov site.

3. At the government corporation site, find the LLC link that takes you to the LLC forms for your state.

4. There may be a lot of forms listed, but you only need a few and there will likely be links to instructions on how to fill out the form. Choose the forms you need. Most of the forms are for changes you may need to make, such as changing an address or correcting an error. For Arizona, I found the ones I needed were:

    a. Articles of Organization

    b. Articles of Organization for an LLC in the state of Arizona. Put in the name of your company—be sure to do a search to make sure your name is original in the state, otherwise the form will get bounced back and you'll need to resubmit with another fee. Input in your name and address, and unless you have the startup funds to open your own office space, the business address will be your home address. If the LLC has a planned limited duration, you will be asked to provide dates. The rest of the form will typically have a place for the name and address for everyone who is a partner in the LLC.

    c. Manager Structure Attachment

      This form simply lists the name and address of the partners in the LLC. If you don't have any partners, then you will write your company name and your name and address. I check off everyone as a manager since we have equal power and stake in the company.

    d. Statutory Agent Acceptance

      You will need to sign off as the legal representative of the company. There needs to be one person who accepts the legal responsibility for the company, and is the contact for it. You will not have the A.C.C. file number if you're just creating the company, so leave this blank. You'll be given the number after you file.

    e. Cover sheet (under miscellaneous forms)

      Arizona has a cover sheet that goes on top of your other documents and is the checklist for your payment. This requires you to check off everything you're doing (with a different form for each). I check off the Articles of Organization and include a $50 fee (each state will be different) for regular service. If you need it before 30 days, pay the expedited fee. Include the name of the company and your email, as well as your name and contact information.

Click on each one and download them, as well as the instructions.

Every state will have different types of forms, but the principle and ideas are the same. You're forming a company, naming it, and you're telling everyone that you're in charge of the company, and where it legally exists (address). In addition to the state forms, Arizona law requires an LLC to place an advertisement in a local newspaper, so that there is a public record of it. Many newspapers will have a standard fee and a form to fill out.

CONTRACTS

Contracts are what keeps your company legal. Andrew Hutcheson at Zandrak hired a lawyer to review his contracts. Once he had a set of contracts that legally cleared, he didn't need to go back and clear every new contract with a lawyer. Online, I supply a set of contracts (courtesy of Zandrak) and other forms that can be used for your work. You may adopt them for your own use, but it is your responsibility to hire a lawyer to make sure the contracts will do what you want them to do for your business. These are offered as educational models.

At Zandrak, Andrew Hutcheson explains, if the client likes the idea and approves the budget, "we make a treatment, this goes hand in hand with the production agreement that we'll make for the client once they like everything. We'll put all of that into a contract, and include deadlines, the schedule, and we make a treatment that portrays everything, the entire idea, how we're going execute it, style, storyboards." Chapter 6 will cover writing and pitching proposals and treatments, but the key point, here, is getting the contract settled.

See **http://kurtlancaster.com/contracts-and-forms/** for the following downloadable contracts and forms:

- **Location Release Form**

  In most—if not in every—case, you will want permission to shoot on location. This form provides it. It also emphasizes that the location is not liable for the production—which is why the production must have liability insurance, and the insurance will go a long way in securing permission from the property owner.

- **Production Agreement**

  The sample production agreement contract provides a strong foundation of protection, understanding, and scope of what a project could entail with a client. If you don't have a limit on the number of edits, for example, a client could keep taking advantage on many edits. But agreeing on three edits with new charges for additional edits protects you from a project that never ends. In either case, you will want to put this material in a contract.

- **Independent Contractor Agreement**

  The parameters of a person's role on a job. Use this if you're hiring someone for a particular task. You can also use it as the basis for a freelance job.

- **Performer Agreement**

  Similar to the Standard Release Form (which covers everyone appearing in your project, including extras and those with nonspeaking roles), the Performer Agreement lays out the specifics for performers you hire for your projects, such as actors. It's tailored to detail their duties, your expectations, and what their expectations are as to schedule, meals, travel, and so forth.

- **Standard Release Form**

  This is key for any documentary interview or any shot that captures a recognizable person in the background of a shot. Get permission from anyone you shoot, so that there are no hassles when it comes to finishing the project. If you don't have a person's permission, you may run into legal issues, especially if you're using it for film or broadcast distribution. When Zandrak produced "Still Life" in New York City, Charles Frank and Jake Oleson shot great-looking footage. Andrew Hutcheson followed in their footsteps, going up to every person they shot and getting a release form signed.

- **Production Quote Form**

  Zandrak's quote sheet. Use when submitting an estimated budget to a client, and include it in your bid.

- **Budget Form**

  A standard film budget. Use it to show what you need to run the budget for a particular project. Some material may not be needed, but it'll cover nearly every type of role in a production.

- **Call Sheet**

  Provided by Stillmotion, this template allows you to set your daily shoot schedule, contact information, and location for your talent and crew.

- **Budget Expense Worksheet**

  This will allow you to calculate your monthly expenses and so determine the cost of doing business. Change the Excel spreadsheet as needed.

In discussing a production agreement, Patrick Moreau of Stillmotion emphasizes that you want to "have a lot of clarity around revisions and process. You can do a wedding, for example, where a couple can have you doing revisions for months if you have not set the right expectations." Building the right relationship and setting proper expectations in writing marks you as a professional. "So if you've done the right communicating and set the right expectations" then everyone is happy, he explains. "We're done when you're happy; we're done when we all come to that same place." This might mean "a big detour and seventeen more revisions than you thought, but sometimes it also means there's absolutely nothing." By putting the expectations in place and allowing room for revising those expectations in the contract, then there's no hidden charges.

Patrick mentions how, "We've done projects where we've turned it in and there's been zero revision—they just love it." But "if we think somebody's being unreasonable or excessive with requests for changes or not improving the story, then we'll make it clear on the limit to revisions that are allowed." In short, he notes, "We'll do one more round of edits and we'll start talking about billing" for additional edits. For Stillmotion, this makes the client aware and encourages them "to get all their thoughts down and make all their changes." By putting it in the contract, then there are no surprises between you and the client.

Furthermore, Patrick explains that in most cases, "Nine times out of ten, if you tell somebody they have to pay a nominal fee of $500 for changes, they'll walk away." This tends to wash out the real suggestions from surface suggestions. "They just don't understand the process and they don't know how easy or hard it is," Patrick says, "and that's really on you as the studio to set the right expectations and process of how this communication is going to go and how we're going to handle changes." Again, this kind of material goes into a contract.

In addition, Patrick notes, there really "shouldn't be a lot of changes because we've all looked at storyboards and we know exactly what it is we're trying to do." If you set the expectation that you make something and they think there's room to "collect everybody's thoughts and meet all of the requested changes"— that's a beginner's mistake. But by writing out the treatment, storyboards, and other expectations, and getting approval on them, then, Patrick explains, "we're not even talking about changes because we're going to operate on the assumption that you love it." By setting that expectation in the production agreement, then there's no expectation for significant changes. The other contracts in the Appendix provide a similar level of expectations for location, performers, and independent contractors.

MUSIC RIGHTS

An additional legal element to think about is the use of music. Most production house projects use some form of music. Not every moment of a project needs music, and I feel that it should be used judiciously and in support of emotional shifts in the story. There are five ways to source music:

1. Original compositions from yourself, friends, or even approaching a local band—but be sure to get the proper rights in writing. Payment will be negotiable, but be sure the rights are perpetual.
2. Sound libraries in music editing software (usually not that interesting), but may be useful for certain sound effects or moments.
3. Track down the rights holder to a song you like (usually the publisher). For example, I wanted selections from several songs from Michael Stearns, who has done sound tracks to some Omnimax films (such as *Chronos*). I was directed to his lawyer and then I negotiated the rights for film festival use and paid a fee of $700.

4. Creative Commons (https://creativecommons.org/). This is where you may find free music. Each song will show the types of rights it offers. For example, you may be allowed to use some songs for free—but only for noncommercial purposes, so be sure to understand the legal code, which is located at:

    a. https://creativecommons.org/licenses/by-nc-nd/2.5/legalcode

    b. A short "readable" version is located here: https://creativecommons.org/licenses/by-nc-nd/2.5/

    c. Websites that offer Creative Commons music are listed on their site, here: https://creativecommons.org/music-communities. They include SoundCloud.com, FreeMusicArchive.org, CCMixter.org, among others.

5. A music licensing site, such as MarmosetMusic.com, MusicBed.com, Sound Reef.com, among several others. These usually include a database where you can search for moods and/or genres of music. You can select the usage and determine the fee.

INSURANCE

Another piece of legal concern is insurance. One of the key ways you can distinguish yourself from the amateur is to get insurance—it'll make you come across as a pro. Moreover, you'll be protecting yourself and your investment, and most importantly, covering any liability (including third-party damage, passerby, talent) in addition to covering your equipment. You may have your equipment covered through renter's insurance or a homeowner's insurance, but once you're running a business you'll need different coverage. Don Pickard of Tom C. Pickard & Co. in Hermosa Beach, California, says that when you're shifting from "that personal status to the commercial, business status, a homeowner's or a renter's policy is either going to exclude it completely or give very, very little coverage."

Even if you start a production company without owning any of your own gear and decide to rent equipment as you need it, you still need insurance. "The very first instance where that person has to go rent camera equipment they are going to walk in and immediately the person behind the counter is going to ask for their certificate of insurance," Don explains. He says that even if you enter someone's property or even try to get a permit to shoot on public property, they may ask for evidence of insurance because of the key need to cover any liability for damages to someone else's property and any possible injury to your talent, crew, or passerby. This is why places you shoot (a business, a public place, venues, and so forth) require proof of insurance—they don't want to be held liable for your project, so you need the coverage to protect them and yourself. Without that protection, you could get sued and depending on the circumstances, potentially lose your business.

Your Legal Rights

Understand your legal rights when it comes to permits. Shooting in a public space, for example, may be supported as a right, especially if you're shooting solo or with a small crew. It's not recommended that you shoot without a permit, but at the same time you should understand what you can get away with, legally. Some filmmakers shoot guerilla style, not worrying about getting permits. For example, as a journalist or freelance journalist, you're allowed to shoot material in public spaces, but if you have a large crew and are impeding traffic (pedestrian or street traffic), you'll need a permit. There are resources such as the website, Lawyers for the Creative Arts (http://www.law-arts.org/) and the advocacy page of the National Press Photographers Association (NPPA) (https://nppa.org/page/advocacy), which offer information, for example about drone use. Municipalities and the federal government (such as the National Park Service) have clamped down on photography and video use, including some bans at different locations and increases in the price of permits. Being aware of these costs and your rights is key in understanding what you will need to do to work on certain projects.

Don feels that there are three elements to think about when considering the motivations for getting insurance as a production company:

1. Protection for your own personal equipment.
2. Protection for rental equipment. Even if you have your own gear, you may need more equipment for a particular shoot. Maybe you realize, "'Oh, shoot, I don't have the right grip equipment, I don't have enough power packs, I don't have enough back drops,'" Don says, "and they go to rent that equipment, then boom, they are faced with having to get insurance."
3. Protection for your own financial interest, which is covered by liability. On another note, this liability also protects locations and by extension, your clients. Most places won't give you permission to shoot in their location unless you have liability insurance, because they don't want to be in a position where they get sued and your production isn't covered. It also protects your clients. Your company is doing the work and you're responsible for the actions of your crew and talent. You're liable, so make sure you have liability insurance.

Choose whichever insurance company best suits your needs. Shane Hurlbut's company uses Insurance West (http://insurancewest.com/spectra.html), and Lydia Hurlbut says this is because they have garnered a strong reputation as well as offering outstanding service for them.

Below, I lay out the step-by-step process for getting a quote from TCP Insurance Agency. These steps are similar to those you would encounter in any insurance process, and I choose to use this company as an example since it covers startup production companies and offers online quotes. As Don explains, "I actually developed an insurance program specifically for a person who is just starting out. Yes, we insure the largest companies but also we insure the guy that is just starting out. Literally in under two minutes they can get a four-page insurance proposal just by typing in a few things. So to find out what their cost is going to be for the year is really, really simple." From there, an agent can refine the quote based on the questions and needs of their clients. "That is when our people advise and help them along in this process," Don says.

In addition to a standard insurance package, Don says there are other aspects they can cover, such as "hiring assistants, or talent, which is a workers' comp exposure. You can get into stock photography or stock video or distribution and that is an errors and omissions conversation. And no two production companies or people are exactly the same. I mean they might be in fashion, they might be in advertising, they might be web-streaming, they might be music video. You know there are a lot of people doing drone work right now. Everyone has their own nuance that affects how their insurance coverage is written for them or not written for them. There is really no blanket statement that says, one size fits all. It's all very individualized." Filling out the online form is the first step in finding the kind of coverage you may need.

At the very least, you'll have an online quote in minutes. Below, I will also go through the big picture, but not every detail, of the quote, as well as the other forms required to submit an application after getting a quote, including the video coverage checklist, equipment list, an online application, and an annual certificate processing fee of $350 (which will be rolled into the cost of the annual premium).

The video and film section of TCP Insurance (http://www.tcpinsurance.com/hd-film-video/) presents a brief introduction, explaining what they can provide for services, including general liability (important in covering negligence while on production), certificates of insurance (which you will need to rent gear and prove to clients that you're covered, such as shooting on location in a public or private space), coverage of your own gear or equipment you rent, errors and omissions insurance (for coverage of material that is put under distribution or broadcast), and workers' compensation (for coverage of employees, work for hire, and talent). This will be similar to any other insurance company quote.

1. Click on "Video & Still Production" to go to the quote request page. This quote will tell you how much your insurance will cost per year, but it does not include workers' compensation if you want to cover talent, for example, nor does it cover errors and omissions (for distribution and broadcast of your work).

2. Video & Still Production Quote. Fill in all required fields and then submit.

3. Ideally, you'll complete this after you've completed your LLC forms and have your LLC accepted. Put in your name, address, phone number, company website, email, the value of your gear, and the estimate of your business income (likely to be the $0–$75,000 category). Submit and you'll receive an email summarizing your quote and listing required forms to fill out before purchasing the insurance. My quote comes to $1,704 per year (which means

I will need to budget $142 per month into my costs of doing business, covered in Chapter 5)—which is reasonable based on the coverage and protection the insurance provides. The required forms include:

a. Equipment Schedule

b. Online Application

c. Insurance Checklist

d. TCP Certificate Processing Fee.

4. Equipment Schedule. List your gear, describe it, including serial numbers, and lay out the replacement cost for a new one. Include all the gear, and be sure to update your insurance agent right away when you get a new piece of gear.

5. Online Application. Fill out all of the required fields, including your name, your LLC name, address, phone number, email, and business website. If you're living in an apartment, don't worry about the premise or premise type unless your agent requires this.

The next section covers the type of work you do or plan to do. I include video production and postproduction (since I do post on my clients' work), listing it as a 50–50 split. If I'm doing more post work, then I would increase the percentage.

They also want to know if you do any specialty work, such as stunts, music videos, drone work, and so forth. I choose none, since I don't plan to engage in anything on the list.

The company also wants you to write a brief summary of the types of work or projects you do, such as weddings, commercials, promotional projects, and so forth.

The next section is a straightforward set of questions that you should just fill out and answer the rest of the Yes or No questions.

6. Video Coverage Checklist. This summarizes insurance coverages that are included or coverages you've selected not to purchase at this time, such as props, workers' compensation, and so forth. These items may be added at anytime during the policy period. The "Pro Pack" includes material you may or may not want. Discuss each item with your agent and how much additional coverage will cost. Each one covers a different element of production and your standard policy will cover your gear and provide liability. The digital film/data covers memory cards and data while faulty stock will cover defective cards.

Note that there is $10,000 coverage of props, sets, and wardrobes—if you need this, then talk to your agent. It's not a bad idea to make sure third-party property damage is covered (especially if you're shooting on location), so if you or your crew break something, then you're covered.

Typically liability would cover this, but "unless an insurance broker understands this coverage, most agents get this wrong," Don explains. General Liability (GL) policies exclude "Property Under your Care, Custody or

Control," Don explains. For example, during a shoot in a home grip equipment is placed on an expensive rug and destroys it. A general liability policy would exclude this; however, third-party property damage may be added to cover such a loss. Don also recommends you ask questions of your agent.

For example, Don adds, "The section on additional coverage will increase your premium, but discuss the importance of each one of these with your agent. Workers' compensation, for example, would cover your talent and people you hire as contract workers (such as a second shooter, PAs, hair and makeup etc.). When production companies purchase general liability and workers' compensation together, 99 percent of workplace liabilities are covered."

After going through theses steps (whether online, over the phone, or in person with an agent or company of your choice), you'll receive a detailed quote. These steps may vary a bit from company to company, but are a form of communication and understanding of your insurance needs. I've include the quote I received from TCP, below (Figures 3.1–3.3).

Notice the liability coverage of $2,000,000 with no deductibles. If you had damages on a shoot and you were sued, you're covered for up to $2,000,000 for any one occurrence with $4,000,000 for all general liability claims during the policy period. Don said the largest general liability claim he's seen in 30 years was for $450,000. Don't limit the need, however. Keeping it high is important.

If you plan to rent equipment for a specific production, such as a Phantom camera for slow-motion shots, then you can purchase rental coverage for 30 days at a time. For example, you can have a high-end camera covered for up to $100,000 for a cost of $250 for that 30-day period (this will have a $1,500 deductible if you did indeed damage it). If you're hired to do an expensive production, which includes a set, props, and wardrobe that is high budget, then you can get coverage of up to $100,000 for $250 for a 30-day period (with a $1,000 deductible). Talk to an agent about each one of these and weigh the costs in the context of your production needs. The rule is, you're better off paying for the protection than not. Roll the insurance expenses into your production budget.

This page also includes optional policies, such as workers' compensation, errors and omissions, employment practices liability (if you have people you've hired and you face a sexual harassment suit, for example), and a cyber liability endorsement (which gives you up to $25,000 on a high-end laptop or several laptops, for example, as well as data protection, among other types of online protection). Take a close look at each of these and discuss them with an agent.

In any case, your client will want you to have the protection to cover the production. You don't want to face a situation where you don't have the coverage and you lose your business because you didn't have the necessary protection. Don't skimp on your insurance needs, even for low-budget productions.

Tom C. Pickard & Co., Inc.

820 Pacific Coast Highway * Hermosa Beach, CA 90254
Tel: (800) 726-3701 * Fax: 310-318-9840
Email: info@tcpinsurance.com

TOM C. PICKARD & CO. INC.
INSURANCE AGENCY
Lic.# 0555411

Video & Still Production Quote

Quote Date: March 3, 2015

(Quote Valid for 30 days)

Kurt Lancaster

Flagstaff, AZ 86001

Phone:
Email: kurtlancaster@gmail.com

Business Operations: Production

Name of Business: Lancaster Productions

Estimated Annual Premium: $1,704

Coverage Type		Limit	Deductible
General Liability:	Per Occurrence:	$2,000,000	Nil
	Aggregate:	$4,000,000	
Owned & Rented Video Equipment: *(Schedule Required)*			
	Owned Video Equipment	$15,000	$1,000
	Rented Video Equipment:	$0	
Business Personal Property:		$5,000	$1,000
Computer / Laptop:	On Premise	$25,000	$1,000
	Off Premise	$10,000	
Identity Recovery		$15,000	$250
Advertising Agency Reshoot:		$15,000	$500
Portfolio:		$5,000	$500
Owned Camera Equipment Rental Expense:		15% of Owned Equip. Coverage	
Rented Camera Equipment Vendor Rental Expense:		15% of Rented Equip. Coverage	
Business Income & Extra Expense:		Actual Loss Sustained (12 Month Limit)	
Civil Authority:		Actual Loss Sustained (30 Day Limit)	

Requirements to Issue Coverage:	Payment Information:
1. Equipment Schedule	Premiums
2. Online Application	Under $2,500: 25% Down, balance divided into 3 quarterly installments.
3. Annual Certificate Processing Fee $350.	Over $2,500: 25% Down, balance divided into 9 monthly installments.
4. Insurance Checklist	

FIGURE 3.1
The first page of the quote lists the estimated annual premium as $1,704. (Courtesy of TCP.)

Optional Coverages

Coverage Type		Limit	Deductible	Premium
Hired & Non-Owned Auto Liability		$1,000,000	Nil	Not Included
Pro Pack				Not Included
Digital Film/Data		$15,000	$1,000	
Faulty Stock		$15,000	$1,000	
Extra Expense		$15,000	$1,000	
Props/Sets/Wardrobe		$25,000	$1,000	
Third Party Property Damage		$1,000,000	$1,000	
Hired & Non Owned Auto:	Per Auto:	$125,000	10% of Loss, Subject to: $1,000 Min;	
Physical Damage	Aggregate:	$250,000	$7,500 Max.	
Workers Compensation:		$1,000,000	Nil	Not Included

Estimated Annual Payroll $0

Short Term (30 Day) Coverages:

Coverage Type	Limit Increase	Deductible	Premium
Miscellaneous Equipment	$50,000	$1,000	$150
	$100,000	$1,500	$250
	$250,000	$2,500	$500
	$500,000	$5,000	$1,250
Third Party Property Damage	$1,000,000	$1,000	$250
Props, Sets & Wardrobe	$100,000	$1,000	$250
Non Owned & Hired Auto Physical Damage	$125,000 per auto/$250,000 agg.	10% of loss subject to $1,000 min. $7,500 max	$1,000

Recommended Coverages:

Workers Compensation (A Separate Policy)

This coverage is required by state law for all temporary or permanent clerical, assistants or production crew members. The policy provides medical, disability or death benefits to any person who becomes ill or who is injured in the course of employment. Independent contractors or subcontractors are usually considered as employees for Workers' Compensation purposes. Failure to carry this insurance can result in paying benefits plus penalties. Even though a payroll service is the employer of record, the production entity must have its own Workers' Compensation policy.

Errors & Omissions (A Separate Policy)

Legal liability coverage, including defense costs, for claims alleging unauthorized use of titles, format, ideas, characters and plots; plagiarism and unfair competition. Also provides coverage for alleged libel, slander, defamation of character or invasion of privacy.

Employment Practices Liability (A Separate Policy)

Provides defense and indemnity insurance for claims arising from the employer/employee relationship. The policy shields employers from claims of harassment, discrimination, failure to hire, wrongful termination, and includes all current, former and prospective employees, directors and officers, even the corporate entity.

Cyber Liability Endorsement ($300 per yr)

This Endorsement provides coverage for Website Publishing Liability; Security Breach Liability; Replacement or Restoration of Electronic Data; Extortion Threats; Laptops Coverage (increased to $25,000); Business Income & Extra Expense Extension due to "e-commerce incident"; Public Relations Expense; Security Breach Expense. Contact TCP for additional information, limits of coverage, exclusions, terms and conditions.

FIGURE 3.2
The second page allows for optional coverage, including Pro Pack items, such as coverage of film stock, props/sets/wardrobe. You may not need or want any of these items—each one you add will increase your premium, so be sure to talk to your agent about the need for each based on your production parameters. (Courtesy of TCP.)

Included Coverage(s)	Limit
Accounts Receivable	$100,000
Accounts Receivable - Off Premises Limit	$25,000
Advertising Agency Reshoot Expense	$15,000
Airline Tickets: theft supplement	$2,000
Animal Mortality	$20,000
Arson & Theft Reward	$10,000
Blanket Additional Coverage Limit	$150,000
Building Glass - Tenant	$25,000
Business Computers	$25,000
Business Income & Extra Expense - Business Computer	$25,000
Business Income Web Site Extension	$50,000
Business Income-Dependent Properties	$25,000
Certain Property at Other Premises	$10,000
Computer Fraud	$5,000
Contract Penalties	$2,500
Employee Dishonesty	$25,000
Expediting Expenses	$25,000
Fine Arts	$10,000
Fire Department Service Charge	$25,000
Forgery & Alteration	$25,000
Garages, Storage Buildings & Others	$5,000
Jewelry, Precious Stones/Metals, Antiques & Art Coverage	$5,000
Laptop Computers - Worldwide Coverage	$10,000
Loss Data Preparation	$10,000
Loss Key Coverage	$2,500
Money & Securities	$10,000
Money Orders & Counterfeit Paper	$10,000
Personal Effects	$50,000
Personal Property of Others	$25,000
Pollutant Cleanup & Removal	$10,000
Portfolio	$5,000
Power Supply Interruption - Extra Expense	$20,000
Salespersons' Samples	$5,000
Tenant Building & Equipment-Req by Lease	$25,000
Transportation in Custody of a "Carrier"	$25,000
Unauthorized Credit Card Charges	$5,000
Utility Services - Business Income	$25,000
Utility Services - Direct Damage	$10,000
Valuable Papers and Records	$100,000
Valuable Papers and Records-Off Premises	$25,000
Water Under the Ground	$25,000

Disclaimer: This is a quote only. It is not intended to represent full insurance coverage. This is not an insurance policy or a contract of insurance coverages. Policy limits, coverages, exclusions and terms of conditions may vary from your actual insurance policy.

FIGURE 3.3
The third page of your quote lists all of the included coverage. If you're not sure what any of these are, discuss them with your agent. Is there anything missing? If so, you may be able to add it. (Courtesy of TCP.)

The included coverage page lists additional areas the policy will cover. You may want to discuss this in detail with your agent, so you understand how each works. For example, Don explains that the Advertising Agency Reshoot Expense "applies to a direct physical loss to photographer/video operations. For example, a camera is damaged or stolen on set, or a power pack is dropped and damaged, the Ad Agency goes and rents additional equipment. If the image did not come out due to damaged lens or the production couldn't get shot as a camera was stolen, or lighting was off due to a damaged power pack, then a re-shoot is needed—and this covers the production up to an additional $15,000 to complete the re-shoot."

GEAR RENTAL COMPANIES AND INSURANCE

Many rental companies are based in large cities, but there are now several companies that allow you to search and rent gear online, which is then shipped directly to you. Most of them will offer damage waiver policies (their own limited insurance), but owning your own insurance will protect you better than most rental companies' policies. Here's a quick overview of some of these web companies and what their rental policies require when checking out gear:

TABLE 3.1

Insurance Policy for Gear Rental Companies

Name of company	Production insurance requirement	Damage waiver	Cover loss or stolen gear
http://borrow lenses.com	No (except on expensive gear)	Yes, for unintentional damage to main item only, not lens caps, for example, and no water or sand damage or intentional damage.	No
http://lens rentals.com	No (except on expensive gear or a high volume of inexpensive gear that adds up to a high cost)	Yes, but it does not cover "theft, water damage, intentional damage, or any other situations which leave you unable to return the items you rented."	No on the standard plan. However, their optional Lenscap+ plan covers theft and loss of items with a 10% deductible.
http://thelens depot.com	No	Yes, but it does not cover "loss, theft, negligence in return packaging or any type of liquid or sand damage. Lens hoods, filters, chargers, cables, missing pieces, and other accessories are also not covered."	No
https://lens protogo.com	No	Yes, responsible for paying 10% of value of equipment should damage occur during the rental period. The optional protection plan does NOT cover complete loss, theft or water damage.	No
http://camera lensrentals. com/	No	No. Customer is fully responsible for repair or replacement retail value of items.	No

As can be seen, due to the limited nature of their coverage, it is important that you have your own coverage to better protect the gear.

WORKING FROM A COFFEE SHOP

A brick-and-mortar office tends to lend legitimacy to a business, but in the age of multistage communication channels through mobile devices, you really don't need it. Meetings can be scheduled in coffee shops and restaurants. If you're working from home, you can write off a percentage of your rent or mortgage, since a part of your dwelling is being used for your business.

Charles at Zandrak pursued a client by researching a list of startup companies that were building apps for smart phones. "We found that startups have a really great openness to new styles of promotion, because they are just trying to do whatever they can to get into the world," Andrew says. While he found that it is more difficult to break down the wall of traditions of how to approach production storytelling with big businesses that have been doing the same thing for decades, with a startup "it's very much they're just building the foundation, they're at a point where they're more open to newer forms and more current forms of advertisement because they can start fresh." David found Moodsnap (see Chapter 9), and Charles emailed the owner, David Blutenthal, "out of the blue, a coldcalling email from his contact form on his website. I pretty much told him that I had connected deeply with what he was creating, I thought that images and music being tied together and finding playlists based on emotionally driven choices is something that is really beautiful and something we exercise as a company." He mentioned that their "philosophies were really in line and that I think it would be worth it just meeting up and chatting." Andrew sent the potential client a link to their best work and he agreed to meet. And this is the point: they didn't meet in an office.

"Only get an office when you can pay the office rent four times over per month," Andrew says. "Nobody cares if your office is out of your living room. It is about your presence and what your perceived values are. We could have met at a coffee shop and you would never have known that we didn't have an office." Because, he adds, "My goal is to build a relationship and build a connection." Since the client was in Boston, it was convenient to meet locally. "I met up with him for pizza the next day. Super casual. We went out and we started chatting and immediately, it clicked and it made sense to him. And we both understood each others' philosophies and that translated well into actually doing work together." And it wasn't "necessarily about a product or a project or how we are going to make money together, but just sharing that philosophy and being on the same page: It was just a really strong foundation for us moving forward as a collaborative group."

You can work from home and meet clients at restaurants and coffee shops. And if you're meeting for business, you can write off the meal (but not alcohol), but you can't write off regular meals, unless you're traveling. It's about making a connection and building a relationship. If you can't afford wireless right away, you can work a few hours at a coffee shop which has free wireless internet. (Although it's recommended that you do get high-speed reliable internet. You'll want it long term, especially when you're uploading large files.)

This chapter has looked at the heart of your business—it's the material that protects you, the people you work with, and your clients. All of this information is designed to give you the tools to get started, to take you down the path in setting up your business. When it comes to insurance and taxes seek out experts in the field. Don't shortcut or shortchange this process.

Now that you have created a legitimate business, you need to make a website with presence and put up a strong portfolio example, so clients can understand your style and see that you do compelling work.

CHAPTER 4

Creating Presence

The Portfolio Reel and Website that Reflects Your Style and Vision

With the business legalities covered, and the actual legal entity of your company registered as an LLC, this chapter shifts to how to create presence for your company on the web and the importance of using the right portfolio sample(s) that expresses your style. Potential clients want to see who you are, the vision of your company, and the professional-level work you've done. The quality of the website and film may make the difference in winning over a client.

THE IMPORTANCE OF PRESENCE

When Andrew and his team (Charles, Kyle, and David) started Zandrak, they developed a philosophy. Andrew tells me: "We didn't really have a presence. And we didn't really want to go out into the world and say, 'Here we are! We are Zandrak hear us roar.' Not until we had a website and an online presence that reflected that body of work. It reflected who we were."

When considering your website—which is the potential client's point of contact—you need to do it right. It's the public face of your work and it must be professional. Andrew believes that "your website and the presence you put out there for yourself is your story—and if someone is hiring you to do storytelling in any capacity, then they're going to expect that you know how to tell a good story. So you should put a lot of care into presenting what your own story is. Why do you do what you do? Everything about your business should reflect that. It should be the embodiment of your eternal philosophy, and your motivation. That's going to come across a lot more effectively, a lot more charmingly, than putting together a top-notch state-of-the-line facility."

In the end, Andrew explains, people don't care "about statistics, no one cares ultimately at the end of the day about what something does for them. They care about how it makes them feel. That's the fundamental law of advertising. You don't appeal to someone's pocketbook, you don't appeal to their brain—you appeal to their emotions."

The danger in trying to make your business unique is realizing that "everyone is aware that they're being sold all the time." If you want to do commercial work, then you need to "convince people that your advertising is entertaining." It revolves around emotions. If you're "trying to land a client or trying to establish your brand," Andrew says, "the more you show your vulnerability and your honesty with your passion behind why you want to do something. The more you try and actually connect with this client, this potential donor, this investor, emotionally, the stronger chance you actually have of making it happen."

When shaping your vision, this can become your brand. Those who start a business "know what the service they are going to offer is, they know what their competition is, they know what differentiates them from their competition, and they know who they are." That's easy, Andrew continues. "But what your brand is—that's more difficult. "It isn't just, 'We are the most cutting-edge, innovative, quirky production company in town'—that's anybody. Rather, ask, 'Why are you doing it?'" Andrew says that if you're networking at a party, "don't ask someone what they do, but ask them what they like to do, or why they do what they do too. A 'what they do' question is closed. 'What do you do?' I'm an author. I'm a teacher. Great, end of discussion. We've just answered the facts." But when you ask the why question, then you get deeper. "Our goal at Zandrak," Andrew explains, "was to not just make commercials or not just make films, but to tell a story in 60 seconds—to do branded storytelling."

Ultimately, "you should find what you're good at and scale it down. So if you live in any city in the world, there are small businesses, there are startups, you can look at the incubators, these are companies that get grant money to help seed the business"—these are potential clients, he says. You can help "build that new business with a video."

WEB-BUILDING RESOURCES

This chapter isn't about how to build a website—there's no space for that, and there's plenty of resources online. One easy-to-use site that allows you to create a website with no coding while maintaining a clean and cutting-edge design is Squarespace.com. It provides free access to a blog-style site, but there are many others. The Grid is another option (http//thegrid.io). The scrolling parallax style found on many cutting-edge websites integrates text, images, and video in a visual way.

Ultimately, there are two options if you're trying to make your life a bit easy when getting a website built:

1. Hire a professional web designer who can execute your vision, your story, through the web design.

2. Use one of several noncoding, but design-friendly, website builders:

- Pagecloud: http://pagecloud.com
- Squarespace: http://squarespace.com
- Wix: http://wix.com
- The Grid: http://thegrid.io

With these tools, you do not need go beneath the hood. Pagecloud requires no coding and utilizes visual tools to create cutting-edge designs. (You can even copy another web page, then replace it with your content. You can also drag and drop designed images from Photoshop.) The Grid uses artificial intelligence algorithms and creates a compelling design for you. Wix uses HTML templates, so you can tweak them if you want, while Squarespace engages in visual design elements from templates. All of these will be cheaper than hiring a designer if you're on a tight budget. Look at good examples of websites you like and find ways to utilize some of the design concepts.

Let's look at Stillmotion's website as a case study.

CASE STUDY: STILLMOTION WEBSITE

Let's review Stillmotion's mission statement, describing who they are:

STILLMOTION IS A FILMMAKING AGENCY AND CONCEPT HOUSE.

By partnering with our team, you are engaging a strategic collaboration of psychologists, authors, social media experts, engineers, educators, and Emmy-Award-winning filmmakers.

We don't make commercials.

We don't sell your product.

We tell stories that make the right audience fall in love with you.

http://www.stillmotion.ca/about

If we look at Stillmotion's smartly and beautifully designed website, we can see how it integrates storytelling with their portfolio—it's one and the same. It tells their story as they show their work. Page one (Figure 4.1) reveals an arresting image (http://www.stillmotion.ca/). This page has since been updated, which most nimble companies do in order to stay current and not come across as stale.

By stating, "Bold stories for those who want to be remembered"—along with a strong, bold image in the background, the site grabs your attention. It tells us that these are image makers and they know how to tell stories with images. There are three menu items below the text—Who we are, Our process, and View films. These will branch you off to new pages, but if you scroll down you find their portfolio (see Figures 4.2 and 4.3).

FIGURE 4.1
The opening page to Stillmotion's website, as of fall 2015. (Courtesy of Stillmotion.)

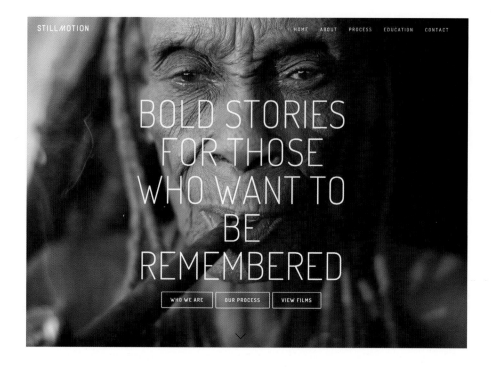

FIGURE 4.2
Stillmotion's portfolio is integrated into their home page and as you scroll down you can see a still from each film along with a link to the film. (Courtesy of Stillmotion.)

5-TIME EMMY-AWARD WINNING FILMMAKERS

TRUSTED TO TELL THE STORIES OF LEGENDS.

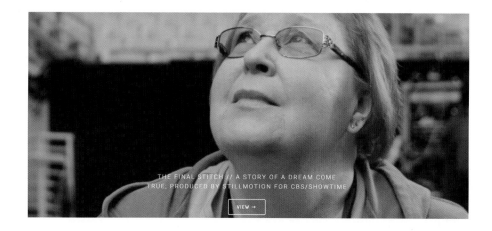

FIGURE 4.3
Stillmotion's book trailer project, *My Utopia*, detailed in Chapter 8. (Courtesy of Stillmotion.)

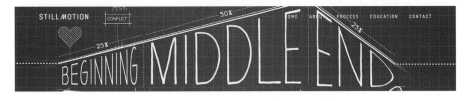

FIGURE 4.4
Stillmotion summarizes their storytelling process through several scrollable pages, beginning with this one, which highlights their MUSE storytelling process..
(Courtesy of Stillmotion.)

SPEAK TO THE HEART TO MOVE THE MIND

We believe that story is based on 4 P's: People, Places, Plot, and Purpose.

The 'P' you put first, or prioritize, determines the type of story you'll end up telling.

Lead with Plot and you have an action movie. Lead with Purpose and you have a commercial. But when you lead with People, we have the potential for an emotional, character-driven story.

We believe that you need to let the story move you, before you try and move the story. And so we start with listening. To the people, places, plot, and purpose that exist within any story.

This is why we feel that the best storytellers are the best listeners - they see and hear what others don't and allow the story to come to them.

As we start in discovery, we are listening for that perfect character to be the heart of the story. The person whom you'd run home and tell all of your friends about. Somebody who can carry the story through their great complexity, uniqueness, and desire.

By listing their major awards (five Emmys), they're establishing themselves as award-winning filmmakers and they place the logos of some of their major clients—from AT&T and NFL to Toyota. They describe the film, "The Final Stitch // a story of a dream come true", a project that they produced for CBS/Showtime.

Scrolling down, the site continues to another project, "The haunting true story of a 10th grade English presentation from 1981," which is a book trailer for a nonfiction book.

By designing their site around strong still images from their film projects, Stillmotion establishes themselves as those who know how to tell stories through compelling visuals. They profile several projects in this way, while at the same time showing their awards and their film education tools, and discussing their project MUSE, a worldwide outreach of their storytelling process (under the tab, process).

"Speak to the heart to move the mind" is a key statement about their storytelling approach and how they educate other filmmakers and students about this approach, which revolves round People, Places, Purpose, and Plot. Their website reflects their storytelling style.

PORTFOLIO FILM CASE STUDIES

Portfolio films should represent the best that you can do, while at the same time defining your cinematic style. In both of the examples below, these are strong films made on very low budgets and may not be as polished as the Chevrolet commercial, "Maddie," described in the Introduction, but they are examples that define their respective companies. At the same time, notice how each film utilizes different forms of the cinematic techniques explored in Chapter 1.

If you don't have a strong portfolio piece, then you will need to create one. When creating a portfolio piece, you're either doing something that's a work for hire, as a volunteer, or as a school project that you did before opening your business. Choose wisely. Make sure the piece is flawless and directly reflects your storytelling style. (I'll discuss the idea of a "sizzle" reel in the worksheet section at the end of the chapter.)

Stillmotion's "Old Skool Café" (https://vimeo.com/42108559)

Stillmotion's "Old Skool Café" video was created as a volunteer piece. It gave Stillmotion a way to practice their storytelling skills, while at the same time drove home their approach and style to attract an audience and potential clients.

We can see a strong sense of visual storytelling revolving around a documentary style—it would set the tone and style of everything Stillmotion stands for. Let's break it down (it's under six minutes) to see what elements worked for them. I provide this analysis not so you can mimic Stillmotion's style, but to get you thinking about how you approach your portfolio film. This should bring home the point that the level of detail and story planning needed to make a good piece doesn't just appear. It takes intention.

The film tells the story of several young adults who have faced hardships—from abuse to selling drugs to violence—and were taken in by Teresa Goines, who opened up a dinner club in San Francisco, run by these young people. It profiles each youth and briefly tells their stories and how this café gave them focus and turned their lives around. It reveals strong interview lighting with key, fill, hair, and background lighting, adding to their sense of strong cinematography. It includes environmental shots of the neighborhood as well as detail shots of the youth working at the café. It reveals the cinematic style that defines their approach to filmmaking and story, showing why this is a strong portfolio film.

The close-ups and detailed shots—beautifully composed and well lit—help define Stillmotion's storytelling style. Story is revealed in action and through the emotional expressions on people's faces. The interviews are not expository and boring, but emotional and engaging.

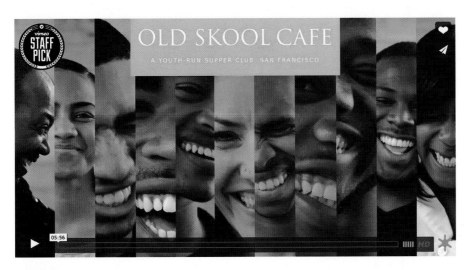

FIGURE 4.5
One of Stillmotion's earlier works, "Old Skool Café"—a project that they did for free—reveals the tone and style of Stillmotion's work. It reflects their mission to tell stories about those who change the world in a better way. (Courtesy of Stillmotion.)

FIGURE 4.6
Tammy Vaitai, the youth general manager and entertainer at Old Skool Café. Notice the composition and beauty of the shot through lighting (the placement of light and shadow). The hair light in the upper right helps separate her head from the dark background. The key light is soft and shapes her face with soft shadows. The background light adds color to the scene and provides depth on a two-dimensional surface. (Image courtesy of Stilllmotion.)

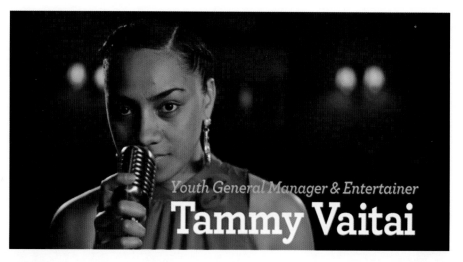

FIGURE 4.7
Stillmotion shows Tammy in her performer role at Old Skool Café. Again, we see the classic lighting setup (hard light on her left, defining the edge of her face and shoulder), a soft key light from the front, classic rule-of-thirds composition, lights on in the background providing depth. (Image courtesy of Stilllmotion.)

FIGURE 4.8
Daniel Bermudez, a former gang member, in the kitchen at Old Skool Café. Notice the shallow focal depth of field—a strong cinematic image that softens the background, making it pleasing to look at (when lit properly) and placing our focus on Daniel. The key light comes from the front right, while a hair light (or kicker) comes in from the left rear as a harder light source defining his cheek bone and separating the black shirt from the background. (Image courtesy of Stilllmotion.)

FIGURE 4.9
Daniel putting on his chef outfit in Old Skool Café. This is a detail shot, revealing his hands as he ties his apron—the detailed action shot placing us into the working atmosphere of Daniel's work life. (Image courtesy of Stilllmotion.)

FIGURE 4.10
A meal is prepared in Old Skool Café. Notice the soft background of the chefs working. The focus is on the food, and the color and texture reveal how Stillmotion wants the story told in a certain way—a point-of-view shot of the food with workers prepping in the background. (Image courtesy of Stilllmotion.)

FIGURE 4.11
As part of the Old Skool Café story, Stillmotion includes shots of the environment, the streets these youths grew up in, to remind us that this environment is part of the story. (Image courtesy of Stilllmotion.)

Patrick Moreau, co-founder of Stillmotion, considers this one of his favorite pieces Stillmotion has ever done. It goes back to the basic storytelling principle which became their vision/mission statement: "Let the story move you before you move the story." He feels that this approach is "very much inspired by anthropology, ethnography, the idea of participant observation, immersing yourself in an environment, living with people, being them, so it's about living, breathing, and doing everything they're doing." He feels that they did this to some extent with "Old Skool Café"—"You go to dinner there, you meet all the kids."

Music plays in the background, but very little ambient sound—if any—is used. This purifies and allows for control of their image and story. (But at the same time, a well-crafted ambient sound design can be a powerful storytelling approach.)

Zandrak's "Still Life" (https://vimeo.com/92040599)

One of Zandrak's earliest portfolio pieces, a project that began as a spec video for Nikon produced after their Hasbro commercial, "Still Life" was co-produced with their friend Jake Oleson, who also co-directed the film. In the end, Nikon didn't accept the work, but that only forced Zandrak's creativity down a new path. They rewrote their narration and decided to use the work as a portfolio piece. The snapshot moments of people's lives around Greenwich Village in New York City—shot with the Phantom Miro camera—combined with a compelling narration script written by Kyle Harper, places this film into a poetic category all of its own. It is one of the "wow" films that make you want to keep watching and helps define what a portfolio film brings to the table when trying to win over clients.

I want to examine this film a bit more closely, since it uses a narration script[1] to help set the tone (as opposed to the Stillmotion piece on Old Skool Café that utilized a documentary style).

The piece opens in silence, with the low angle of a photographer looking up at skyscrapers. The audio builds as the noise of New York City gets louder, then cuts to black as we hear, "How do we hold a moment?" Then we see a shot of a piano player in Washington Square Park and the soundtrack builds around this music. The shots include slow-motion moments and stills as we see a variety of people in New York, including people listening to the piano, a man playfully tossing a baby up in the air, a couple kissing, taxi cabs driving by, a youth on a skateboard, and so on as we hear the narration:

How do we hold a moment?

Is it a sight, sound, sensation?

Does it have weight you can support with an outstretched palm?

Does it have distance you can travel on restless feet?

Or do moments hold us in that instant when we let the universe drip from our soul, seep through our skin, and teach us to feel the difference between existing and living?

How can you capture something that is meant to capture you?

Swimming against the currents of time, unwilling to surrender.

We are concerned with every modern proof of experience and have cheated ourselves out of lives well lived.

Time was always meant to linger, to wrap around us in beauty that captures our minds, astonishes our souls.

The anthem by what we think we know is always changed and what we hoped to find is ever realized.

To hold such moments is to unearth the discoveries of a lifetime.

If only you lived them.

This text sets the philosophical and emotional tone of the piece. Kyle says that the script itself "developed throughout the production, but was primarily written after we had shot (but before we had a complete, locked edit)." This allowed him to focus on the writing and not be "too influenced by what was shot—instead, we wanted the editing to naturally work with the voice over," Kyle explains.

FIGURE 4.12
A photographer looks through his lens and captures emotional moments in "Still Life," one of Zandrak's early works that represents their storytelling style. (Image courtesy of Zandrak.)

FIGURE 4.13
A man plays a piano in Washington Square Park in Zandrak's "Still Life." (Image courtesy of Zandrak.)

The story captures a documentary style and reveals strong composition—and more importantly, emotional moments through that composition. This helps build their soundtrack, as music increases throughout the piece, setting a rhythm that reinforces the visual content of their work, which we can see in two additional shots from the film:

FIGURE 4.14
A man playfully tosses a baby in the air in Zandrak's "Still Life." The emotional beat drives home some of Zandrak's specialty of capturing a story in moments. (Image courtesy of Zandrak.)

Notice how the aspect ratio changes between a 4:3 and 16:9. The 4:3 is used when the photographer is looking through his lens and taking shots, while the 16:9 is used when the photographer is observing with his eye.

FIGURE 4.15
A couple about to kiss in Zandrak's "Still Life." Most of the shots are in slow motion (shot with a Phantom camera), which forces the audience to slow down and absorb such moments. (Image courtesy of Zandrak.)

By highlighting this film as a key portfolio work, Zandrak shows off their creative talent in composing shots, editing, emotional story beats, and writing revolving around a documentary-style shoot. (In Chapter 9 we look at how Zandrak engaged a narrative fiction to tell a story for the app, Moodsnap.) The shots show strong poetic moments revealing a cinematographer who feels the streets and people of New York City. The work forces us to slow down and appreciate moments, to live moments fully, and Zandrak is about finding such moments in stories, to reveal deep moments of appreciation for others—and the fact that they can do this and still sell a product directly reflects their mission as to why they love storytelling in the first place: "Films are how we speak. Collaboration is how we find words. Zandrak is how we have a voice," as they state on the early version of their website before they would become Voyager Studios, LLC.

Kyle's words have power on their own, but in collaboration with Charles Frank and Jake Oleson's directing and shooting, they bring it to another level of visual storytelling (and a compelling musical sound design), and drive home why it makes such a strong portfolio piece. The sense of collaboration comes through when Charles talks about how he let Jake trust his own instinct when shooting the footage documentary-style:

> There were so many instances where we would be in the city and Jake would see something and he would want to capture it. And instead of me questioning or trying to rip that vision from him or push mine onto him, I would completely let him. And in that way he would capture these really organic moments. He would then trust me when I found a shot as well. It allowed us to be real and authentic in those moments. A lot of it wasn't staged and a lot of it was the result of us trusting each other to just capture what felt right for each of us.

Kyle explains how he, Charles, and Jake were "all inspired by an idea called 'sonder,' which is the feeling you get when you pass someone you do not know and realize that they have a fully detailed and deep life that you will never know." After thinking it through, Kyle says, they wanted to focus the project to be "experiential rather than narrative, and the rest was just the result of exploring and shooting in New York City over a weekend."

"Still Life" represents their story, their discovery and honing of their craft, where words and visuals stayed in balance. "Ultimately, people really connect with the piece," Kyle explains, and "some connect more with the visuals, others more with the writing. It's this mix of appeal that I think displays a consistency between our visual and written expectations and execution of the work."

Ultimately, the story of Zandrak is a story about a young group of men creating a cinematic-style production house and being specific in how they would create branded commercials using techniques from narrative filmmaking. The most important take-away is how they establish this information through their website (see http://voyagercreative.co) and portfolio pieces. Andrew agrees, "We established a brand identity and not just a gallery of really cool-looking photos and films that we shot, but rather a philosophy." They want to help build a brand around a story. "We're bringing their brand to life," Andrew explains. They will also be there after the work is completed to help promote it, including providing behind-the-scenes photos. "We do our best to push that spot to get awards, for it to get seen," he continues. In the end, they want to be a creative partner and not just a team that executes someone else's top-down vision. "If they just want to hire someone to do a spot that talks about their new health care, for example, in 30 seconds and put it on TV, we're not interested in it," Andrew states. As a company, he knows what makes Zandrak unique. "We found our niche, and we are continuing to explore that and we think there are a bunch of different ways to do creative branded storytelling," he says. "There are a bunch of different ways to work with companies in a creative way."

And this creativity is revealed in "Still Life." Kyle says it "is one of our favorite pieces largely because of the way it came together. We got an idea, pulled it together super quickly, and had a lot of fun staying up late, traveling, and shooting all weekend to make it happen. All because we wanted to. The love of making films is really what 'Still Life' was constructed around, and that it happened to turn into something compelling for viewers is a direct result of that. This is really why we include it in our portfolio—because 'Still Life' speaks to what we're capable of doing when we love what we're doing, and we want that to be at the center of all of our work."

In the final section of this chapter, several questions will help provide focus to approaches to your website and portfolio.

Worksheet: Creating a Website

1. Write down your mission/vision statement (revise it if needed).

2. Describe your story, which should be tied to your mission/vision statement.

3. Outline your home or welcome page. Is it mainly visual? Which shot will you use? Will you rotate the shot every few weeks to make it look fresh? List several images (ideally, compelling stills from your projects). What text will you use on the welcome page?

4. List your menu items, such as Welcome, About, Portfolio, and Contact. If you have one portfolio film, you might place this on the welcome page and not have it has a separate menu item. Do you want to include a bio? Perhaps you want to include that on the About page. Be honest and show emotional vulnerability.

5. Describe your website style. Do you want a traditional page or a parallax scrolling page? As you scroll down the page, what information, images, or films do you want to provide? Describe them in detail. Draw it out or use examples from other pages and take screen grabs to give you a source of inspiration.

6. Describe the content (words, images, films) on each of your other pages: About, Portfolio, and Contact, or whatever pages you feel you need.

7. Can you design this website yourself? If so, use Pagecloud.com, Squarespace.com, Wix.com, or thegrid.io.

8. Choose a hosting site, such as Bluehost.com, Godaddy.com, etc.

Worksheet: Your Portfolio

I feel that the best samples show complete short works, since clients can see what you can deliver. Creating a sizzle reel, where you show clips from many projects compiled into one short film, may be an alternative or an addition to a portfolio piece. But, says Wes Pope, a photo- and video-journalist who teaches multimedia journalism at the University of Oregon, be sure it tells a story, or "meta-story about who you are as a storyteller." Use your strongest clips and edit them into a piece that expresses strong rhythm and pacing with its own beginning, middle, and end.

1. What is the strongest film you've ever made? Why do you think it's strong? Are there any weaknesses?

Remove the weaknesses. If you want to create a clip or sizzle reel, then gather together your strongest clips and arrange them into a story in your edit. Make sure it expresses strong rhythm and pacing. If the cut feels long, then make it shorter. Using music may help.

2. Describe how it fits with your mission vision.

3. How does it show off the kind of projects you want to do?

4. Screen it to people you don't know. Does it grab their attention? If they're excited, your potential clients will likely be excited. If not, do it over.

PART II
Running an Independent Production House Business

CHAPTER 5

Making Money

The Cost of Doing Business, Generating Income Streams, Setting Up Invoices, and Planning Your Taxes

The web presence and portfolio film helps get you noticed. Before discussing how to get and work with clients, including developing pitches (covered in the next chapter), it's important to know how much you should be charging for your work. It's one thing to do a pro bono project for a nonprofit, but if you undersell yourself with a client you won't be able to stay in business. Knowing how much to charge, thinking about different ways to generate income, submitting invoices, and planning for your taxes all revolves around the daily operations of your business.

THE COST OF DOING BUSINESS AND CREATING A MINIMUM BUSINESS BUDGET

Andrew of Zandrak recommends that you determine achievable goals for your company. "What are the milestones along that map? And when do you want to hit them? And what are the costs?" he asks. "You need to factor in your own life and not only know how much you need to live on, but how much you want to be living on." Once you know that, he says, you can determine how much you need to make per job. What are your expenses? "With the numbers, make a map for how much you need to be making and figure out what to charge your clients," he adds. This section tells you how to make that map.

How much money do you need and how can you generate income? What will it cost you to do your business? You will need to budget for camera and audio equipment, rentals, computers, software, and subcontractors (if not going solo).

One way to calculate the amount of money you should charge for a project is based on how much money you need to live on and how much money you need for expenses. Vincent Laforet, who started the DSLR cinema movement with his piece "Reverie" (see https://vimeo.com/7151244), and now runs his own production house, says that this is fundamentally the cost of doing business (C.O.D.B). He argues in his blog that you need to be making enough money to break even based on the days you work. Using fundamental ideas of accounting—adding in your income and subtracting expenses, then dividing that by the number of days you'll work, you can determine your day rate.[1] This will provide your minimum break-even point, he adds. "If you make more per day on average than your C.O.D.B. you are profitable," Laforet continues. "If you match your C.O.D.B but work fewer days than what you've expected, your business is in the red, *and you're on a path to being out of business.*" And that's when you're in trouble.

In fact, Laforet is surprised by how few people, even freelancers, don't know the minimum amount they need to break even or make a profit. Without that number, he explains, you'll never know what you should be charging clients. Part of determining your day rate, he counsels, is understanding that shoot days are different from preproduction days. If you're only getting paid for shoot days, then you need to roll into your rate the preproduction planning elements of research, story development, phone calls, and so forth, as well as including postproduction time. He continues:

> In other words, if you get paid three shooting day rates, but you actually worked a total of twelve days between pitch, prep, shoot, and post—you need to QUADRUPLE your DAY RATE (or daily C.O.D.B. day rate) to break even for those three shooting days you are actually being paid for.

A company like Zandrak will charge a $1,000 per day for writing a script, for example. So you need to determine if you're rolling everything into shoot days or breaking it down for the client. Stillmotion will sometimes charge a $2,500 or a $5,000 dollar retainer just to do the research, Patrick Moreau says, giving them the time to conduct pre-interviews, do the research, "come back with keywords or what we're trying to say in a concept."

The amount you charge will also reflect the amount you need to run an office— therefore if you're running an office from your home or even a coffee shop (rather than an office space you rent), that will reduce your expenses. You also need to consider the costs of not only getting gear, but updating it. Below is a recommendation based on low-level startup costs. Laforet breaks down the costs based on shooting days over a year, but I prefer to look at it from a monthly budget perspective (so you know what you need to earn per month)— and I include cost of living expenses. Then you can set your day rate based on your monthly expenses depending on the project you work on per month. For some equipment, such as a camera or a large hard drive, you may be able to spread the cost of the gear over two to three years. If that's the case, then divide the annual expenses for these items by two or three, depending on the number of years you want to amortize the payments (I did this for some of the gear, below). I've also divided the chart into two sections—one for the business side of things and the other for personal cost of living expenses. Use this and fill it in based on your actual expenses. I use the numbers below as an example. I've included an Excel spreadsheet that you can download on the forms page of my website: see the Budget Expense Worksheet (http://kurtlancaster.com/contracts-and-forms/). It'll include these figures, so adjust them as needed.

1	Description	Category	Annual costs	Monthly costs
2	Cost of gear and business expenses			
3	Laptop computer @3 years	Business	$2,500	$69
4	External hard drives (12T + several field drives) @2 years	Business	$1,500	$63
5	Software @2 years	Business	$300	$25
6	Camera @2 years	Business	$3,500	$292
7	Lenses @2 years	Business	$1,500	$63
8	Recording media	Business	$500	$42
9	Audio gear @3 years	Business	$1,500	$125
10	Tripod and monopod @3 years	Business	$800	$67
11	Website hosting	Business	$150	$13
12	Mobile phone	Business	$1,200	$100
13	Business cards	Business	$100	$8
14	LLC fee (varies): 1 year only	Housing	$200	$17
15	Legal (as needed)	Business	$500	$42
16	Insurance	Business	$2,000	$167
17	Rent (may be business portion of home)	Business	$3,000	$250
18	Accounting (taxes)	Business	$400	$33
19	**Subtotal for business expenses**		**$19,650**	**$1,374**
20	**Cost of living expenses**			
21	Rent or mortgage	Housing	$9,000	$750
22	Clothing	Personal Care	$1,000	$83
23	Food (including eating out)	Food	$8,000	$667
24	Electricity, water, and heat	Housing	$3,600	$300
25	Car (including insurance and gas)	Transportation	$6,000	$500
26	Grooming	Personal Care	$300	$25
27	Medical	Insurance	$1,000	$83
28	Student loans (varies)	Loans	$4,000	$333
29	Retirement account	Savings or Investments	$100	$8
30	Insurance (renters or home owners)	Transportation	$1,500	$125
31				$0
32	**Subtotal for living expenses**		**$34,500**	**$2,875**
33	**Total expenses.**		**$54,150**	**$4,249**

FIGURE 5.1
Example of an annual and monthly budget expense worksheet.

So, using these figures, you would need to make $4,300/month to turn a small profit. If you plan for ten working days in a month (and include days for preproduction, production, and post), then your day rate would need to be at least $430/day. I would then set it at $500/day, so you turn a profit. You would need to maintain 120 shooting days per year to maintain this. You may need to charge more for a project, of course, when you hire a crew, so doing a production budget is important. This chart tells you what you need to make in order to maintain a real business that covers your expenses. Also, be sure to set aside 25 percent for quarterly taxes, so you will need to add 25 percent to the monthly income to compensate, subtracting out business expenses. This is why you will need a CPA or tax attorney.

TABLE 5.1

Explanation of Expenses

Expenses	Explanation
Laptop computer/three years (MacBook Pro for editing)	You can get any computer, but for video editing getting a high-resolution screen with a fast processor and high memory is a must, and a strong graphics card with dedicated video RAM is key. See Chapter 7 for more detail.
External hard drives (12T home drive + several 1T field drives)	This should cover you for the long haul. Keep a backup of client work until you know for sure you'll never need it again. Some companies sell 4T field drives and these are worth the investment.
Software	Final Cut Pro is $300, but you can also get Adobe's Creative Cloud subscription with Premiere for $30/month, although this will actually cost more over the long term. Avid Media Composer can be purchased for $50 per month.
Camera	We'll look at more options in the equipment chapter, but if you're on a tight budget the Canon 70D costs only $1,000. Ultimately, whatever your primary choice of camera, the fundamental question is whether or not you can get earn back the value of the camera during its lifespan (two to three years). Some people starting out will have one base camera (perhaps the Canon 70D or 6D), then rent additional gear, lenses or cameras, as needed, and charge that rental cost back to the client. Many professional cinematographers take this approach.
Lenses	This price will vary based on the quality of the lenses and how many you need. You can get one 50mm f/1.8 Canon lens for $125, but a set of Rokinon Cinema lenses for about $1,500 will give you more variety. You will probably add more lenses each year as your needs shift. You can also get a Canon 17-55mm zoom lens (f/2.8) for $850 which can cover a range of focal lengths. Renting specialty lenses for particular shoots is also another option.
Recording media	Memory cards are pretty cheap, but fast cards are more expensive, especially the CFast 2.0 cards needed for the Blackmagic URSA Mini, for example.
Audio gear	If you're shooting on a DSLR, then the Tascam DR-70D is a good piece of low budget gear. You'll want a wireless lav (we recommend the Sennheiser G3 series), as well as a solid shotgun mic (such as a Sennheiser or Rode).
Tripod, monopod, and slider	This is standard gear. Adding a slider will give your production cinematic quality with camera movement.
Website hosting	You'll want your own website and a place to host it, such as bluehost.com or godaddy.com.
Mobile phone	You don't need a separate business line. Just use your personal cell phone. If you end up using it half the time for your business, you can actually write off half the monthly bill for your taxes.
Business cards	Good to have when networking.
Creating an LLC (varies per state)	Type in LLC and the name of your state and go to the government website. There, you can get forms and find out the cost.
Legal	You can draft your own contracts, but it's a good idea to have a lawyer look them over, so you may not need to hire a lawyer every year—but keep a record of your contracts and practice due diligence in the legal realm.

continued . . .

TABLE 5.1

Continued

Expenses	Explanation
Accounting (taxes)	You can do your own taxes, but a good accountant (CPA) will know best about laws on how you can write off expenses covering the amount you may owe.
Rent (or mortgage) for living.	Your cost of living is your biggest expense. Know where you want to live and research what it costs to rent a room, a studio apartment, one bedroom, a house, etc. Do you want roommates? What is the size of your family?
Food	Groceries and eating out. If you spend about $30 per day, then $900 is your food budget. If you're thrifty and plan meals from your groceries, you can probably cut this in half.
Bills (electricity, water, heat)	This varies according to city and rate of usage. Do some research and come up with a rough estimate.
Student loans (over ten years)	If you graduated university without students loans, then this is a big saving on your budget, but if you're like me, then you need to factor in a ten-year payoff (or more). Also, you may be eligible for a discounted rate based on your income. Use student loans to get gear if you're still at university.
Car, insurance, gas	This price will vary depending on whether you are buying a used or new car. If you're getting a new car and factor in gas, $500 is a good estimate. You can write off over 50 cents per mile for your travel for production and research, so log your miles. If you're traveling by air or rail, then you can write off those expenses as well.
Monthly income	Set aside ~25% of your income to be safe. You'll be able to write off expenses so hopefully you'll get some or most of this money back. You also may need to pay taxes quarterly.
Insurance	Find out what it costs to fund your own health insurance and put this in your monthly budget, just in case.

With your monthly budget in mind, you'll know exactly what you need to make per job in order to get by month to month and determine if you can run a viable business. As your income stream goes up, then you can expand and grow the company. If you need to, hire subcontractors to do a job right. Simply roll that cost into your budget (you should never be paid less when taking on a crew).

There are several ways to generate income from your creative business.

GENERATING INCOME STREAMS FOR CREATIVE WORK

Don't rely on one income stream, unless it's paying all the bills. Even if it is, it's always good to make extra money in case you have a slow month. Realistically, you may need to have a second job to cover your expenses until you get enough steady clients to make it work. In either case, there's several ways to earn money doing shoots and/or editing and/or sound recording. Another way of securing an income stream is to license your footage. This section will cover all three of these methods:

1. Client work
2. Freelancing
3. Licensing footage.

Client Work

This is pro level—doing full projects for clients, including the entire process of developing clients, writing proposals, giving pitches, shooting footage, editing it, sound design, and delivering a rough cut and a final cut on a variety of projects. Such projects might include commercials, weddings, promotionals (nonprofits, book promos, apps etc.), business profiles, documentaries, and multimedia journalism.

The next chapter will examine bidding, client development, and proposals, but the idea of client work is really what running a video production house is about. If you're a one-person crew, it's possible to work on smaller projects, but as projects become more complex, you may want a crew—and once you hire one, you'll need to increase the budget to cover the cost—so it should impact your bottom line.

As mentioned above, Stillmotion began as a two-person company that shot weddings with stills and video (one person on each). The video was shot in a cinematic style, and as it evolved it focused more on characters and story. Now, Amina Moreau says, they do mostly commercial work, including promotional films. They have not given up on doing weddings, however, although they now only do a couple a year. Furthermore, they're applying the storytelling concept to the promotion of businesses through film, which is one of their goals—"to really tell stories of people doing some sort of good," Amina adds. "Our preference is to work with companies whether they're for-profit or nonprofit that are somehow making the world better. That's where our heart really lies." This is what they look for in clients, she explains. They still do weddings "because they have a certain something—an emotional quality. And the kinds of couples that we now attract are people that end up becoming life-long friends a lot of the time, so we truly do love weddings." Although you will likely end up doing projects which you may not fully love in order to pay the bills, this sense of love and respect for the client is all important to the Stillmotion team.

However, as Patrick notes, when they do the larger promotional projects and commercials, it's something that does need a bigger team than for weddings. "You need producers, you need directors, you need a director of photography (DP). In a wedding you can get away with two people." And the person on camera, the DP in this case, is also "the director and is also the gaffer and is also the production assistant"—which, of course, impacts the bottom line.

Patrick explains: "If we were doing weddings for x amount, then when we shoot a commercial-type project, it become x times five." The budget changes and how you approach the work changes.

To engage in a cinematic storytelling style—and to make your work competitive —then conceiving of a project from the outset differently than a conventional one, requires you to think like a cinematic storyteller. When they were conceiving the book promotional, *My Utopia*, Patrick describes the initial research (after reading Stephanie Henry's autobiographical *If Only I Could Sleep: A Survivor's Memoir*, Emerald, 2014). The typical approach of such a book promo would be to get contacts from Stephanie Henry for the Stillmotion team to interview, and deciding who they might interview to get the story. "It would be a traditional interview," Patrick says, "a whole bunch of people talking about who Stephanie is and why she's awesome and how good her book is, show some b-roll of her and her family and put it together." But they decided not to go the traditional route. When Patrick got to the section of the book that included a high-school essay that Henry had read to her class in 1981, he changed the direction of the project, making the story cinematic at the same time.

"That essay is what would become your trailer," Patrick told Stephanie. "We're not interviewing people, we're not doing anything else, that's too safe, that's too easy. What we need to do is to rebuild that day she read her essay in 1981," he explains. In cinematic storytelling, pushing the boundaries becomes important. This project is detailed in Chapter 8.

Freelancing

In many ways this is the simplest way to run your business. Freelance your skills to other production companies, whether it's in editing, shooting, sound recording, or even sound design or audio mixing. They get the clients and they hire you as part of a team. Make sure your skills are strong and that your work is professional in every way. You can freelance solo projects, like multimedia journalism, or be a subcontractor on a crew-based project for another production house. With this approach, you don't need to worry about getting clients, since you're being hired to do a particular job for another company (including doing freelance video for a newspaper).

Eléonore (Léo) Hamelin started out as a television reporter in France. Eventually she grew tired of the television news gig and she applied and got accepted to graduate school in journalism at Columbia University in New York. Since then she's done some teaching, as well as working as a freelancer, shooting documentary-style short work. As a freelancer, she thought she could just pick and choose her stories. "You're like, 'I'm freelancing I'm going to do what I want,'" she told me, "but in reality if no one see your stories you're losing your time." She warns that you should not commit to a potential story until you know you have a place that it can be picked up and screened. She had a difficult time with that, but, she adds, "As much as you have a bright idea if no one wants to publish it it's not really the way to go, because a) you are doing work for your own hard drive and it's going to stay there, and b) you're also not getting any money." Don't take on a project unless you know you're going to get paid (unless you're doing it for your portfolio).

"It takes self-discipline to make a good pitch," Léo says. You have to make the time to dig into a story and "figure out a main character, get access, and discover why the story is exciting. After that you need to wait and see if anyone's interested in it. And then go ahead with the story." But she feels it's worth it, because it fires her passions:

> The fact that you could do something interesting but also just hold the camera and have so much fun with shooting and editing, it's such a creative process in the end. You know it's a whole new world. I felt like this is what really attracted me to it at the very first. You can still do something that has a lot of meaning and people will watch to know what's going on in the world or to learn about something and yet you can still be very creative about it.

Léo feels that as a one-woman operation, she has full creative control over her material—especially when editing. By editing your own work, she realized, "you are accountable to yourself to get all of the shots. And it makes you a much better shooter in the end because you come back and you're like, 'I can't build a scene with this!' You really just spent the whole afternoon shooting

Freelancing for the BBC and AFP

Dave Eckenrode, Durango, Colorado

I think there are all sorts of different ways you can go about it, but if you really want to go the local video production route, the best thing to do is get your advertising out there (such as the Yellow Pages) and hit the streets and get your face known.

I chose a different model. My model is that of word of mouth for getting local shoots. But I try to farm my work from vendors or employers out of town and the best way that I've found to build that is through networking. My feature-length documentary, *El Inmigrante*, was a success and that allowed me to go on the film festival circuit. Along the way I met several people that worked for different outlets such as the *Agence France Presse* (AFP), and that led me into the network. Right now I shoot commercially for an ad agency and that just came all word of mouth, as well.

I freelanced for AFP for about a year, year and a half. Then I got in with the BBC and I've been freelancing with them for about a year and a half. I produce content for their magazine series which is all online. And they want three-and-a-half minute stories, maximum. Now they want to knock them down to about two-and-a-half minutes. I love working for the BBC because it focuses a little bit more on what I was trained to do in documentary film. And I find the BBC is such a massive, huge corporation, they tend to allow their producers of content to be a little more creative and more flexible than when I was working with the AFP—they were very strict. You had to follow their guidelines to a "T." And basically AFP stories were 90-second news stories that were pretty much like an NPR report with video.

this one thing that was funny and you didn't capture anything else that was going on. It makes you realize that you need a huge variety of shots, but you also need to keep continuity and you need to get good sound."

Working as a crew member is different, since you're ultimately responsible for doing a great job in your one role, whether as a shooter, sound recordist, or editor. In either case, the ability to be a part of a crew or do solo work is something you may need to juggle as you take on different types of freelance work.

Licensing Footage

There are many places where you can license footage. For stills photographers, Getty is one of the large ones, but unless they receive a large volume of licensing requests for your images, this is certainly not a viable income stream—especially as a sole means of support. Approach licensing as something extra, and if it eventually pays well through large volumes, then it'll pay off. Otherwise, make sure your primary strategy is getting clients and setting up freelance gigs. Film Supply (http://filmsupply.com/) provides stock footage that includes cohesive multiclip scenes and prices that revolve around the specific project a client may need. You can apply to have your portfolio reviewed as a potential contributor at: http://filmsupply.com/#modal.

Story & Heart is another example of a site where filmmakers and talented shooters can upload story-driven and authentic footage for worldwide licensing. It's a multifaceted business extension of Stillmotion. In fact, Patrick Moreau explains, it'll become bigger than Stillmotion. It includes an education arm called the Academy of Storytellers as well as a community of filmmakers. Patrick Moreau explains how it's a natural evolution and an important next step for Stillmotion: "It is taking what is best about what we have created over the past number of years with Stillmotion" and turning it into a business model: "Connecting with filmmakers, sharing ideas, collaborating, and then trying to help people be better at what they do. It's evolving that model exponentially. Other people teach through the Academy and collaborate on projects through the community." It goes back to their fundamental mission: Story first and being "connected to what you do through collaboration to a much greater degree." You have to own the rights to the footage and, if you're using client work, you need to put that into the contract.

"I'm going to work really hard shooting a project, so I don't know if I want to give up my rights to all of it," Patrick says. "For example," he adds, "there's a project that I just submitted a creative estimate for and they came back and said, 'You know we love you guys, we love the philosophy, and we think we are a really good fit, but it's above our budget.'" When that happens, Patrick explains, then they'll work with the client. They can cut things out of the budget in order to lower it. "We can cut here, that's what it's going to result in, or we can give you an overall X percent discount if you let us retain the copyright, and they went for it . . . Because they wanted us enough and they also wanted the price brought down enough that they were willing to forego ownership of the footage," Patrick explains. "They get a great film out of it, and they get no compromises in the quality of their work. Since in this case we don't own the footage we will relicense footage to earn additional money." But that doesn't mean they want to use the footage *carte blanche*. "We won't necessarily show their product in the footage or create anything like it," Patrick says. "We're not going to relicense interviews, but we will use b-roll from the city that we're shooting in. We're starting to encourage other filmmakers in the city to think about ways to earn money from licensing footage."

Why is that important? It allows the client to get their film on a lower budget, Patrick explains: "You can hopefully make the money back you lost with the lower budget, while at the same time creating new relationships from the process in licensing your footage."

Why did they decide to go this direction? To help filmmakers. "As a filmmaker 95 percent of what I shoot sits on a hard drive and nobody ever sees it and that is stuff that I have poured my heart and soul into. I have no revenue coming back in." Moreau feels that's not a viable option, nor is it sustainable. "It's hard to have something this physically demanding as filmmaking, this many hours, and after 30 years of my life I'm going to put my camera down, and then what? How do I do that? I better hope that I've saved enough money for retirement!" He feels that Story & Heart will allow people like him (as well as many other filmmakers) to "create a way that all of this stuff that I've cared and lovingly poured over can not only create revenue for me but can also help other storytellers." Despite the fact that the revenue stream may be small, the hope is that it'll get bigger.

But Story & Heart also engages a collaborative approach to filmmaking, beyond just licensing footage. Traveling the world shooting stories and giving workshops, the team at Stillmotion discovered something important. "One of the biggest things we learned," Patrick tells me, is "nobody wants to be an island. Everybody wants a team. They want to work with people." But rarely do they know how to make it happen. Through Story & Heart, "we can bring people together and really celebrate that idea of sharing our ideas, sharing our stories, sharing our footage to all."

And this is the collaborative element. If you need footage from across the world for a commercial, for example, which could cost a lot of money, then "rather than me having to go out and film it," Patrick believes, "I can actually save money to get footage that was shot by you that you cared about, that has story in mind, that is intentional, and if it fits with what I'm doing, we both win in this situation." In fact, he feels that it "lets everybody win", because it "helps the storytellers using the footage, it helps the storytellers selling the footage, and it brings people together in a new way so that we can collaborate on projects."

They claim it's the "world's first story-driven platform," and the website (storyandheart.com) states how the client can "compare clips with similar lighting, characters, and settings to determine which work best for your project. Even better, sequence them together to tell a cohesive narrative that looks like a custom shoot."

Justin DeMers, who worked early on with Stillmotion when Patrick and Amina were still doing weddings, now runs Story & Heart. He feels the Story & Heart model works for freelancers, studios, and as a work for hire. He feels that its soul revolves around the needs of filmmakers in a world where concepts like saving for retirement, vacation, childcare, don't exist for them. "And they don't exist because it's the nature of the industry to be largely a work for hire, where you work for a project, you get paid, you go onto the next project." Justin adds, "It's amazing to know that someone else has made use of something you put your heart and your blood and your sweat and your tears into in order to help bring another story alive."

Placing footage online and collecting licensing fees from footage you've already shot can be an additional revenue builder. "Very few filmmakers haven't even thought about or haven't even been introduced to the idea of footage working for you long past it's been delivered to the client," Justin explains in their office. So they want filmmakers to submit footage to them so that they can join a community of other filmmakers, being involved in that community so you can help and be helped by others when you need it, and to "have your work constantly work for you." It's a great feeling to get an "email at two in the morning saying you've licensed some more footage, and you had to do nothing for it. It's constantly working for you." However, you need to make sure you own the footage if you're working on a project for a client. While the footage may be only generating a small income, over the long term it may pay off as an additional, albeit modest, source of income. (Don't expect to give up on getting clients as you won't be living off the royalties of licensing your footage!)

INVOICES

When charging clients for your work—and after the proposal process and a contract that lays out the payment terms—invoice them. Use an online form for invoicing or get an app such as FarmersWife.com (which also includes scheduling and management tools). There are many sites that set up invoicing and some are free. Invoice-generator.com is one such site. Some sites require a monthly fee—but many of them will allow you to use Stripe and PayPal for payment processing. Most provide a template allowing you to upload your company logo and include your name and address as well as the client's name and address. Add an invoice number, date, a date due for payment, as well as a description of the service, the rate, taxes, as well as additional notes and terms.

Keep track of all invoices (and all expenses). It will be much easier if you have a separate checking account and credit card dedicated to your business than trying to sort through personal checks and accounts. You will want all of these for tax purposes.

TAXES

When you're generating money, you'll need to pay taxes, which is another aspect of running your business smoothly. This book does not profess to offer professional advice on taxes. The information provided here is for representative purposes only. You will want to hire a certified public accountant (CPA) or tax attorney to work with you on your taxes. For many years I filled out my own taxes and estimated my work and I didn't realize I could have written off more expenses and actually could have saved money. Seek and use experts when it comes to taxes—even if you're a one-person operation and not making that much money. For example, as a side business I made just under $4,000 in video work in 2014. My expenses (supplies, purchase of an EVF for my Digital Bolex, trips where I can write off my mileage, and airline fares exceeding $5,000) meant I took a loss—no net income from the business—so I did not have to pay taxes on that income. If I didn't write off expenses, I would have owed over $1,000. Also, be careful that you are generating income and not doing work that looks like a hobby (which cannot be written off and may lead to an IRS audit). Your CPA will give you forms to fill out and then he or she will fill out your tax forms.

So the first step to take is to hire a good CPA or tax attorney. They will save you money. You will need to pay taxes and if you're contracting out your services and/or operating as a single business owner, you will have to pay estimated income taxes (the money you make) and self-employment tax (social security and Medicare taxes) on a quarterly basis (see http://www.irs.gov/Individuals/Self-Employed). Ask your CPA for details.

The good news revolves around all of your expenses—travel (including car mileage), research, wi-fi, mobile phone, equipment and gear purchases, postage, supplies (memory cards, printer cartridges), business meals—everything relating to your business can be written off in your taxes. Every piece of gear, supplies, percentage of your mobile phone used for business—everything. It could mean the difference between owing money and getting a tax refund.

If you work from home (such as an apartment), a part of your space can be used as a percentage of your rent or mortgage and can be written off as an expense against your taxes. If you have an 800-square-foot apartment and it costs you $1,000 a month in rent, you could say you use 25 percent of the space for your business, and write off $250 per month, which comes out as $3,000 for the year. Same with your phone, wi-fi, electricity, and other utilities. If your calls are about half personal and half business, then you can write off half of your mobile phone bill. If you travel to a shoot, whether driving or flying, or make an overnight trip (hotel expenses and restaurant expenses, the *per diem*), you can write that off, too. I wrote off my ticket to Jordan at $2,847, which offset my income of $3,500.

You can even write off part of your car. If you're driving to locations to shoot and meeting potential clients, you can keep a log of your miles (from your odometer) and write these miles off against your income. If you're using the car for personal use, then you'll compute a certain percentage for work and personal use respectively. Some gear and computers can be depreciated over several years. As long as the life of the property is more than a year, you may use the value of the property as "an annual allowance for the wear and tear, deterioration, or obsolescence of the property" (http://www.irs.gov/Businesses/Small-Businesses-&-Self-Employed/A-Brief-Overview-of-Depreciation). A good CPA or tax attorney will know all the ins and outs of what you need and what you can write off, and they will likely save you a lot more money—worth the fee they will charge.

The key point—keep your paperwork organized. Keep your receipts (even records of purchases with your credit card, which can be found online on your credit card's website), invoices, a log of your miles for travel in your car, a list of your *per diem* (the amount you can write off for food and hotel stays), airline ticket purchases—everything! Put this material in a folder. I tend to put everything together for each project and staple it all together (including all receipts, maps, travel log), as well as all equipment and software purchased during the year.

For example, if you made $30,000 from your production house work (gross income), and you had $12,000 in expenses, you would only be taxed on earning $18,000. If you paid someone $1,000 to help out on a shoot, you can subtract it as contract labor and you'll need to fill out a 1099 form, unless they're an hourly worker, and then you'll need a W2 form. However, if you placed that in your budget and was paid by the client, then you wouldn't be able to include it.

One such company that does accounting for film projects, documentaries, internet projects, commercials, industrials, including low-budget productions, is ABS Payroll (http://abspayroll.com). They cover employment and payroll taxes (useful if you have a staff and/or a crew for a particular production), information about hiring independent contractors, and information about engaging in loan out companies (subcontractors with their own businesses). Their services also include production accounting, payroll, and workers' compensation insurance. Their forms include a SAG form, request for a duplicate W2, a W9 form, employee time card, weekly crew time card, direct deposit form, request for contract services letter, and employment of a minor (see: http://www.abspayroll.net/industry-forms.html).

Here are some other recommendations:

- Open a separate business account at a bank or credit union distinct from your personal account.
- Use a credit card that's dedicated to business use only.
- Balance your accounts every month.
- Keep all of your receipts, checks, invoices, and any paperwork related to your business.

- If you have a staff, you may want to consider subcontracting payroll (if you're legally allowed to do so).

Taxes can be complicated and laws change every year—this is why it's important to budget in a professional CPA or tax attorney and let them advise you on your legal rights when it comes to writing off expenses for taxes.

Worksheet: Running a Business

1. What are your startup costs?

   This includes camera gear and accessories, mobile phone, computer (powerful enough to edit projects), and so forth.

2. What are your living expenses?

   Scope out the cost of renting a room, house, apartment (studio, one bedroom, two bedrooms), utilities, phone, food (groceries, eating out), clothing, car, gas, insurance, public transportation, and so forth. This is the minimum you need to break even and make it work for you. If you're in deficit every month, then you don't have a viable business. If you're making a profit, that's good news and you should save money to cover deficit months.

3. What is the cost of doing business?

   What's the bottom line on what you need to make per month to cover your cost of living and the cost of your gear?

4. Income stream plan.

   a. Client-based work

   - Be sure you have at least one strong cinematic storytelling sample on your website (see Chapter 4). It should be flawless, compelling, and representative of your style. If you don't have one, then find a nonprofit that needs a video and talk to them about making one for free. This will give you legitimacy and perhaps through word of mouth you will get several additional paying clients.

   - Potential clients. What kind of work do you want to do? Can you do a strong wedding video, a nonprofit promotional film, a film promoting a local business, and so forth? Think about the type of stories you want to do and research and make a list of potential clients. Look up their websites and see if they have a video on their homepage. If not, then show up in person and talk about the potential of putting together a video for them.

   b. Freelance possibilities

   What skills do you excel in—shooting, editing, sound design, sound recording? It's possible to get hired on existing projects with bigger video production houses. Some may not have a full crew and need to hire out services (subcontracting). Research other production houses and meet them. Talk to them about your skills and your availability to work.

   c. Licensing footage

   You've got footage. Research licensing companies and find the best one for you. Story & Heart may be the one, but there are others. Choose the one that best suits your needs.

   - Identify your best footage.

   - Send footage to licensing business.

CHAPTER 6
Developing a Client's Story
Making a Connection, Finding the Story, and Writing a Pitch, Proposal, and Budget

Now that there's an understanding of what you need to do to stay in business, we now shift, in many ways, to the heart of this book—the reason you have your business in the first place. This chapter starts out with Amina Moreau discussing how to interact with and treat clients, followed by what Stillmotion uses in their bid and treatment process. I also explore how Stillmotion use keywords as a way to communicate with a client. It also includes some ideas on brand strategies that you can apply to your clients (making you, in many ways, a person who will help brand a client's product or service through your video). It then moves into a workshop on the use of keywords (developed by Stillmotion) and utilized by Zandrak in helping them develop a story for the Moodsnap app. Shifting to a visual pitch model, the book examines the one Zandrak created for Moodsnap, which led to a successful contract, including a discussion with Charles Frank on his process in creating the visual document— and how the project ultimately changed from the initial pitch. This is followed by a script that Zandrak's Kyle Harper wrote for a promo video developed for Northern Arizona University's Honors Program. Lastly, I describe the process of creating a production budget quote.

MAKING A CONNECTION AND WAYS TO FIND A CLIENT

The foundation for your business revolves around the ability to make connections with people. This is why you need to put yourself out there and network. (In some cases—especially when you get established—you may end up getting clients through advertising agencies.) In either case, networking is the process by which you put yourself out in the world and let people know who you are and what you do. It's where you engage with others at a real level. You can't tell a client's story if you don't talk to a client. And if you're superficial or don't care, then you'll end up finding no clients or getting clients who are also superficial and don't care.

Alex Buono, Director of Photography for the *Saturday Night Live Film Unit*, in an interview in *Film + Music*, gives this advice about networking:

> The way you can control your career is by getting to know people, actively going to film festivals, watching films, engaging with the filmmaking community, sharing your work, helping people. When I was first starting out I worked for free all the time just to meet people. It's absolutely better to be working on something for free than to be sitting around doing nothing waiting to get paid.[1]

There's three aspects to networking, according to Amina Moreau of Stillmotion:

1. "It's being involved and making the effort to know what other people in the industry are doing. Whether they're fellow filmmakers or they're manufacturers, we have a lot of close relationships with manufacturers of gear because we use them first of all. But then second of all we can provide feedback, and third, if we can support them through helping them market their stuff because we honestly believe in it, then why not?"

2. "Develop friendships in the industry." You're not just treating a shoot or people like a tripod. Connect to people as people.

3. "Kindness goes a really long way," Amina adds. "I think when you develop relationships with people that are more than just as a business but you actually care about them and you make the effort to follow up a week later, and ask, 'How are you feeling? How are you doing?' It's amazing. I'm not saying I do it as a business tactic, because I do care. When you put the effort into caring about people the way that you do about your own family—they notice. And that means in the future they want to work with you more, or they want to help you more if you're in a bind, or if you need a favor, such as needing exposure or something like that. This is what Stillmotion is founded on—this idea of let's do something that makes the world better. I almost don't care in what way, let's just make it better somehow. Let's leave our mark and not do something for ego's sake. People need to start caring about things that will improve it and not just selfishly do something just to get ahead. A lot of people feel like if they can't do everything, then why do anything? Nobody can do everything, but if everybody did a little bit of something, it can make a difference."

Ultimately, if you're trying to run a business and get clients for that business, you need to be excited about your work and about your client. "Excitement is contagious," Amina exclaims. "Engage in something you truly believe in, something you live and breathe," she adds.

Where can you find potential clients? You could place a standard ad in Yellow Pages or its online equivalent and people may call you. In some ways you need to go to conventions and networking parties for the types of business you might want to do.

Andrew Hutcheson at Zandrak recommends that you look at startup companies. "There are dozens of these in every city, and sometimes they're on college campuses, sometimes they're in financial districts, universities might have some business incubators. These will have potential clients that are just getting started, and if you're just getting started any business knows that it needs an online presence and it needs a video presence. It's still the most effective form of marketing. That's an opportunity for you to meet someone and make a connection. They probably won't have all that much money, but it's a place where you can get started. You can help out a nonprofit, or a local business that wants to expand to a certain extent. You need to market your services."

But the key point isn't to just tell people they should hire you to do their video. "They're probably not going to buy it," Andrew states. It turns them off. "But if you discover what their problems are, and how this video will solve the problem, people will pay for a solution," he explains. Take time to figure out how to sell yourself and your services to people and how to do it "in a way that it's in their best interest to do a video with you," he explains. "A cornerstone of media is just making people feel convinced that they're actually getting the better end of the deal paying for this service."

To make it happen, you must find out why they want a commercial or a promo. "Ask that question," Andrew says. "Why do you want to make this commercial?" They will give you a reason, he continues, "then it's your job as an artist and a storyteller to interpret that need and discover the emotion behind it." This is one of the key points that might set you apart from others. "You are not selling someone on a shoe that's lighter and that's made from a more durable rubber," Andrew contends. The factual stuff. "You are selling them on a shoe that makes them feel that at any minute they could be doing parkour. You are not selling somebody on the car that has the V8 turbo engine. You are selling them a car that makes them feel badass. Find the emotion and then you sell them on the emotion in the commercial." That is how Zandrak approaches their branding projects. "We work with a brand and it's our goal to find out what their agenda is, what they want to accomplish, and then we translate that into a commercial that is emotionally appealing."

DEVELOP A RELATIONSHIP FIRST, THEN DEVELOP A STORY

Before Stillmotion gets to the money aspect—the estimated budget—they "put people first." As Patrick Moreau explains, "We're not talking about prices and production and a lot of that stuff at first. We're getting to know the people. What makes them different? Whether it's a product or it's a service, we want to know, why does it need to exist? Who created it?" He would rather, as he says, "get at some of those deeper questions, as opposed to just getting a call from a coffee shop who wants a commercial and asking them such business questions, as 'How long do you want it to be? Where's it going to air? What's your time frame? What's your budget?'" That's taking the tripod approach. Rather, Patrick says, they take this process in steps, because "nobody wants to be a tripod, nobody wants to be told where to stand and how to shoot and what to do. We are storytellers and we want some sort of creative vision. And we can gain that by agreeing not on what we are going to do but what we were trying to say," he explains.

So instead of those types of generic questions, they're more interested in asking:

- Why did you open a coffee shop?
- Why do you love coffee?
- What is this about for you?

In this way, they're making a connection with a client, developing a relationship. "We get to know them and explain to them what makes our process different and what we believe a story can do and how we would approach it," he adds. "Those are really our first conversations. It's about putting people first, moving people emotionally, how we'd approach it, and that so much of this work is in preproduction." In addition, if they're local, Patrick says, they prefer to meet clients in person. "Amina will often Skype with them if they're not local, and try to make it as personal as possible."

The questions that ask "Why?" and "What's in it for them?" comprise the first steps in getting to know clients—and it's the process that determines whether or not the Stillmotion team clicks with the potential client. If that process goes well, they start talking about their coffee shop video, for example, and provide rough estimates based on what they think the preproduction and production process will be. "We provide rough estimates with wide ranges because we try not to pigeon hole ourselves without nailing down the story first. So we might give somebody a range that's going to be $25–40,000 and explain that we need to dive in and really get to know what the story is before we can be specific with the budget."

"We definitely don't want to just develop a concept or idea until we know what the story is," Patrick adds. "So the first thing we do is develop keywords— which helps us determine what we're trying to say with the project." (The keyword development is explored later in this chapter, and in Chapter 8 in the case study on Stillmotion). They'll work with and present these ideas to the client. "After we agree on what we're trying to say," he adds, "then we'll come back with the creative." Getting into this development phase may take a while, and with a large client Stillmotion will ask for a $2,500–5,000 retainer just to do the research, just to come back with these keywords or what they're trying to say in a concept, Patrick explains.

At this stage, Patrick says, "If they love the concept and the direction of it and if it's within their budget then we'll go with that concept." Of course, they have the initial conversation about what their budget is so they can see if the concept (along with the preproduction and production planning) is reasonable for the client's budget. However, Patrick tells me, "If in doing our research we feel like the story needs something completely different, then we'll just be completely up front with them." If they have a certain budget, and Stillmotion feels they can do it for less, they'll let them know. In some cases it may be more. It depends on the parameters of the project.

Because of the step-by-step story process they have developed—how they make it "tangible and clear on the process and expectations," Patrick says, "clients tend to feel great when we come back and say here's the keywords based on what we discussed, about what you want to say in the video, and this is how we'll approach it. For example, we might tell the client," he explains, "If one of your keywords was global and you guys have offices everywhere we can't just shoot here, we need a large travel budget. We'll provide different options and that kind of thing. That's how we work through it."

Patrick brings the point home about the importance of approaching the project creatively based on story—and why they emphasize the importance of their MUSE story development process (outlined in Chapter 1). It's a tool for working with clients, to get clients on board with a creative vision shaped by the Stillmotion team's passions. Because there's a shared vision there's little to no conflict with a client when you go into production. By going through these steps, Patrick says, "there really is a lot less room for disagreement on how you're going to approach the film creatively":

1. Developing keywords.
2. Setting expectations.
3. Clarifying what is trying to be said with the project.

If you listen to the story it really has one shape, one form, and so then the debate becomes, 'Do I really want to tell this story in an authentic way because we are going to listen to keywords and come back to you with the best way to express this for you?'"

What may happen, however, is getting a CEO of a company telling you that they want the story done in a different way, even after you've developed your creative vision for it. "They want to put a spin on it," Patrick says, and when this happens we know that "we're getting sold something, we're getting told something"—these "are not the stories we want to tell." These are the standard commercial projects that fail to engage storytelling in the cinematic style. "Our job," he explains, is to try to "go back to the idea that people are going to connect with something that has substance for them, that has purpose, that offers them value and if you're trying to shift or spin or add another slant to it that is not authentic, people are going to sense that and you're wasting our time and your money."

If a client doesn't want to utilize Stillmotion's storytelling approach, then they won't do the story. That's rare, however, Patrick explains, because they're so clear in the storytelling process—using keywords—and developing what they're trying to say in the project. Even when they run into issues with clients during the planning stages, they can use those keywords as a "filter" through which they can run every decision.

For example, a client might say, "'Hey, why don't we interview this person or why don't we do this?'" Patrick says. "We would reply, 'Okay, well, how does this express your keywords? Does it or does it not?'" Sometimes they'll have ideas the Stillmotion team hasn't thought of, but sometimes they may just revert to an old concept, such as interviewing the CEO. Patrick explains that they would push back and say, "'One of your keywords is flat, meaning you don't have a hierarchy so we probably shouldn't have the head person . . . we should probably have people that are all on the same level, and then they might realize, 'You're right, we don't have to do that' . . . And that's exactly how those conversations go when we use our tool to drive [the] creative and get agreement and communicate why it is we're making those decisions."

Before looking at a case study, let's discuss what it means to help a client deliver their product, message, or service. As Andrew Hutcheson noted at the beginning of this chapter, you are discovering a client's problem and offering them a powerful solution through your film. Let's dig deeper into this.

HELP YOUR CLIENT BE THE BRAND THEY NEED TO BE

Be the thought leader in how you approach client-based work. Lead your client down a path that will allow them to be leaders and visionaries. In this way, your work will help their work and this is where your creativity, your mission, your vision can help coincide with your client's need for a solution—and this is the real reason why client interaction is *the most important thing you will do with your company*. It's not about how cool your gear or video is. It's about how cool you'll make your client. In this way, you are helping your client brand their product or service through your video.

Glenn Llopis, President of the Glenn Llopis Group, discusses six brand strategies in his *Forbes* article, "6 Brand Strategies Most CMOs Fail To Execute".[2] He feels that if you copy what others are doing, you're failing to be creative and will fall behind by just doing what has already been done. If they need to "reinvent" themselves, Llopis says in the first step of his brand strategy, be there to guide them. If you or they are always reacting, then you and they are not on the cutting edge. Below, you'll see how Stillmotion and Zandrak are thought leaders in the video production house business through their approach and style of work. You need to help set a vision for your client that puts them on the cutting edge through the messaging that occurs in the film you're creating.

In addition, is your video—and your approach to communicating your vision for the client—relatable? A potential client shouldn't be trying to figure what you want to do. You should express laser focus. So, Llopis feels that that identity should be "deliberate" and "forward thinking," a key point of Llopis' second brand strategy. So when you're creating a piece for a client, whether it's a work that highlights a product or a service from a nonprofit—whatever your video is meant to do—be sure it helps your client *with their identity*. Remember, you're trying to do two things with your business:

1. Let potential clients know who you are and what you do (your vision)— and this should be communicated through your website (from Chapter 4).
2. Help solve a client's problem—your video should be the solution for their needs in getting their product, message, or service out. They're looking for clients or customers through your video.

In this way, we move to Llopis's third point, that you're helping to inspire and communicate hope—and this will make that message last. What does this mean to the production house leader? Create projects and attract clients that inspire people through the work you create for the client. In the case study with Zandrak below (and in Chapter 9), we can see how the video they did for Moodsnap helped reveal the lifestyle of a young couple on a road trip that reflects the hope and lifestyle of Moodsnap's app. If your client sees you engage in such work, they will likely want you to help discover message strategies that inspire and give hope to their clients through the stories they want you to create for them.

In his fourth strategy, Llopis argues that you should be willing to continually innovate and be proper with your timing. Again, if you remain innovative you will support your clients in being innovative as well. In many ways, this is why you cannot be a tripod, as Patrick Moreau emphasizes about Stillmotion. You have to be a brand strategist for yourself to attract clients, and then be a strategist for your client through the video you create. If you're doing your job right, showing your excellence, then your potential clients will begin to know you for your excellence and they'll take note. As a visionary for audio-image storytelling, you should be helping your client tell a story that puts them on the cutting edge, and if you're trying to help them with the release of a product, service, or message, you should deliver on that promise.

There's an element of "corporate social responsibility" that you and your clients should think about, says Llopis in his fifth strategic point. If your projects are able to help improve the world then more opportunities will open up. This kind of approach, where you are thankful and socially responsible, will likely attract other clients who appreciate such stewardship.

Llopis's sixth and final point discusses the idea of brand legacy—how does it impact the business or lifestyle? In other words, does your vision and mission for your company really do what you want it to do? Is it designed simply to start or run a business so you can do any type of job, or does it help sustain the businesses and nonprofits, the lifestyle your clients are trying to shape through their product, service, or message?

If you can apply these concepts in a visionary way to the film you're trying to create for a client, you'll be in a position of leadership in helping them set that vision. You're the professional storyteller. Help guide your client through your creative and visionary process. After making a connection, developing a shared vision with the client, the next step usually begins with a treatment as a way to communicate your initial vision.

WHAT'S IN A TREATMENT?

There is no one way to create a treatment, proposal, or production quote bid. Each production house company approaches it differently and each project may require a different type of template—there is no one formula. Zandrak utilizes different types of styles and content in their work. A project I did for the American Community School in Amman, Jordan required just a brief outline and a budget. Stilllmotion uses the following elements in a bid and treatment in their projects:

- **Concept:** A brief overview of the concept for the project, to be expanded upon later if necessary as a treatment.

- **Pre-production:** Casting, pre-interviewing, scouting, and learning the story.

- **Production:** Days required for production, and a list of resources—the Director, the DP, a second camera, major pieces of gear should be listed.

- **Post-production:** A list of the deliverables—"one 3–5 minute film in HD, web ready," how many rounds of editing are required, color correction, sound mixing. . . . all these things you should mention briefly.

- **Soundtrack:** Here you might want to give some options, with the estimated costs for licensing music. A song with a one-year lifespan is going to be cheaper than a song with a perpetual lifespan, and that's a choice they'll have to make. We list the cost for both the one-year and the perpetual lifespan, usually indicating the cost for anywhere from 1–10 songs.

- **Travel:** "We'll make all the travel plans . . . you give us this much money."

- **Rights:** A brief statement of the ownership/rights to the material, and that we reserve the right to show the material (when applicable—this isn't always the case).

- **Project Estimate:** No fluff—just the estimated cost of the entire project.

- **A Final Note:** We don't want the last thing on our bid to be a big dollar sign and nothing more. Here we'll make a note about why we're excited to work with them, and why we believe in the project.

http://stillmotionblog.com/bid-and-treatment/

KEYWORDS AND STORY DEVELOPMENT

As part of Stillmotion's vision they have created story development tools as a part of their education outreach, showing what they have learned from over ten years of experience, and teaching at workshops around the world. (See Chapter 1 for a summary of the entire MUSE process.) It involves the four Ps and keywords:

> ## "We Believe that Story is Based on 4 Ps: People, Places, Purpose, and Plot"

The 'P' you put first, or prioritize, determines the type of story you'll end up telling.

Lead with Plot and you have an action movie. Lead with Purpose and you have a commercial. But when you lead with People, we have the potential for an emotional, character-driven story.

We believe that you need to let the story move you, before you try and move the story. And so we start with listening. To the people, places, purpose, and plot that exist within any story.

This is why we feel that the best storytellers are the best listeners—they see and hear what others don't and allow the story to come to them.

http://www.stillmotion.ca/museprocess

See http://kurtlancaster.com/contracts-and-forms/ for a sample creative brief from Stillmotion. It includes a space for keywords, characters, treatment, and storyboard based on the MUSE process.

To summarise:

- People represent the *who* of a story.
- Places are the *where* and *why*.
- The purpose is the *why* of a story. It revolves around the five keywords by which they become "a lens to filter every decision."
- The plot is the beginning, middle, and end—the *how* of a story.

What follows over the next few pages is a transcript of a fast-moving discussion by members of Zandrak as they utilized Stillmotion's keyword technique in developing the foundational ideas for their Moodsnap short. Note that the Zandrak team members have already talked to Moodsnap in order to get a sense of how the app works (and they've recreated this discussion for the author). The discussion occurred among the four members of the team: Andrew Hutcheson, Kyle Harper, Charles Frank, and David Brickel. Since it moves fast, I do not designate who is talking, but rather highlight the fact that the four of them are operating as a team. They push and challenge each other as they develop a consensus. It's like being in a writer's room or the locker room before a game—ideas flow fast and may appear jumpy at times, but the overall control revolves around what they feel are the best words to describe what the Moodsnap app will be like and how they can translate that into a short film. I provide the transcript in order to show that ideas don't just pop into place by magic. The dynamic conversation reveals the creative process in embryo, gestating to completion over time. It also shows the potential power of Stillmotion's process. It's a process I have my students engage with in my production classes at Northern Arizona University. Even when they do nail down these keywords, it's just the beginning step to writing a storyline or treatment (which I examine in the next section). Remember the keywords are drawn from their research and pre-interviews with their subject—they're not flying blind, but drawing from previous conversations they've had with the client.

Andrew writes and erases words on a whiteboard in their small office in Boston and they jump right into the process, trying to discover the best words to define the appeal of the Moodsnap app.

Moodsnap is accessible, definitely.

Personalized.

Great.

Well, it's about discovering new music, isn't it?

Yeah, it's good for discovery.

Discovery, adventure. Exploration is probably better than adventure.

Exploration, what about—

Context.

It's also introductory, introduces you to new music.

It captures emotionally driven material.

I think it's capturing a moment, it's convenient.

Enhances what you do, enhances the moment.

Nostalgic. Memorable. Relevant. Innovative

It's communal. What else we got?

Something about the music relating to the context. Like pairings.

Relatable.

Fitting.

Fitting is better, yeah.

Anything else?

Motivated.

Nostalgic.

Something about having the right music for the right place for the right experience.

Fitting, pairing, contextual.

Yeah.

FIGURE 6.1
Andrew of Zandrak writes down some keywords on a whiteboard in their office. (Photo courtesy of Kurt Lancaster.)

Anything else, or do you want to cut it down?

Let's start to cut down.

We'll see what we're missing when we start to get rid of some sort of . . .

So, this point you know we'll cut down the words that don't fit.

Motivated.

Agreed.

Relevant.

Yeah.

Accessible.

Mobile.

Introductory.

Maybe not mobile.

Capture.

Relatable.

Yeah.

I think music goes.

Yeah, I don't think we need it.

How about visuals?

I think adventure.

Discovery.

I also liked multi-sensory and emotional.

Yeah those are good. I don't like personalized.

I like user-curated. It gives an important element of it as well.

That's fair.

And contextual I love.

So we like contextual, we don't like fitting. Don't like experiential. I think it's summarized like it's an app. It is experiential by nature.

There's some apps that aren't experiential.

When I think of experiential, I'm thinking of what it does outside the app. The app is a catalyst.

That's a good point, I didn't think of that. Let's lose elegant and inspiring, though.

Yeah.

Convenient.

Yeah.

Pairings.

What about emotionally-driven, is that like, could that be a hyphen?

I think just emotional.

Let's start getting rid of some of these words. I think we lose feelings and I think we lose music, because it's not just about music.

Nostalgic and mobile.

FIGURE 6.2
Kyle, David, and Charles discuss with Andrew keywords for the Moodsnap app. (Photo courtesy of Kurt Lancaster.)

What do you like about mobile?

Yeah.

I think that the problem is it doesn't distinguish itself.

Yeah you're right.

So now we have these guys to look at: emotional, experiential, user-curated, contextual, and multi-sensory.

Wait, how is it multi-sensory?

Because it's visual and music, so multi-sensory stays, definitely, so does discovery.

Does discovery stay? Is it about discovering new music? Or is it about finding the perfect playlist?

Alright, yeah.

Is contextual important?

Yes.

I feel like we have only one word about the visual aesthetic for the app. Being elegant, which has been cut. I wonder if there's maybe something that can tie into it.

I think experiential would tie in the fact that it's like the experience of using it, as a part of it.

I would keep experiential and lose emotional, personally, I think emotional—

Is covered under what?

It's covered in Moodsnap.

I think it's pretty essential to the brand.

Or we write them both and just admit it's a middle ground.

What's the difference between experiential and emotional? Inspiring?

I think about emotional and driven is kind of like that.

But I don't think that's experiential. I think emotionally driven talks about it. I think that's just emotional, expanding off it.

I see. My only thing would be that if it's emotionally driven, then it's causing an experience.

How user-curated is it?

That's a big part.

They submit the songs.

Yeah, there's an image then all the users submit songs onto that and then through the algorithms it finds it.

I would be more inclined to lose contextual and keep emotional and experiential.

I think that contextual—

Emotional is the context though. If you remove the term emotional it describes both the idea of pursuing feeling, but also describes the context in which you're choosing things.

He talked about it so much in his brief about how this app is really about context.

Okay, in which case we can hold onto that.

I think it's an important element. I would almost say that emotional is covered in contextual.

We can do that, then we keep experiential, those are the five.
Okay.

Before we solidify them, we can see if there's any gaps that we feel are missing.

Yeah, I don't see any. What about you guys?

Let's see them all up first.

They're all up: **Experiential, user-generated, discovery, multi-sensory, and contextual**.

Alright, we've covered the soul of the app. That's core. We've covered some of its functionality.

What it does for you?

We've addressed users a bit by talking about being user-curated, and how they'll interact with it.

I think that's good.

Okay. So we have to come up with one 90-second spot based on these five words, and it's going to be for online use.

What's clear in this ping-pong style discussion is how Zandrak members make the work stronger when they let go of egos and push for what's best for the client, the story, the app—and this would get filtered through the five keywords they collaboratively generated: Experiential, user-generated, discovery, multi-sensory, and contextual. After the keywords are completed, they start brainstorming. Andrew Hutcheson says, "Everyone goes home that night and they think about some ideas, come in the next morning, we all have two or three ideas each, bring them up, put them on the board, look at all of them. So we can see what they are, and take the best parts of each and turn them into the final idea." It's a collaborative approach. "Usually what ends up happening is everybody comes in with their ideas to talk about and in the process of talking about the ideas we come up with either a middle ground or an entirely new idea that everybody just loves," Kyle Harper adds. Charles says that, "We all have pretty full narratives in mind, and we're all willing to let go of them so long as they are for the betterment of the full piece."

After brainstorming and coming up with the ideas, Kyle explains how "we get these ideas together, we flesh one of them out and write a synopsis for it. And we're trying to put that together and send that to the client. And after that point it's going to be about developing that treatment." Charles says, "Once we create the synopsis, the outline of what the piece is, we'll contact the client with just a general overview of what it is, whether it be a Skype call, a phone call, or just an email with the synopsis. If they like the direction in general, we'll create a fuller treatment that talks about the execution, contains some visual samples, and then in the case of Moodsnap we also talk about the rollout plan, what other kinds of pieces we would link to a campaign in this style, as well as an estimated budget."

Andrew adds that the budget is important. "Because if we get the idea and the client likes it and it's all going great, then the client says we have ten thousand dollars, and we say we can't do this for that, no way. We'd end up walking away with maybe a hundred dollars, if anything." So they need to shape the budget realistically. Sometimes it might cost more than a client has budgeted. "That's why we make clear the defining parameters of the project," Andrew says. "Here's the idea, here's the budget, and they come back and say we have a third of the budget, and then we can say, 'Okay, well you still love the idea, how can we scale the idea, adapt it to fit your budgetary constraints.'" This process can be just as creative. "It is fun," Andrew adds, "that's the creative brainstorming, using creative budgeting constraints."

THE VISUAL PITCH

Written pitches or proposals are normal in the industry. But Zandrak isn't normal. Since videos, or short films, are visual, why not make the pitching and proposal process visual? It still contain paragraphs, but it doesn't focus on a lot of text. Once Zandrak discusses keywords and develops story ideas from that, Charles develops a treatment for a client that "portrays the visual aesthetic of the piece. I just like them to match the aesthetic of what we are doing so that they get a sense of who we are and we are not just presenting them a Word document with a bunch of copy, because I don't think that is representative of our style." (See Figure 6.3.) Charles hopes that this approach shows clients that a visual document proves "that we go above what their expectation is so they know we are invested in what they are doing."

Charles says that, "The thing that takes the longest and it might look super in-depth, is finding images that are really fitting for the piece. We want to do a road trip so the opening page show this road trip. This is how he received it." This is not a still from the film. It's concept art, providing the client with a possibility or potential look for their film. It allows the client to sense the mood of the piece, which Zandrak says is much more difficult to convey with words. When they do words, such as in their synopsis, it's sparse, it's poetic (see Figure 6.4).

The synopsis, Charles explains, is "just a minimal approach with the texture on the page and the elegant font." When comparing the finished product with the original, Charles admits that "the original concept is a lot more involved. It was a lot more complex. I had the boyfriend and girlfriend framing up these moments together and then based on the frame they create, they make a song together that represents that frame. And that was very much in line with exactly how Moodsnap works. But as we were getting closer and closer to shooting, I just had trouble imagining in my head that process being natural and organic."

As Zandrak did their research, such as scouting locations, casting and meeting the actors, Charles started to see the edit of the film in his head. "I start thinking about pacing, I start seeing visuals, I start seeing the wides, mediums, and close

FIGURE 6.3
Moodsnap—the cover page to their treatment. (Courtesy of Zandrak.)

FIGURE 6.4
Zandrak's visual treatment for Moodsnap, page 2, the synopsis. (Courtesy of Zandrak.)

——SYNOPSIS——

We want to create a 90 second short film that embodies what it feels like to seek out music using Moodsnap. To do this, we want to tell the story of a musician and his girlfriend going on a road-trip together. Along the way, we see the Musician frame up various scenes with his fingers, take in the feeling, and set about writing/playing music. From simple, intimate activities like cooking over a campfire or waking up in the morning, to grand experiences beneath waterfalls or gazing at a brilliant night sky, the couple's journey is constantly expressed first through finger-frame, and then given full emotional context in song. The world is singing- this story is a glimpse of how one couple shares in the song.

shots and how they're cutting together," he explains. "I start seeing the interactions of the couple because it's all starting to materialize and be real." For Charles, the pressure of a looming shooting date helps fire his imagination. "And when it got closer and closer I imagined the performers having natural interactions and then one of them pulling up one of their hands and taking a fake snapshot. And every time I imagined it happening I thought, 'That's going to look fake. It's not going to look real. It's going to look like this is for the app.'" He felt trouble looming with the original vision that Zandrak and the client had worked out. But rather than meticulously follow the plan, he decided to listen to his intuition and confront his fears. "So finally the night before shooting I called the client and said, 'Listen I know this is so last minute and it's crazy, but I just don't see the original idea for the piece working.' I told him that I know I should have thought of this sooner but now that it is here in my head, I can't make it work."

Charles' intuition and passion paid off. The client, Charles says, replied, "'It's okay, I trust what you see and I want you to do what you think is right.' So we ended up going in and we decided to shoot it both ways. We shot them doing all the frame-ups with their hands just in case I was wrong, and we shot every interaction authentically without the finger framing. And after editing it, I am glad that we took the new approach because it's stronger not having had them do the frames." (See Figures 6.5 and 6.6.)

For Charles, projects shouldn't be cemented in stone and it's why it's important to build a good relationship with a client. The Moodsnap example shows how

FIGURE 6.5
The last frame of action from Zandrak's Moodsnap promo. It contains the only actor frame-up with his fingers culminating in the representation of memory. (Courtesy of Zandrak.)

a project can evolve. He says, "If you have a client that trusts you, and you have a good relationship about the philosophy behind what you are doing, they are probably going to be willing to take a panicked call at midnight the night before you're shooting, saying, 'I want to take a change in direction,' and they might even be okay with it." It's also an example of the type of clients they like. "It's this kind of relationships we are looking for," Charles says, "and when the client came in and looked at the footage he was really happy with the shift in direction as well."

After the synopsis, there's the execution page (see Figure 6.7).

This explores their approach to capturing the feel or the sense of direction or style in which they want to take the work. "We talk about the way we want to capture the piece," Charles says. "And in this case it was very much centered around the POV perspective, looking through the frames. We wanted to do a visual style where when they brought up their hands and did the frames, we would be actually seeing from their eyeballs through the frame to what they were seeing." It revealed their visual style, but when it came to thinking about how to shoot it, Charles realized it wouldn't work. "It was a cool visual style," he explains, "but once again, it was something hard to incorporate organically that we couldn't have predicted until we really got closer to the shoot."

FIGURE 6.6
Zandrak's Moodsnap as it appears on an iPhone in the final moment of their promo. It contains a shot of the couple we see in their film. (Courtesy of Zandrak.)

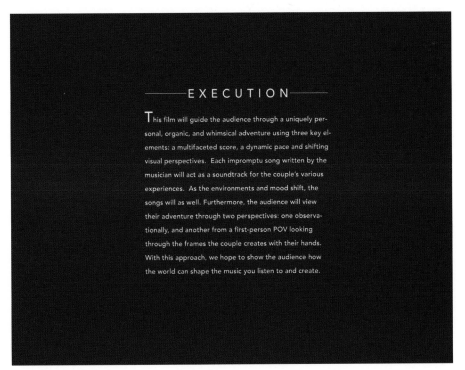

————— E X E C U T I O N —————

This film will guide the audience through a uniquely personal, organic, and whimsical adventure using three key elements: a multifaceted score, a dynamic pace and shifting visual perspectives. Each impromptu song written by the musician will act as a soundtrack for the couple's various experiences. As the environments and mood shift, the songs will as well. Furthermore, the audience will view their adventure through two perspectives: one observationally, and another from a first-person POV looking through the frames the couple creates with their hands. With this approach, we hope to show the audience how the world can shape the music you listen to and create.

FIGURE 6.7
The pitch or proposal from Zandrak, includes an execution page. (Courtesy of Zandrak.)

Ultimately, the pitch or proposal is a draft and it sets the tone, even if you don't literally follow all of it when you execute it. "But this is what we pitched to him and he liked that, and we even made a page, called Mood." (See Figure 6.8.)

The mood page is a visual way to set the tone of the work. "We went out and we shot frames, with Chris, the actor, and a friend of his and then we shot it through their hands so we could see what that would look like," Charles explains. "It gave the client a visual reference for what those points of view shots would look like. And we even developed a bit of a campaign around the idea of framing the music, because you are literally framing your music. In the end, it's something that didn't hold up, but we did pitch it originally."

The budget provides a brief outline of the cost for the project (page not included for privacy purposes. See Zandrak's Moodsnap Budget Estimate in Figure 6.10, below). The budget, Charles says, breaks out all the list items of what everything would cost. This is where you might add a note about the number of editing revisions allowed before additional charges to your client. There's also a "future" page, where, he explains, "we talk about the continuation of our collaborative relationship and types of projects we could do that could continue to help

FIGURE 6.8
Zandrak's mood page from the Moodsnap pitch. (Courtesy of Zandrak.)

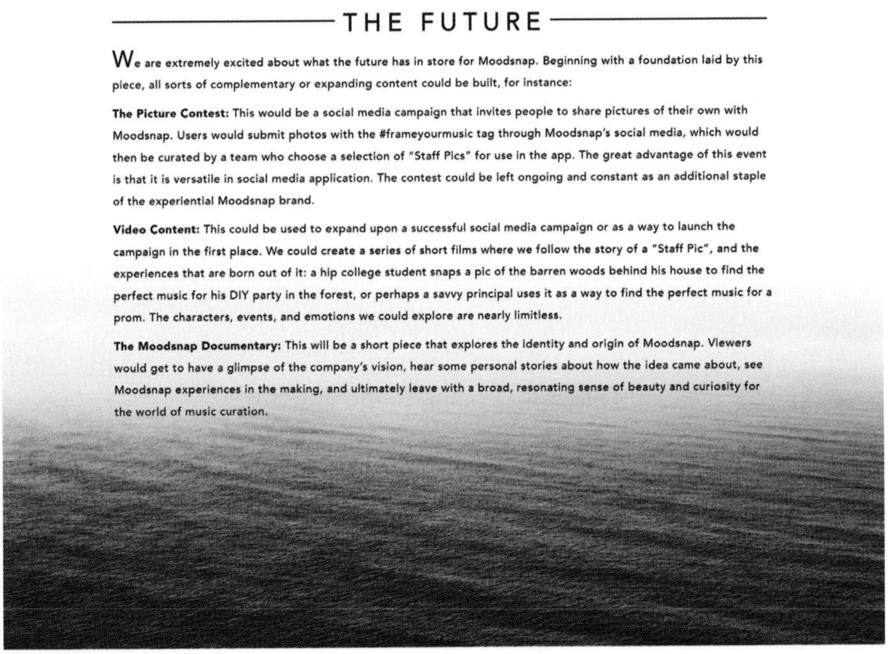

─────────────── **THE FUTURE** ───────────────

We are extremely excited about what the future has in store for Moodsnap. Beginning with a foundation laid by this piece, all sorts of complementary or expanding content could be built, for instance:

The Picture Contest: This would be a social media campaign that invites people to share pictures of their own with Moodsnap. Users would submit photos with the #frameyourmusic tag through Moodsnap's social media, which would then be curated by a team who choose a selection of "Staff Pics" for use in the app. The great advantage of this event is that it is versatile in social media application. The contest could be left ongoing and constant as an additional staple of the experiential Moodsnap brand.

Video Content: This could be used to expand upon a successful social media campaign or as a way to launch the campaign in the first place. We could create a series of short films where we follow the story of a "Staff Pic", and the experiences that are born out of it: a hip college student snaps a pic of the barren woods behind his house to find the perfect music for his DIY party in the forest, or perhaps a savvy principal uses it as a way to find the perfect music for a prom. The characters, events, and emotions we could explore are nearly limitless.

The Moodsnap Documentary: This will be a short piece that explores the identity and origin of Moodsnap. Viewers would get to have a glimpse of the company's vision, hear some personal stories about how the idea came about, see Moodsnap experiences in the making, and ultimately leave with a broad, resonating sense of beauty and curiosity for the world of music curation.

FIGURE 6.9
The future, a page from Zandrak's Moodsnap pitch. (Courtesy of Zandrak.)

promote the client's brand and would give us continued work to exercise creativity" (see Figure 6.9).

The page for the future, Charles says, "Buttoned up the initial visual style that we saw in the beginning. We see the car on the first page. It's a road trip and now we are ending on an empty road implying the future has in store but still along the same theme of a road trip. It took a lot of time to find images that contained little representations that matched our aesthetic, but I think it is little details like that that helps sell what you are doing."

And it worked. The client approved it. "He had notes and thoughts about it," Charles states, "but that was what it took for him to sign a contract, and say, 'Let's do this thing.' And even though it evolved from there, it was just that initial starting point that we needed to really get him on board. And I think had we just sent him a Word document it wouldn't have been as compelling and we wouldn't have seemed as committed to it."

There was no formal script for the shoot, rather Charles developed scenarios and developed the storyline as they shot. The final work, "Our Songs," as seen on the client's page is located at: http://moodsnap.fm.

CREATING A SCRIPT FOR THE HONORS PROGRAM AT NAU

To show the process of developing a script from keywords involving story intention, I include a project that I oversaw at Northern Arizona University for University Marketing. I led a team of students in the creation of a promotional video for NAU's Honors Program. As we discussed possible story concepts with the director of the program, Wolf Gunnerman, how it would show off visually the different classes and activities, including livings spaces, outdoor adventures, classroom interactions, community building, I knew we needed Zandrak involved somehow. I wanted Kyle Harper, the writer for Zandrak, the writer of "Still Life" and the Hasbro commercial. I got approval for a payment for Zandrak to cover the cost of the writing and talked to Kyle about it. He developed a short script. Gunnerman requested a few minor changes. Kyle revised it and it was approved.

The project began as an open discussion of intent and the development of keywords (following Stillmotion's MUSE model). Marteen Cleary, Reed Robertson, and Mariah Soer (and later, Michael Kerbleski)—the student team for this project—developed the following keywords with me: Community, adventure, unique, and engaging. The University Honors Program revolves around honor, distinction, and community (http://nau.edu/honors/)—also were the video is embedded. The thrust and purpose of our project revolved around the fact that many potential incoming first-year students are turned off from the Honors Program due to the demands put on them from AP honors programs in high school. The university program is more fun, Gunnerman says. It's about the unique class content, interactive participation in the classroom, and engaging in outdoor activities in some classes (such as experiencing art and creative writing at Vermillion Cliffs in northern Arizona). In addition, since the program focuses on leadership, teamwork, and interpersonal communication, many students with this skillset are offered jobs after graduating.

Reed came up with the idea that there should be a student who enrolled in the program from the beginning, show students in the different phases of classroom, housing, and outdoor activities, graduation, and then at a job. We developed this concept and called Kyle Harper at Zandrak, giving him the information we had developed. The questions involved intention and sharing the keywords and the purpose of the recruitment video, as explained above. He created the following script from our discussion (this version of the script includes minor changes requested from the client):

NAU Honors Video (Kyle Harper)

Note from Writer: The opening action/scene is only written in for context of how the professor starts speaking—obviously feel free to change it or just exclude it entirely. I have not included any other scene suggestions, so as to leave as much room for creativity from the students shooting the film. The speech itself, beginning at the VO, currently runs about 1:15 seconds. (Which should be just enough wiggle room for you to edit a 90-second spot comfortably.) If you would like an example reading, let me know!

INT. CLASSROOM. DAY

A class of COLLEGE FRESHMEN are milling about in a classroom while the PROFESSOR arranges some papers on his desk. The students are setting down their backpacks, settling into seats, chatting with their neighbors. The Professor casually addresses them.

PROFESSOR First day of class, welcome everyone! If you would please, grab your seats.

The students settle down in their seats, pencils, notebooks, and attentive smiles at the ready. The Professor looks out at all of them, considering. Then, he begins to speak.

PROFESSOR (Start of the voiceover)

What makes you a student?

Is it your desk? The notes you take? The tests you pass?

Maybe. But I think there's more.

Outside of this classroom, you need more than your notebooks or papers to learn.

You find people and places that capture your imagination, causes that stir you to action, challenges that push you and excite you all at once.

Your goal isn't just to know more, it's to step outside the box, to do better.

And maybe even change your world in the process.

This makes you more than just students.

This makes you explorers and leaders, innovators and visionaries.

You are influencers and game-changers in the making.

All because you don't let learning stop at the end of your textbook.

You are not students because you learn in this classroom, you are students because learning is everything you do with your life, and this will enrich you far more than anything I could ever offer you.

What will you discover this year?

What will you try that has never been tried before?

Who will you be afterwards?

(I imagine this would be an excellent place for a longer pause.)

I cannot wait for you to find out.

Welcome to real learning.

Welcome to NAU Honors.

Notice how Kyle doesn't utilize the formal script template. He is trained as a creative writer and you can see his technique of poetry informs his style, providing the project with a fresh approach. With the script in hand, we shot different angles of one of the Honors Program's instructors, Kevin Ketchner, introducing himself to a class and interacting with students from his classroom on Sherlock Holmes. He improvised the opening dialogue and then we had him read the script. We edited the visuals around the words he performed. We also gathered trips outside the classroom, our team gathering footage in Mexico and northern Arizona, for example.

Some marketing films at NAU utilize improvised dialogue based on focused questions (similar to a documentary style)—very few projects use a scripted narration, but we felt this one could use the words and we wanted one of the teachers to do the performance rather than a hired professional performer. But as a part of the process, Director of Marketing Sandra Kowalski, who made a couple of minor changes to the script as well, said that she didn't want a professor reading it—it's a marketing tool for students and she wanted a student performing it (we changed the script to reflect this). We assigned Marteen, a student, to read the script, recording it line by line in a multi-hour recording session until we got the tone right. Furthermore, after the project was approved by Kowalski, Gunnerman sent it out to his team of professors and instructors and some of them gave feedback and additional changes were made (not every suggestion was taken, but there were a couple of changes made).

This example shows how different people with a stake in a project will require changes, but the original vision and feel of the project was never lost since we had held onto keywords, which evolved into Kyle's script. The completed University Honors Program video is located on their homepage: http://nau.edu/honors.

WRITING A BID OR PRODUCTION BUDGET QUOTE

Woody Biomass Project

The production budget quote—or bid—is tied to your cost of doing business, covered in Chapter 5. Be sure you're meeting your financial need when you create a quote and base it around your day rate. (The Production Quote Form is online at http://kurtlancaster.com/contracts-and-forms/) This sample form was provided by Zandrak (see Table 6.1). The opening section provides the contact info for the production company and client. If needed (you will likely want to use it on larger productions), use the Film Project Budget Form online to lay out the entire budget and use it to fill in the estimated production costs in the bid.

Let's walk through an example of a budget quote for a project that I submitted to Arizona State Forestry. (I'm leaving out personal contact info.) Patrick Rappold approached the School of Communication at NAU, wanting to develop a short documentary about the use of excess wood for word-burning power plants—it's a way to use leftover wood parts and for forest thinning to help control potential wildfires. His division won a grant of $15,000 for the project, so that's the non-negotiable budget.

Here's a brief breakdown of each section:

- Preproduction: The planning stage which includes onsite pre-interviews, scouting locations, story development, storyboards, scripting, shot lists.
- Production: The actual time spent in the field shooting. I set it up for five days at $600 per day, which will cover two cameras and a sound person.
- Deliverables: What file are you delivering? Is it a DVD or web link, a memory stick with a ProRes file? In this case it will be a web file for streaming.
- Editorial: Editing of the film. I include six days of editing plus up to three revisions (which is what you would put in the Production Agreement).
- Audio postproduction: Mixing audio and fixing audio issues. In this case, I roll the costs of audio postproduction into editorial, since I will do the audio mix myself—you would put in the cost of an outside postproduction studio for one day of work (anywhere from $500–1,000 would be typical).
- General and Administrative: Covers the cost of your time doing emails, contacts, communication with the client, setting up meetings, and so forth. I'm also rolling in the cost of hiring student production assistants for the shoot into this administrative cost.
- Travel: Include miles for car travel, or train or plane fare, as well as *per diem* and hotel costs.
- Notes: Rewrite the notes as needed.

TABLE 6.1

Production Budget Quote for Woody Biomass Utilization in Arizona Documentary

Production Co: Kurt Lancaster	Client: Arizona State Forestry
Address: NAU School of Communication PO Box 5619 Flagstaff, AZ 86011	Contact: Patrick Rappold Wood Utilization & Marketing Specialist
Telephone:	Product: Website file for streaming
Date: July 28, 2015	Production days: 5
Exec. Producer: Kurt Lancaster	Timeline: 10 months

Estimated Production Costs	Estimate
Preproduction (onsite pre-interviews, scouting locations, story development)	$3,000
Production (5 days)	$6,000
Deliverables	$100
Editorial postproduction	$3,000
Audio postproduction (in editorial)	$0
General & Administrative (including production assistant and university overhead costs)	$2,000
Travel	$900
Total	**$15,000**

Notes

This quote estimate was prepared for Arizona State Forestry under the pretense that Kurt Lancaster with NAU's School of Communication will produce one spot based on preapproved storyboards and script, to come in at a running time of 5–8 minutes, for public promotional use. This includes preproduction, 5 days of production, a production crew and equipment package. Kurt Lancaster with the School of Communication will provide postproduction services, including editorial, audio mixing, stock music, and finishing. Kurt Lancaster will act as the client's point of contact throughout all phases of the production through final deliverables.

This is a rough quote and was made under the assumption that Kurt Lancaster with the School of Communication will manage the project to completion, consulting with client, and that client will have the option of being on site for production and postproduction. The client will have three revisions of pictures for editorial.

Upon completion of the shoot, we will deliver the final video as a QuickTime ProRes 422 file and a file for the web. Additional deliverable file types and still frames for promotional use are available upon request.

This form is key in laying out the initial expectations for the client. Once this is agreed upon, you would issue a production agreement contract for signature.

Zandrak's Moodsnap Budget Estimate

The budget below in Figure 6.10 reveals the estimate that executive producer Andrew Hutcheson delivered to their client (the final budget is confidential). Note that personal information has been blacked out. This is provided to show what a higher budget estimate looks like at a professional level.

ZANDRAK

PRODUCTION QUOTE

Production Co:	**Zandrak LLC**		Client:	
Address:	1260 Boylston St. Suite 204		Contact:	
	Boston, MA 02215			
Telephone:	(908) 619-2047		Project:	
			Production:	3 Weeks
Exec. Producer:	Andrew Hutcheson		Timeline:	Due Mid-September
Director:	Charles Frank		Duration:	1.5min

SUMMARY OF EST. PRODUCTION COSTS	ESTIMATE
01-00 Pre-Production	$2,700
02-00 Production	$16,000
04-00 Equipment	$7,151
05-00 Logistics	$8,487
06-00 Deliverables	$750
07-00 Editorial/VFX	$12,500
08-00 Audio Post/Music	$4,900
09-00 General & Administrative	$1,200
SUBTOTAL	$53,688
DISCOUNT	$0
GRAND TOTAL	$53,688

Notes

This estimated quote was prepared for _____ under the pretense that Zandrak will produce one spot based on pre-approved concepts, content, and treatments for online and promotional use. This includes creative collaboration with the client, storyboard and treatment development, pre-production, casting, location scouting, two days of production, a professional production crew, and a digital cinema equipment package. Zandrak agrees to provide post-production services, including three rounds of edits, color correction, audio mixing, music, and finishing. A producer or director from Zandrak will act as the client's point of contact throughout all phases of the production through final deliverables.

This is an estimated quote and was made under the assumption that Zandrak will finish the videos to completion, consulting at all turns with client. Director and/or producer from Zandrak will be present throughout all of the post-production process.

Upon completion of the shoot, Zandrak will deliver the final videos as QuickTime ProRes files, along with any additionally requested file types.

FIGURE 6.10
Zandrak's budget estimate for Moodsnap video, "Our Songs." (Courtesy of Zandrak.)

Zandrak's estimated budget for the Moodsnap promotional film includes a specific breakdown of preproduction; production; equipment rental; logistics; deliverables; editorial and effects; audio postproduction work, including music; and administrative costs. The production project is set to revolve around a three-week shoot.

Worksheet: Developing a Pitch, Treatment, and Bid

1. Who is your client?

2. What is their need and how can you solve their problem?

3. Research the client:

   a. Websites

   b. News stories and magazines

   c. Existing interviews

4. Interview the client(s) in person, if possible, and note what they really need—you will develop keywords from these notes to discover their needs and how you can solve their problem.

5. Stillmotions's four Ps and five keywords (or, even better, use the full worksheets if you sign up for MUSE)

   a. People

   b. Place

   c. Purpose (including keywords)

   d. Plot

6. Write a bid proposal. Use a. or b. below.

   a. Here's what Stillmotion uses, modify as needed:

      i. **Concept:** A brief overview of our concept for the project, to be expanded upon later if necessary as a treatment.

      ii. **Preproduction:** Casting, pre-interviewing, scouting, and learning the story.

      iii. **Production:** Days required for production, and a list of resources—the director, the DP, a second camera, major pieces of gear should be listed.

   iv. **Postproduction:** A list of the deliverables— "one 3–5 minute film in HD, web ready," how many rounds of editing is required, color correction, sound mixing. . . . all these things you should mention briefly.

   v. **Soundtrack:** Here you might want to give them some options with the estimated costs for licensing music. A song with a one-year lifespan is going to be cheaper than a song with a perpetual lifespan, and that's a choice they'll have to make. We list the cost for both the one-year and the perpetual lifespan, usually indicating the cost for anywhere from 1–10 songs.

   vi. **Travel:** "We'll make all the travel plans . . . you give us this much money."

   vii. **Rights:** A brief statement of the ownership/ rights to the material, and that we reserve the right to show the material (when applicable—this isn't always the case).

   viii. **Project Estimate:** No fluff—just the estimated cost of the entire project. (Reference the Production Quote Form).

   ix. **A Final Note:** We don't want the last thing on our bid to be a big dollar sign and nothing more. Here we'll make a note about why we're excited to work with them, and why we believe in the project.

   b. Zandrak uses a visual proposal that typically includes:

      i. **Title** page (based on an image)

      ii. **Synopsis** (short and poetic)

      iii. **Execution** (how they will approach the project; a description of the visual style)

    iv. **Mood** page (a series of stills that show off their visual style and approaches—this should reinforce the written execution in a visual way)

    v. **Budget** (what will it cost?)—attach or insert the full Production Quote Form here.

7. Submit the above bid, including the production quote.

    a. Accepted as is.

    b. Make additional changes negotiated with the client.

8. Submit Production Agreement contract for signature (forms online at http://kurtlancaster.com/contracts-and-forms).

9. Go into full preproduction and develop a formal treatment, script, and storyboards.

10. Submit treatment, script, and storyboards (see Stillmotion's Creative Brief, online, http://kurtlancaster.com/contracts-and-forms/).

    a. Accepted as is.

    b. Make additional changes negotiated with the client.

11. Submit initial invoice for first third of payment as stipulated in the contract.

12. Go into production.

13. Submit second invoice for second payment as stipulated in the contract.

14. Go into postproduction.

15. Client reviews the final cut of film.

    a. Make additional changes as requested by client.

    b. Repeat up to contract limit (usually three).

16. Deliver final product to client.

17. Submit final invoice for final payment as stipulated in the contract.

CHAPTER 7
Cinematic Gear on a Budget
What You Need and What it Does

Now that you've built a business and gained some tips and techniques to working with clients and writing a pitch—hopefully leading to a signed contract—you'll want to think about what kind of gear you may need to shoot and edit your projects. You don't need to break the bank to get professional results. A basic gear package with a Canon DSLR can yield strong cinematic results.[1] You can get professional results with minimum gear if your production house is on a tight budget.

For some people, throwing a lot of money at a problem is the only way to find a solution—but this isn't usually the best option. Being challenged with limited gear can result in creative solutions that may actually lead to better work. The challenge arrives from the fact that when you're on a tight budget you must still put together a great-looking film.

But the gear is only part of it. A person with a $1,000 Canon 70D can get better results than with a $20,000 RED—if the person on the RED doesn't know as much about cinematic storytelling—the professional skills—as the person on the 70D. Andrew Hutcheson of Zandrak feels that the most important element of your business revolves around your skills and professionalism. "The client's impression of you is all that matters, it doesn't matter how you do it. It doesn't matter where you are so much, but it's really how they see you as being valuable. Did they see the work they get from you as being professional? Is it giving them what they need? Which is why it's so important to find a client that's right for you."

In the end, those facets are more important than what camera you own, for example. "Most people aren't going to be impressed by what camera you have," Andrew adds. "Like most dates aren't going to be impressed by what car you drive, because they're dating who you are." So, yes, you need to shoot high definition and if you can't afford the camera you want, then rent it. Andrew says, "The industry at a certain point is a renter's market."

But renting can have its limitations, such as lack of versatility in being able to have the gear on hand when you might need it. "If you're going to get your own gear," Andrew says, "you should get a piece of tech that you think is going to not just be the best thing right now, but it's going to hold up for some time." DSLRs are perfect examples of how they have come a long way. "There's a lot you can do to upgrade them. Shane Hurlbut, ASC is a perfect example as to how you can really professionalize these cameras. *Escape from Tomorrow* was a feature film recently shot at Disney World all on DSLRs, and it was a Sundance film that got distribution."

"The point," Andrew adds, "is to show that it's not the tools that define the job—it's you." What skills, vision, and passion do you bring to the project? "Anyone can buy the tools," Andrew explains. He heard a story from Vincent Laforet—who helped instigate the DSLR cinema revolution by using a Canon 5D Mark II as a cinema camera. An executive for a potential job asked him, "Why should I hire you to shoot my project when my daughter has a 5D?" Andrew says it goes back to the vision statement: "What you need to sell people on is your style, the same thing that you've always had as an artist":

- What's your style?
- What's your story?
- What differentiates you from someone else?

"And that's the most important thing to establish in the beginning, before you go into business." (You should have explored this vision in Chapter 2.)

"In addition to that," Andrew explains, "you should get business cards printed. Accessorize your camera package, more lenses, more media cards, more batteries. Maybe a tripod, or maybe a shoulder rig if you're more about handheld. Monopods are the most common tools we use. And I'd make sure within all of that, find out how much it will cost you to get a website and factor that in. That's almost more important than anything else. It's your baseline for your business."

Furthermore, when you invest money (or credit) in your gear, you should calculate your return on the investment. Will spending money on a RED Epic give you a return on your investment over a few years? Or does it make more sense to spend $1,000 for a Canon DSLR and accessorize it for a couple thousand more, knowing that once you've gotten a couple of jobs your gear is paid for? And if you need to shoot a project with a RED Epic, you could rent one.

Rather than recommending one piece of gear over another, below I describe what features you need to consider when getting a computer, editing software, camera, and audio gear. Getting the cheapest PC or Apple's MacBook Air, for example, is not the way to go when faced with gigabytes of video data that needs processing and editing, but I'm also making an assumption that someone starting a business isn't going to invest $50,000 or $100,000 in getting gear. A startup should be wise with their funds (unless you happen to have that kind of money laying around). Andrew at Zandrak recommends that if you have an equipment budget of around $5,000, then the first thing he would do is buy a DSLR camera, whichever is the best for you at the time. "You get a DSLR, you get a laptop, and you get a copy of Adobe Creative Cloud (monthly subscription), since you have access to multiple apps, from color grading to Photoshop or retouching, as well as After Effects, Audition for music, and there's a storyboard visualization software you'd want to get."

Even though I do list a few items of lower-budget gear (such as cameras under $5,000), I'm not going to provide an exhaustive list. Rather, I delve into the details, explaining what some of the equipment does and what features you may want to consider when purchasing or renting certain gear. Too many shooters, for example, don't know what 8-bit compression means and how that limits postproduction work when compared to a camera that shoots Apple ProRes or a camera that shoots 12-bit raw. Therefore, the heart of this chapter is really about what features and specs you should be looking for, so when you look at a camera, you can see if it has what it takes with regard to image and audio quality, and if it doesn't, what you need to compensate for it.

WHAT COMPUTER SHOULD I GET?

The merits of a laptop and a full desktop system cannot be understated. If you're starting out and need the portability to edit or at the very least back up files in the field, you'll want a laptop. It's your choice whether you should get an Apple or PC—and that will depend on what software you want to use for editing. If you want to use Final Cut Pro, then you must get an Apple computer. If you choose Avid or Premiere you could buy an Apple or PC. If you want to use Sony Vegas, then it's PC only. To keep the budget reasonable, I'm not going to get into the Mac Pro description, but when your budget increases you may want to go for the top-of-the-range model if you really want serious computing power (it'll cost upwards of $10,000, but you'll have 12 core processors, 64GB of memory, dual AMD graphics card with 6GB of video memory for each)—this kind of setup will be good for 4K and raw video assets, so that's something to consider.

Whatever you end up choosing, these are the kinds of specs you'll want:

- **Processor:** This is what will render your projects, including special effects and graphics. The more processors you have, the faster the render times. Quad core processors are a minimum. Apple's MacBook Pro has a 2.5GHz speed with turbo speeds up to 3.4GHz in the high-end mid-2015 model, but there are high-end PCs clocking in at 4GHz, and you can choose more than four cores (6, 8, 12, or even more). (The Mac Pro tower will allow you to go up to 12 cores.)
- **Memory:** 16GB RAM (minimum). This allows you to run more apps at once, or for video purposes, less refresh of your timeline.
- **Graphics card with dedicated video memory**: Make sure you have a dedicated graphics card with at least 1GB of dedicated video RAM (2GB is

better, but the higher this number the better off you are—especially if you're running 4K and/or raw video files). Some models I describe below, such as the PC laptop, offer up to 8GB of video memory.

- **Display:** You want this to be high, preferably 4K (not what's called full HD 1920x1080). Apple's Retina display on a MacBook Pro is 2880x1800 (in the 2015 model). I would say this is the minimum you would want since you need to have good real-estate area on your screen when editing.

- **Storage drive:** This is where all of your software goes. Hard drives spin and you want at least 7200RPM. You can also get more expensive SSD (solid state drive), which contains no moving parts and is faster than hard drives in general. I use Apple's MacBook Pro with a 500GB SSD, which makes the bootup times fast and increases performance. All of my software goes on this main drive. However, I don't store any video or audio here; use dedicated drives instead (see below).

- **External storage drives:** Get dedicated hard drives to store your footage. We're talking terabytes, not gigabytes. The onboard base drive for your computer should be 500GB—this is for your software. Don't store your footage on your main drive. Use additional drives. You can get large array drives or stand-alone portable drives. If you're getting a hard drive, you'll want a minimum of 7200RPM spin speed with a USB 3.0, eSATA, or Thunderbolt (Apple only) for high-speed connectivity. For field drives, look at LaCie's 4T RAID drive with USB 3.0 and Thunderbolt cables and G Drive mini (1T USB 3.0). For large storage bays, look at CalDigit and G-Drive.

Here are some example computers you should use as a representative baseline when choosing a later model (prices will stay relatively the same, but the specs will just get better):

- **MacBook Pro (laptop) ~$2,500** (~$120/month for 24 months through Apple financing)

  Get the highest-end model with a Retina display. Anything less, and you're not getting the full power you need for editing. The lower-end models and 13-inch models are really not worth it. See http://store.apple.com/us/buy-mac/macbook-pro. Here's the specs as of mid-2015:

  - Processor: 2.5GHz Quad-core Intel Core i7, Turbo Boost up to 3.7GHz
  - RAM: 16GB 1600MHz DDR3L SDRAM
  - Graphics card: Intel Iris Pro Graphics and AMD Radeon R9 M370X with 2GB of GDDR5 memory. The AMD Radeon (or NVIDIA) graphics cards with the 2GB of memory is the key component you want here.
  - Storage drive: 512GB PCIe-based Flash Storage
  - Display: Retina (2880x1800 resolution)
  - Storage drive: SSD (500GB)

- AppleCare Protection Plan for MacBook Pro (recommended so you can get your computer repaired or replaced if you run into issues with it).

- **iMac with Retina 5K display (desktop)** ~$3,400 ($163 for 24 months through Apple financing)

  This is the top of the line iMac. The lower models aren't really worth it. With the 5K display, this is one of the best computers for video editing you can get from Apple. For the price point, you're getting a lot of computer power without having to spend over $9,000 for a full-spec Mac Pro tower. See: http://store.apple.com/us/buy-mac/imac-retina. Specs as of mid-2015:

  - Display: 5K (27″, 5120x2880 resolution)
  - 4.0GHz Quad-core Intel Core i7, Turbo Boost up to 4.4GHz (don't do the standard i5 core—pay more for the i7)
  - 32GB 1600MHz DDR3 SDRAM—4 x 8GB
  - 1TB Fusion Drive (SSD for bootable software fused with a regular hard drive)
  - AMD Radeon R9 M295X 4GB GDDR5 (pay the extra money for this card with 4GB of dedicated video/graphics memory).

- **PC (Windows) laptop** ~$2,800

  Priced about the same as the MacBook Pro, there's more bang for your buck in this work horse from Titan Computers. Do not get an $800 laptop for video editing. This is where you do not want to skimp on your budget. The fact that this model has a 4K display, with high memory and a strong video card makes this a great workstation for editing. As you shop around for PC laptops, take note of how the specs outperform Apple's MacBook Pro. But also note that by putting this kind of power in a laptop, the weight of the computer comes in at 7.5 pounds (as opposed to the less than 3.5 pounds of the MacBook Pro):

  - Display: 4K, 15.6″ Samsung (3840x2160)
  - Processor: Quad core Intel i7-4790K 4.0 GHz (4.4GHz turbo) with 8MB L3 Cache
  - Hard drive: Seagate 500GB 7200 RPM
  - Memory: 32GB (4 x 8G) DDR3 1600 (PC3 12800)
  - Video card: NVIDIA GeForce GTX 980M with 8GB GDDR5

  You can tailor this model with several options, including going up to 12 cores, for example (see: http://www.titancomputers.com/Titan-X4K-Intel-Xeon-E3-1200-V3-Series-Mobile-Wo-p/x4k.htm).

- **PC (Windows) tower** ~$3,000 ($4,200 with recommended display)

  This computer is comparable to Apple's 5K iMac (the iMac is somewhat better and contains the 5K display). See Titan Computers for an example of how you can map out a top-of-the-range PC. See: http://www.titancom puters.com/Titan-X180-Intel-Xeon-E5-2600-V2-Series-Video-p/x180.htm. Specs as of mid-2015:

–   Processor: Six core Intel i7-4960X Ivy Bridge-E 3.6Ghz (4.0GHz turbo)

–   Hard drive: Seagate 500GB 7200 RPM

–   Memory: 32GB (4 x 8G) DDR3 1866 quad channel

–   Video card: NVIDIA GeForce GTX 970 with 4GB GDDR5

–   Display (not included), but a recommend 4K display would be LG's 31-inch 4K monitor (31MU97-B) for around $1,200 (see this link from Amazon: http://www.amazon.com/LG-Electronics-Digital-31MU 97-B-31-0-Inch/dp/B00OKSEVTY/)

Again, these specs are 2015. The secret to computer prices—high-end machines will stay about the same price; what changes are increased specs.

WHAT EDITING SOFTWARE SHOULD I GET?

There are professionals who spend too much time debating the merits and demerits of particular editing software (and cameras, for that matter). The debate tends to revolve around the big three of Avid Media Composer, Apple's Final Cut Pro, and Adobe's Premiere Pro. Avid was the first and in many ways is the most stable when locking in a picture for film out, so it tends to be the most popular among feature film editors. Apple purchased Macromedia's software

TABLE 7.1

Software Comparison Chart

Software	Avid	Final Cut	Premiere
Cost	$50/month ($600 per year)	$299 (additional costs for Motion and Compressor of $49 each)	$49/month (~$600 per year; includes all of Adobe's software, such as Photoshop and After Effects; student price $19/month)
Platform	Apple and PC	Apple	Apple and PC
Cloud or stand-alone	Cloud and stand-alone	Stand-alone	Cloud
Learning curve	High	Low	Medium
Penetration rate	Hollywood and some news outlets; some independent productions	Independent films, production houses, some news outlets	Independent films, production houses

and rendered it into their version throughout the 2000s, making it popular among those in the indie film movement who were attracted to the graphics and Windows-based Macs. But when Apple finally created their own software from scratch with the release of Final Cut X, some were so used to the old interface, they couldn't adjust and jumped over to Adobe's Premiere, which engages a similar interface to previous versions of the now defunct Final Cut 7. Fundamentally, they all do they same thing—allowing you to put together a digital film comprised of digital images, audio, and graphics. If you want the most flexibility as a professional editor, you should learn how to use them all. Each one has a different interface and that's the point of issue for most users, which comes down to personal taste. Table 7.1 summarizes the price points, platform, ease of learning, and so forth.

WHAT YOU REALLY NEED TO KNOW ABOUT DSLRS AND CINEMA CAMERAS

There have been more innovative and competitively priced cameras released over the past two to three years than probably at any time in the history of the industry. Canon, Panasonic, and Sony have released DSLRs and mirrorless cameras that can shoot cinematic quality for low costs, from full HD to 4K resolutions. Blackmagic and Digital Bolex have released cinematic cameras that shoot raw (little to no compression), providing cinematic-quality postproduction capabilities for under $5,000.

No matter what camera you decide to shoot on, what you need to look at is the sensor size, resolution, frame rate, type of shutter, compression codec, and audio quality—I'll describe what these mean below. Some cameras come with different lens mounts (such as Canon EF, micro 4/3, PL cinema, C-mounts, and so forth). Whatever the lens mount, this is clear: cameras will evolve every year with new releases, but lenses and audio gear don't change often—if you invest in lenses and audio, that will be more important than buying a new camera ever year. In some ways, you could invest in a set of good lenses and audio gear and rent new and different cameras for different projects—maybe invest in one cheaper camera to have it for small projects, personal use, and as a backup or second camera on a shoot. I'll also provide a chart describing the key features of several different lower budget cameras in relation to these elements after laying out these definitions.

- **Lens mount:** Different brands contain different mounts. Sony cameras are different than Canon cameras, and then different sensor-sized cameras might have their own types of lenses. Some companies will use other companies' standards as well. And then older cameras will have different mounts than newer ones (such as older Canon cameras with different mounts than their EF lines). Some of the Canon lenses (EF-S) won't work on their full-frame sensor cameras, since they're designed for their cropped-sensor cameras.

In either case, you're looking for focal lengths, speed, and whether it's a zoom (adjustable focal length) or prime (fixed focal length) lens. The speed of the lens refers to how open you can set the aperture (given as an f-stop number), which lets in more light (the wider the opening, the less light you need). The smaller the f-stop number the more open, or faster, the lens is. For example, f/2.8 is considered a fast lens, while an f/4 or f/5.6 is considered slow. Inexpensive zoom lenses will have changing speeds on their lenses, so getting a fixed aperture zoom lens is important, but they are more expensive. Also, cinema lenses are rated with T-stops, which are the same as f-stops, but take into effect the loss of light going through the glass, so the T-stop is accurate, while the f-stop is a mathematical rating that doesn't take the transmission quality of the glass into effect.

- **Sensor** (CCD and CMOS):
  - CCD (charged coupled device) with a *global shutter*. High-end cameras, scientific instruments, and even older model video cameras used CCDs, but they're more expensive to make. Joe Rubinstein, who designed the Digital Bolex camera, says that, "The pixels that are next to each other on CCD sensors affect each other. When one pixel overflows with energy, it affects the pixels around it. The pixels work together as a unit, much the way chemicals on a film plane do. We believe this gives the sensor a more organic look." There is less light sensitivity with CCDs and, due to the expense, most camera manufacturers use CMOS sensors. (The sensor for the Digital Bolex, for example, costs about $1,000.) Does this mean you should not shoot with a rolling shutter camera? No. Thousands of professional projects have been shot with cameras containing rolling shutters. But you need to be aware of the conditions so you know their limitations.
  - CMOS (Complementary Metal Oxide Semiconductor) with *rolling shutter*. (Blackmagic has put a global shutter feature on low frame rates in some of their new cameras, such as the URSA Mini.) These are active pixel sensors. Rubinstein says that, "Active Pixel Sensors read all of their pixels linearly from top left to bottom right while the shutter is open. The pixels don't store any charge, they simply read how much light is hitting that pixel at the exact moment and convert that into an electrical signal. A rolling shutter (as opposed to a global shutter) is always active and 'rolling' through pixels from top to bottom. This can result in the now-familiar motion artifacts often referred to as 'jello.'" These sensors are more light sensitive, are fairly inexpensive, and can engage in high frame rates. (See http://www.digitalbolex.com/global-shutter/.)

- **Sensor size and resolution:** The sensor size is measured in millimeters, while the resolution of the sensor represents how many pixels are being used in a particular shot (in some cameras, such as Blackmagic's URSA Mini you can choose the resolution on their 35mm sensor to be 4.6K, 4K, 2K, full HD, or even less, while the Digital Bolex shoots 2K and full HD on a 16mm-size sensor). The sensor size impacts how the focal length of lenses effects how the field of view gets resolved. Photographers set the standard of the focal length against the full frame sensor, so they refer to the APS-C sensor on a 70D, for example, as a cropped sensor. Thus a 50mm focal length lens will be equivalent to an 80mm on a full frame camera (it has a crop factor of 1.6). (See http://www.abelcine.com/fov/ for a visual reference guide where you can input different camera's field of view based on the focal length of the lens.)

- *Full frame:* Photographers love the full frame sensor. The frame is the size of old-school 35mm film (but not 35mm cinema film!). Due to the larger sensor, filmmakers can get really shallow depth of field when shooting wide open apertures. You don't need a full frame sensor camera and if you're going for a 35mm cinema look, this is really not the camera to get, unless you're going for its unique look—some argue that it actually provides a 65mm film look. The Canon 5D Mark III (and Mark IV), 6D, and Sony's A7s contain this large sensor.

- *Cropped frame (1.6):* This is the APS-C sensor, which is close to the size of the S35mm sensor. Most DSLRs are this size, including the Canon 60D, 70D, and so forth. If you're shooting with a DSLR, this is the standard for getting a 35mm film look.

- *S35mm:* This is the cinema standard, found in the Canon C100, C300, URSA Mini, among others. Cinematographers will not consider this a cropped frame, but if you want the comparison to the full frame, then it's 1.39.

- *Micro 4/3:* A smaller format found on many mirrorless cameras (such as Panasonic's GH4). Crop factor is 2.

- *Super 16mm:* The sensor size found on the Digital Bolex D16 and the Blackmagic Pocket Cinema Camera. Crop factor is 3 (when shooting full HD) and 2.88 when shooting 2K on the Bolex and 2.88 on the Blackmagic.

- **Dynamic range**: The ability of a sensor to record in a range of dark to bright without losing information in the extreme ranges—the contrast ratio. If a camera says that it has a dynamic range of 12 stops, it means that it can capture a range of detail from dark to light within this 12-stop range. If the scene is beyond a 12-stop range, then the values beyond these 12 stops will not be recorded—the darks will either go black (crushed) or the light will go all white (blown out or clipped). Typically in the digital cinema field, you'll want to expose for the highlights, since data can be recovered in the dark regions, while it is impossible with clipped shots. Some cameras can record images in a "flat" mode. These include Sony's S-curve, Canon C-log, and Blackmagic Film setting, a mathematical process that spreads the image data along the full dynamic range making the image appear flat onscreen (see "Raw is Not Magic" at http://prolost.com/blog/rawvslog). It's designed for postproduction work, by which you pull this data out in the highlights and the shadows, recovering a larger dynamic range and allowing for greater color grading. In addition, you can read general exposure data if you use a histogram, which shows the intensity of darks to lights on a scale on a camera's monitor, so you can adjust the exposure if you're clipping values in the whites or crushing the blacks. (Again, you can crush blacks and recover the data, but if you clip the highlights, it's gone forever.)

- **Frame rate:** The film standard is 24fps (frames per second); NTSC Television is 30fps and PAL television is 25fps (these are based on the electrical current rates of 60Hz and 50Hz cycles, depending on which country you live in). High frame rates allow you to create slow-motion shots (since you're getting more data and conforming it to 24fps, slowing down the images and vice versa—shooting at 16 fps, will cause a faster rate). The higher the frame rate, the slower the playback of motion. A 60fps rate will give you a pleasant smooth slow down. For certain scenes and shots, this is an important tool for filmmakers. Frame rates that show 23.97 or 29.97 refer to the space needed for a broadcast signal to carry an audio signal.

- **Shutter angle/speed:** A standard look to your footage will be a shutter angle of 180 degrees or 1/48th per second shutter speed (on a 24fps frame rate). This is half of a circle standard in a film camera as the shutter rotates, letting in half the light in a single rotation. The smaller the angle, such as 90 or 45 degrees (or high shutter speed, like 1/500th), the more staccato the look with minimum motion blur; the larger the angle, such as 270 degrees (or low shutter speed, such as 1/24th), the smoothness or motion blur of the look increases). (See Figure 7.1.) Shane Hurlbut, ASC, describes the shutter angle this way:

FIGURE 7.1
Shutter angle/shutter speed. As the angle increases, you increase motion blur (or when setting the shutter speed slower), and as it decreases you get sharper edges (or when setting the shutter speed faster). (Image licensed under Creative Commons Attribution-Share Alike 3.0.)

What is shutter speed? Imagine a pie, and that pie has 24 pieces. If the film plane or digital sensor in your camera were to always see the lens, this would be shutterless. Nothing is obstructing its view with a 360-degree shutter. To the best of my knowledge, this can only be done on digital cameras, unless you pull the shutter physically out of a film camera. At 360 degrees, you will have a lot of motion blur in your action because as an actor moves his arm or his drumstick you are seeing it on all 24 pieces of the pie. If you were to use a 180-degree shutter, which has become the industry standard at 24fps, you would see motion blur that we have all come accustomed to in the theater. At 180 degrees, the film plane or digital sensor at 1/50 or more exacting 1/48 of a second would be seeing the drumstick on 12 out of the 24 pieces. (See https://www.hurlbutvisuals.com/blog/2013/08/intensity-with-internal-camera-settings/.)

- **Compression:** Every consumer camera, DSLR in video mode, and most prosumer cameras record in 8-bit H.264 codec (compression/decompression algorithm). Eight bits means there are 256 points of data per pixel and the H.264 is a compression standard that engineers created to make the image look great with the smallest file size—which means the image is compressed. It looks good in a small file size, because it is a finishing codec designed to look good as a finished product online or with Blu-ray discs. Manufacturers use these in consumer-type cameras, so a lot more recording can be placed on memory cards. But they're not good for editing, since data is being shared across images. When you import these compressed files into your video editing software, the files are typically decompressed for editing, increasing the file size into Apple's ProRes[2] or equivalent codec (4:2:2—a note about this below). This isn't really a big issue if you get the look of the shot in-camera accurate (proper color balance and exposure, for example). If your color and exposure is inaccurate, you can tweak the image just a little bit in post to correct issues, but the images quickly fall apart if you push it too far, because there's not enough data in the compressed image to recover any details. Treat 8-bit like negative reversal film stock (if you're old school).

High-end professional cameras, and some of the cheaper cameras, such as Blackmagic Design's cameras, can shoot in ProRes at different compression rates. An 8-bit compression contains 256 points of info (4:2:0 and 4:2:2), 10-bits is 1,024 (4:2:2), and 12-bits (4:4:4:4) is uncompressed with 4,096 pieces of data per pixel. The less the compression, the more data you get and more headroom you'll have in post to make corrections and adjust the look and feel of your project during color grading. Other cameras use uncompressed and compressed forms of raw, providing the best quality image, but requiring a lot of recording and storage space (2K recording at uncompressed raw will click in at about 500GB for about 90 minutes of recording).

- **Chroma subsampling:** The eye perceives the nuance of brightness more than color. To take advantage of this, chroma (or color) subsampling compresses color information to save space. In this type of compression, there's one piece of information for luminance (brightness) and two for color (chrominance). The numbers represent the one brightness sample rate (given as a 4) and two color sample rates among a group of pixels (given as a 0—no sample; 2—half sample; or 4—full sample, no compression). The first number (luma) shows how many pixels across are in the group (usually four in each of two rows), while the second number shows how many of these are receiving the color data (chroma) in the top row; the third number shows how many pixels in the second row are getting color data. All pixels get full brightness or luma values, thus these sequences always begin as 4. (When there's a fourth 4, that represents the chroma channel for green screen work.)

  - *4:4:4:* All light and colors are sampled at the same rate. There is no subsampling, so this provides the strongest image for postproduction work. Each pixel contains luma (brightness) and chroma (color) data. Provides for the most headroom in post, especially when doing green screen work, which is called the alpha channel and is represented by the fourth digit. Greatest ability to alter color and exposure values in post color correction and color grading work. This is the 12-bit raw standard.

    When you're shooting an 8-bit compression format, the look is baked in—not much can be done in post. When working with raw or even somewhat in 10-bit workflow, you can shape the look of the film in post. You can either design or apply existing Look Up Tables (LUTs) to a project—which provide color grading to the work, giving it a specific style of film look. This is why raw is so attractive to some filmmakers—you can shape nearly any look you want without destroying the original, so in many ways it's a throwback to shooting on original film stock.

  - *4:2:2:* In a four-pixel sample, all the luma values are used (4), but only two on top and two on bottom are utilized—the pixels share the same color data—resulting in half the sample of 4:4:4 (saving recording space). The image is considered very good and nearly indistinguishable from 4:4:4—except when you need to do heavy post work, when the image will fall apart into blocky, noisy artifacts, and banding across colors. This is the standard ProRes codec, providing a clean image with some ability to change color and exposure values in post. Circumventing the 8-bit compression scheme of many cameras, Atomos and Video Devices make video recorders that allow such cameras as the 8-bit compression found in the C100 and DSLRs to record in 10-bit 4:2:2

with a feed from the HDMI out (the Video Devices PIX-E5 records up to 4:4:4XQ). On the other hand, Blackmagic Design created their cameras to allow for ProRes recording in-camera.

– *4:2:0:* Same as 4:2:2, except the bottom row of pixels in the sample don't get any data—they share it with the top row, therefore they're given a zero. This is the sampling rate found in AVCHD and MPG-4, both of which are a type of package for H.264 compression. The image will fall apart quickly in post if you have to make changes to the image—hence the importance of getting the image right in-camera.[3] Overleaf Table 7.2 summarizes these different types of codecs.

- **Resolution: Full HD, 2K, 4K:** The amount of pixels recorded. The higher the number the higher the resolution. Full HD is 1920x1080 and is the current standard for Blu-ray DVDs and broadcast television; 2K is cinema quality for projection; 4K is the future.[4] Those who are shooting 4K now will not have a large audience see their work in 4K, since most of cinema is still 2K and most television sets are Full HD—although more and more televisions are being released with 4K capability. It will likely become more of a standard by 2020 or a few years later. However, there are increasingly more cameras being released that shoot 4K. There are several benefits to shooting in 4K now:

  – *Future proof:* Store your film or project in 4K so it's ready when there's a market for it.

  – *Cropping a shot:* The editor may want to crop an image and if you have a large area of resolution (such as 4K), then the image can be cropped or recomposed for an HD or 2K project without losing any data.

  – *Fixing unwanted motion in a shot:* There might be a wobbly shot that allows software to fix that motion. If you're shooting in full HD or 2K, that software will share and grab data around the wobbly shots in order to fix it. If there's no space around the shot, then the image will lose some resolution, but if there's a lot of space around it, then it can pull data above full HD and 2K without losing any resolution.

- **Audio quality:** Don't skimp on audio. Poorly recorded audio is the number one killer of a project. For this reason, you must be able to see levels on a meter and listen to the audio being recorded on headphones. Either you're doing this or you're hiring a sound recordist to do this. There are no shortcuts to good audio. Some settings to keep in mind:

  – 24-bit audio should be the standard (as opposed to many cameras still using 16-bit recordings)—more data gives you more headroom in post. It doesn't matter if it's 48kHz or 96kHz, just as long as you have headroom (space to adjust your audio) in post.

  – XLR inputs are a must, which results in low interference, low impedance. It's the professional standard. If your camera doesn't have it, then you'll want a field mixer and/or recorder with XLR connections, resulting

TABLE 7.2

A Comparison of Several Different Types of Codecs

CODEC	Data bit	Data throughput at 1920x1080 24p	Storage space at 1920x1080	Uses
4:2:0 (H.264, AVCHD, MPG-4)	8-bit	18Mb/s	20GB/hr	Finishing for web streaming and Blu-ray DVDs; most lower-end cameras and DSLRs record in this format; files need to be decompressed before editing. Very little postproduction (around 10%) can be applied before the image falls apart.
ProRes 4:2:2 (LT)[23]	10-bit	82 Mb/s	37GB/hr	Shots must be accurate in-camera (proper exposure and color balance); use for extra recording space. Not recommended for professional work.
ProRes 4:2:2	10-bit	117 Mb/s	53GB/hr	A professional codec, but the look should be accurate in-camera; some post correction may be applied.
ProRes 4:2:2 (HQ)	10-bit	176 Mb/s	79GB/hr	A professional codec, but the look should be accurate in-camera as much as possible; some post correction may be applied.
ProRes 4:4:4	12-bit	264 Mb/s	119GB/hr	A professional codec with plenty of headroom for postproduction work.
ProRes 4:4:4HQ	12-bit	396Mb/s	178GB/hr	A professional codec with a lot of headroom for postproduction work.
Avid DNxHD 4:2:2 80	10-bit	80Mb/s	33.6GB/hr	Equivalent to ProRes LT. Shots must be accurate in-camera (proper exposure and color balance); use for extra recording space. Not recommended for professional work.
Avid DNxHD 4:2:2 115	10-bit	116 Mb/s	73.71GB/hr	A professional codec, but the look should be accurate in-camera; some post correction may be applied.
Avid DNxHD 4:2:2 175	10-bit	176 Mb/s	48.7GB/hr	A professional codec, but the look should be accurate in-camera as much as possible; some post correction may be applied.
Avid DNxHD 4:4:4	12-bit	352 Mb/s	147.8GB/hr	A professional codec, but the look should be accurate in-camera; some post correction may be applied.
CinemaDNG (compressed)	12-bit	Varies based on compression level	Varies based on compression level	A professional codec for cinema work; a lot of post correction may be used. Saves space compared to uncompressed raw.
CinemaDNG (raw, uncompressed)	12-bit	357 Mb/s	500GB for just under 2 hours in full HD or under 90 minutes in 2K	Cinema; allows for excellent headroom to adjust when doing color correction and grading in post. Uses a lot of recording and storage space.

in the recording of audio separate from audio on-camera. One-eighth inch inputs found on many DSLRs, the C100 with the top handle removed, and the Blackmagic Pocket Cinema Camera are high impedance, which results in picking up more noise, and are not used by professionals (it's okay to use such mics for reference audio).

– If your camera doesn't have good audio recording, use an external audio recorder to get strong and clean audio. It's best to have a dedicated sound recordist, but when you can't, dedicated audio recorders will give you better audio than the camera provides.

- **Metabones:** DSLRs and the lower-end Blackmagic cameras (such as the Cinema Camera or Pocket Cinema Camera), as well as the Digital Bolex (with the micro 4/3 mount) can greatly benefit from the Metabones Speedbooster. It's a lens adapter that increases the field of view and the aperture speed of lenses. The Digital Bolex, for example, is a difficult camera to get a zoom lens that starts wide. With the EF to BMPCC model, you can place a Canon 17–55mm zoom lens (with a simple modification)[5] and get the equivalent of a 10–32mm lens with a 1 2/3 increased aperture stop. In addition, some of the adapters accept a 5v battery from a mini-USB on the side of the adapter. This allows you to change the f-stop of the lenses that use automatic controls (good for cameras with passive Micro Four Thirds mounts (such as the Digital Bolex and Blackmagic Cinema Cameras). See http://metabones.com for more information. See Figure 7.2 for a comparison of field of view and aperture stop adjustments.

Compatibility List						
EF-MFT Speed Booster Products	Crop factor / Aperture Stop	Cameras				
		GH4	OMD	BMPCC	BMCC *	
Canon EF Lens to Micro Four Thirds T Speed Booster ULTRA 0.71x MB_SPEF-M43-BT4	0.71x / +1	Y	Y**	Y	Y	
Canon EF Lens to BMPCC Speed Booster 0.58x MB_SPEF-BMPCC-BM1	0.58x / +1.66	N	N	Y	N	
Canon EF Lens to BMCC Speed Booster 0.64x MB_SPEF-BMCC-BM1	0.64x / +1.33	N	N	Y	Y	
Canon EF Lens to Micro Four Thirds T Speed Booster XL 0.64x MB_SPEF-M43-BT3	0.64x / +1.33	Y	N	Y***	Y***	

* For the passive MFT mount camera, external 5 Volt micro-USB power supply is required.
** OMD has no AF support.
*** Standard Micro Four Thirds cameras like the Panasonic GH4 have a total of approximately 4mm thickness of filter glass near the sensor, and the Speed Booster XL 0.64x is designed to work optimally with this thickness of glass. The Blackmagic Cinema Camera and Pocket Cinema Camera have substantially thinner total filter glass thickness, which may cause noticeable aberrations when the Speed Booster XL 0.64x is used on Blackmagic cameras at large apertures. For best results on Blackmagic cameras it is recommended that the appropriate Blackmagic-specific Speed Boosters be used.

FIGURE 7.2
Metabones Speedbooster chart comparing the differences to the Canon EF to Micro Four-Thirds adapters. Take note of the crop factor multiplication and aperture stop increase (making your base lenses faster).

- **Ergonomics:** How does the camera handle in your hands? Is it light (too light), too heavy, awkward to hold, designed more for a tripod, and so forth? These questions can only be answered if you go to a store or trade show and handle the camera you're thinking about getting.

- **Magic Lantern:** A necessary tool for those using DSLRs—it provides software on a memory card that the camera can access (you'll need to place it on all of your memory cards to activate this feature). The features of this software comes standard in most professional cameras, but is missing in most DSLRs. Therefore it is one of the most important things you can do to your DSLR to get it to a professional status—providing you with focus peaking, histogram, waveform monitor, spot meter, audio meters, among other features. For installation instructions and updates on what Canon DSLRs are available for the firmware, see: http://www.magiclantern.fm/. The installation guide can be found at: http://wiki.magiclantern.fm/install.

Below Table 7.3 outlines some features in a variety of cameras—from DSLRs to raw capable cameras. All prices are from early 2016.

ADDITIONAL GEAR

Microphones

Without good sound, you do not have a viable project. Your work will never be perceived as professional. While viewers may forgive a compromised image, they will never forgive poor sound. Most cameras with XLR inputs can record clean audio, as long as you record a clean and strong signal—which usually means someone monitors the audio with headphones and observe the meters for a -12dB to -6dB range to make sure the signal doesn't clip, and to allow plenty of headroom in post.

A note about foam windscreens—these come with nearly every mic and they're designed to help reduce pops for people who pop their Ps and Ts. They're not windscreens. You'll want a dedicated windscreen, and if you're really fighting wind, then get a blimp-style windscreen.

- **Shotgun:** These types of mics can sit on the camera with a shockmount (to absorb handling vibration sound), pistol grip, or boom pole. These directional mics may be utilized to pick up dialogue from the direction they are pointed (and always point them at the subject's mouth for the strongest signal) and ambient sound that they are pointed at.

- **Lavaliere:** A clip-on mic designed to pick up dialogue from the person the mic is clipped to.

- **Built-in camera mic:** Never use as primary audio (use only as reference audio that you will replace with an external audio recorder and microphone).

TABLE 7.3

A Comparison of Cinema-quality Budget DSLR and Mirrorless Cameras

Model				
	FIGURE 7.3 Canon 70D. (Courtesy of Canon.)	**FIGURE 7.4** Canon 5D Mk III. (Courtesy of Canon.)	**FIGURE 7.5** Panasonic GH4. (Courtesy of Panasonic.)	**FIGURE 7.6** Sony a7sII. (Courtesy of Sony.)
Lens mount	Canon EF	Canon EF	Micro 4/3	Sony E
Recommended starter lenses	Canon 17-55mm f/2.8 (~$850); if your budget is really tight, the Canon 50mm f/1.8 is a fast lens for ~$125.	Canon 24-105mm (get as a kit with the camera and save ~$400); it's slow for my taste, but if you're shooting outdoors in the day and lighting indoors, it's a versatile lens; if your budget is really tight, the Canon 50mm f/1.8 is a fast lens for ~$125.	Panasonic 12-35mm f/2.8 (~$1,000)	Sony FE35mm f/2.8 (~$800) or Sony FE 55mm f/1.8 (~$1,000)
Sensor size	APS-C	Full frame	Micro 4/3	Full frame
Resolution	1920x1080	1920x1080	4096x2160	1920x1080
Crop factor	1.6	1	2	1
Histogram	None in record mode	None in record mode	No	No
Max frame rate	30fps (1920x1080) 60fps (1280x720)	30fps (1920x1080) 60fps (1280x720)	24fps (4096x2160) 60fps (1920x1080)	60fps (1920x1080) 120fps (1280x720)
Shutter type	CMOS, rolling	CMOS, rolling	CMOS, rolling	CMOS, rolling

continued . . .

TABLE 7.3
Continued

Shutter speed/angle	Shutter speed	Shutter speed	Shutter speed	Shutter speed and shutter angle	Shutter speed
Audio input	1/8"-minijack	1/8"-minijack	1/8"-minijack	1/8"-minijack	1/8"-minijack
Audio quality	16-bit	16-bit	16-bit	16-bit	24-bit
Headphones	No	Yes	Yes	Yes	Yes
Recording media	SDHC card	CF and SDHC card	SDHC card	SDHC card	SDHC card and Sony Memory Stick Pro
Compression codec	8-bit H.264 (91.3Mb/s; All-I mode) 10-bit 422 output via HDMI (with proper external recorder)	8-bit H.264 (91.3Mb/s; All-I mode) 10-bit 422 output via HDMI (with proper external recorder)	8-bit H.264 10-bit 422 output via HDMI (with proper external recorder)	8-bit H.264 10-bit 422 4K output via HDMI (with proper external recorder)	8-bit H.264 10-bit 422 4K output via HDMI (with proper external recorder)
Ergonomics	Hand-size DSLR camera, light	Hand-size DSLR camera, good weight	Smaller camera, light	Smaller camera, light	Smaller camera, light
Additional notes	Best bang for your buck if you're on a tight budget. Shoot in all-I mode (to provide the highest quality image). Get the image accurate in-camera—all the time; there's not much room for fixing it in post!	A standard in the DSLR cinema world, and by the time this book is printed, the Mark IV will have replaced it. Shoot in all-I mode (to provide the highest quality image). Get the image accurate in-camera—all the time; there's not much room for fixing it in post! Will provide a unique full frame look, similar to shooting in 65mm.	Through HDMI out, you can get 10-bit 422 output. You can purchase an "interface unit" for ~$1,000, but if you buy it as a kit on B&H Photo, you'll save $400. The unit provides 2 XLR inputs, audio level monitor, SDI BNC connectors, HDMI out, and Timecode.		This is probably the smallest full frame camera on the market. It has a high ISO and can shoot in low light without a problem. It has a headphone jack, which is nice, and you can get the Rode VideoMic Pro with Rycote Lyre to get usable backup field audio.
Cost (in mid-2015)	~$1,000	~$2,500	~$1,300	~$3,000	

TABLE 7.4

A Comparison of Cinema-quality Budget Cameras

Model					
	 FIGURE 7.7 Canon C100 Mk II. (Courtesy of Canon.)	 FIGURE 7.8 Sony NEX-FS700R. (Courtesy of Sony.)	 FIGURE 7.9 Blackmagic Pocket Cinema Camera (Courtesy of Blackmagic Design.)	 FIGURE 7.10 Blackmagic URSA Mini. (Courtesy of Blackmagic Design.)	 FIGURE 7.11 Digital Bolex. (Courtesy of Digital Bolex.)
Lens mount	Canon EOS	Sony E-Mount	Micro 4/3	Canon EF and PL (separate models)	C, micro 4/3, Canon EF (mounts may be placed on the same camera)
Recommended starter lenses	Canon 17-55mm f/2.8 (~$850)	Get the EF to Sony adapter and use a Canon lens (the Metabones adapter described in the notes is a good option).	Tokina 11–16mm T3.0 ($1,600) or Sigma 18–35mm f/1.8 ($800)	Canon 17-55mm f/2.8 (~$850)	For micro 4/3 mount: Tokina 11-16mm T3.0 ($1,600) This is a manual aperture lens, so you can adjust the T-stops manually. The Bolex will not use an automatic lens. See more in notes, below.
Sensor size	S35	S35	Super 16mm	S35	Super 16mm
Resolution	1920x1080	1920x1080 and 4K with interface unit and recorder	1920x1080	4000x2160 (with 4K model) or 4608x2592 (with 4.6K model)	2K and 1920x1080
Crop factor	1.39	1.39	2.88	1.39	2.88 at 2K and 3 at full HD
Histogram	Yes	Yes	Yes	Yes	No
Max frame rate	60fps	60fps (240 fps at an 8-second burst)	30fps	60fps at 4K	30fps

continued . . .

TABLE 7.4

Continued

Shutter type	Global	Global and CMOS, rolling	CMOS, rolling	CMOS, rolling	CMOS, rolling
Shutter speed/ angle	Shutter angle	Shutter angle	Shutter angle	Shutter speed	Shutter speed
Audio input	2 XLRs	2 XLRs	1/8"-minijack	2 XLRs	1/8"-minjack and XLR
Audio quality	24-bit	24-bit	16-bit	16-bit	16-bit
Headphones	Yes	Yes	Yes	Yes	Yes
Recording media	Built-in SSD with backup to CF cards	CFast 2.0 cards	SDHC cards	SDHC cards and Memory Stick Pro	SDHC cards
Compression codec	12-bit 444 uncompressed CinemaDNG raw	ProRes 420, 422, 444, 444XQ; compressed CinemaDNG raw	ProRes 420, 422, 444, 444XQ; CinemaDNG compressed raw	8-bit H.264 (MPG-4 and AVCHD) and 12-bit 444 2K and 4K raw (via HXR-IFR5 interface and AXS-R5 recorder)	8-bit H.264 (MPG-4 and AVCHD) 10-bit 422 output via HDMI (with proper external recorder)
Ergonomics	Medium size and weight, tripod, monopod; has pistol grip	Large, heavy, tripod or shoulder use	Small, light	Good medium weight	Good handgrip with good weight
Additional notes	A solid 16mm cinema camera that shoots 12-bit raw (CinemaDNG). The SSD is internal (the 1T option may be the one you want if you're doing a lot of shooting in a day). Has the capability to back up files to two CF cards. It comes with a C-mount standard (an older 16mm screw-in mount), but lenses are hard to find; although Kish makes a set with a f/4 primes.	A strong production house camera that provides a lot of codec options when recording, including compressed 12-bit CinemaDNG raw and a range of ProRes formats (from 422 LT to 4444XQ). It is a larger camera, so get the top handle and shoulder mount option if you're planning to do any handheld work. In addition, it comes with a 4K model,	Best features are its portability, size, and the ability to shoot compressed forms of raw and the ProRes settings (already making it a better camera than many others that record in the compressed H.264 codec). Audio is poor, so use an external audio recorder. Uses micro 4/3 lenses. Need to get wide angle in order to get a large	To take this camera to the pro level, get an external recorder, such as the Atomos Ninja 2 or Ninja Star—it's a great workaround on the 8-bit compression issue (recording from the camera's HDMI output), recording in ProRes 10-bit 422 (up to HQ mode). (Records on CFast cards.) This Sony camera packs power with	The Mark II is a nice improvement on the first model. This is a standard camera for many production houses due to its flexibility, including the ability to shoot a flat image, providing more dynamic range/ headroom space in post. Use the MPG-4 format for a higher bit depth (do not use the AVCHD wrapper).

Use an external recorder, such as Blackmagic's Video Assist to record files in 10-bit 422.	the optional interface and recorder allowing it to do 2K and 4K raw. It has built in ND filters. You'll need to use Sony-based lenses, although, Metabones has released a Canon EF mount to Sony smart adapter for ~$400. See: http://www.metabones.com/products/details/MB-EF-E-BM4	field of view, therefore I recommend the Tokina 11–16mm T3.0 lens. The major drawback of the camera is the short battery life. You'll need plenty of batteries on hand or a larger battery pack. See, for example, IndiPRO Tools' Power Grid and XLR audio box designed for the camera (see the products page at http://indiproco.com). This device will give you extra battery life with either Sony or Canon batteries, and the ability to plug in XLR audio. It's recommended that you get the Metabones Speedbooster adapter—it increases the field of view by 0.58x of the lens and makes it faster by 1.66 stops.	using an older sensor, as well as a 4.6K model that Blackmagic designed, claiming a dynamic range of 15 stops.	The better bet is to get the one with the micro 4/3 mount (which can be added to the camera and they'll eventually release a Canon EOS mount). The built-in LCD monitor is okay for going through menus, but weak for shooting (the resolution is too low and it's too small). You need a field monitor that you can attach to the camera. Most of them will have features such as focus assist and a histogram. It's recommended that you get the Metabones Speedbooster adapter—it increases the field of view by 0.58x of the lens and makes it faster by 1.66 stops. With the EF to Micro 4/3 mount, you can use the Canon 17-55mm f/2.8 zoom lens. (But you'll need to remove the plastic flange on the bottom of the lens—zoom all the way out, reach in with your fingers and tug it out. It will now attach to the Metabones adapter.)
Cost (in mid-2015) ~$5,500	~$4,000	~$1,000	~$3,000 (with 4K S35mm sensor with no tophandle or shoulder mount); ~$5,000 with the new 4.6K sensor	~$3,700 with 500GB SSD and ~$4,300 with 1T SSD (get only with Micro Four-Thirds mount).

Furthermore, different microphones use different pickup patterns (what sounds they primarily pick up). Keep the mic less than two feet from the subject's mouth.

- **Omnidirectional:** Audio is picked up from all directions like a sphere. Many lavaliere mics (clip-on mics for interviews) are omnidirectional.
- **Cardioid:** A heart-shaped pattern where audio is recorded mainly from the front, but also some from the side. It'll pick up ambient sound from the sides, while utilizing the strongest signal from the front. Use for dialogue.
- **Hypercardioid:** The audio signal is picked up mostly from the front with very little from the sides and rear. Directional mic used to pick up audio/dialogue from the direction it is pointed.

Video Recorders

You'll want a video recorder if your camera doesn't record in a 10-bit (or 12-bit raw) codec. Nearly every lower budget camera (except for the Blackmagic)[6] records in a compressed 8-bit codec that could lead to unprofessional results. A video recorder takes a camera's HDMI output (or SDI on higher-end models) and feeds it into a specially designed recorder that makes the footage 10-bit, preventing the need to decompress footage in editing.

Preamp Field Mixers

While many people record audio with a microphone attached to their camera—and if they're shooting solo this may be their only option—there are field mixers with dedicated preamps that will provide the best sound in the field. Most of them will have at least two XLR inputs, so professional microphones can be attached. Some of these preamp mixers can be attached directly to a DSLR, the Blackmagic Cinema Camera, and the Blackmagic Pocket Cinema Camera, which do not contain XLR inputs. Because these devices are dedicated to audio, they'll also contain better and cleaner amps than those found in most cameras—the preamps in the Digital Bolex are strong. With the multiple input XLRs, shooters can connect a lav and shotgun mic on two separate channels—the lav dedicated to an interview, for example, and the shotgun mic dedicated to recording ambient audio and acting as a backup to the lav. It will also include phantom power, which will power microphones that do not have batteries (but will also shorten the device's battery).

Audio Recorder

Most professional shoots utilize a sound recordist who will have both a field mixer and an external audio recorder. They may also plug an XLR line into the main camera so it receives the field mixer's feed. There are many field recorders on the market. Be sure to set the recording to 24-bits at 48k (or 96k), so that there's more headroom in post. Make sure the levels hit between -12dB to -6dB. A dedicated sound person is best, because they can monitor the audio and adjust it if the levels get too low or too high. Most devices also contain limiters preventing you from accidently clipping audio. Audio recorders include the Tascam DR-40, Zoom H5, Zoom H6, and the Marantz PMD661. (I don't cover these in this book due to a lack of space, but these are standard recorders for the budget-conscious filmmaker.)

Tripod

You need stable shots. A lot of beginners and amateurs think that they can handhold their camera and get good-looking shots. Very few people can pull off a strong handheld shot, so a locked-off tripod shot is best, because it shows control. Be sure to get a tripod that contains a fluid head and a half-ball leveler, so you're not adjusting tripod legs to get your tripod level. The half-ball leveler will allow you to loosen a bottom handle to the half-ball, adjust it quickly, then lock it off when it's level.

Slider

Provides for cinematically smooth tracking shots without needing to set up a track on the ground. Get a slider that attaches to a tripod. Be sure to make sure the movement reveals something in the shot—that it helps tell the story, rather than providing movement for the sake of movement. Change the way the camera faces, rotating it along the axis to get parallel tracking shots and perpendicular push in and pullout shots.

Cranes/Jibs

Small cranes or jibs will attach to your tripod and allow you to do vertical up and down movements as well as pushing in and pulling out from a shot.

Below, in Table 7.5, I list several lower-budget models of some of the types of gear described above—it is not close to being complete, but reflects a certain budget requirement balanced with a level of quality.

TABLE 7.5

A Variety of Gear to Supplement the Professional Equipment Package

Name	Cost	Notes

Video field recorders

These are necessary if you're shooting with a camera in 8-bit compressed files (an unprofessional file format). The video field recorders will circumvent the compression through the camera's HDMI output, providing professional 10-bit 4:2:2 codec (Video Devices PIX-E5 will provide up to 12-bit 4:4:4:4 HQ)—some will have options for Apple's ProRes or Avid's DNxHD. It also circumvents the file systems of the camera, so you're not limited to a short recording time.

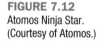

FIGURE 7.12
Atomos Ninja Star.
(Courtesy of Atomos.)

~$300 — This is a small, light, and inexpensive option if you're shooting with an 8-bit codec camera, recording in 10-bit ProRes 4:2:2. It connects to your camera's HDMI port through a mini HDMI cable. You'll want to get a locking cable. It also includes audio meters. You'll need to purchase CFast cards.

The battery will last over five hours, according to the manufacturer. It includes a battery, charger, CFast card reader, and carrying case.

See: http://www.atomos.com/ninja-star/

FIGURE 7.13
Atomos Ninja 2.
(Courtesy of Atomos.)

~$300 — This is a higher-end alternative to the Ninja Star, but has a 800x400 screen that includes over-exposure zebra patterns, focus peaking, and false color readings for exposure. (Some cameras, like DSLRs, do not come with these features that are standard on most professional cameras.)

It can record in 10-bit ProRes or Avid's DNxHD.

It connects to your camera's HDMI port through a mini HDMI cable. You'll want to get a locking cable to prevent it from falling out.

The device records to an internal hard drive or SSD (not included). Be sure to budget $100–400 per drive, depending on size and quality (you'll want at least two).

If you want 4K recording, check out the Shogun model (see http://www.atomos.com/shogun).

See: http://www.atomos.com/ninja/

FIGURE 7.14
Blackmagic Video Assist.
(Courtesy of Blackmagic
Design.)

~$500 — Blackmagic Design's video recorder, the Video Assist, includes a 5" full HD touchscreen and includes such features as a headphone jack, histogram, and audio meters (important for DSLR shooters who are not using Magic Lantern).

Records in 10-bit 4:2:2 ProRes (up to HQ mode) and DNxHD. Uses SDHC cards.

See: https://www.blackmagicdesign.com/products/blackmagicvideoassist

continued . . .

TABLE 7.5

Continued

Name	Cost	Notes
 **FIGURE 7.15** Video Devices PIX-E5H. (Courtesy of Video Devices.)	~$1,200	If you're looking for a rugged housing, then Video Devices, like Sound Devices, is a higher-end alternative. Although coming at a price, Video Devices makes a high-end ProRes 422 recorder up to 4K with 5" touchscreen display. Additional costs are the SpeedDrive USB 3.0 that uses mSATA SDD drives for recording and offloading to a computer. As an option, the PIX-LR device contains two XLR audio inputs that attach to the PIX-E recorder, providing audio preamps and meters for audio recording (so you wouldn't need a second device). See: http://www.videodevices.com/products/portable-video-recorders/pix-e
FIGURE 7.16 Video Devices PIX-E5. (Courtesy of Video Devices.)	~$1,400	These are designed for 4K cameras, but they can be used for lower-res cameras, too. This model records up to ProRes 12-bit 444HQ (in 4K) with 5" touchscreen display. Otherwise, similar to the PIX-E5H. Take note of additional costs described above. See: http://www.videodevices.com/products/portable-video-recorders/pix-e

Audio mixers and pramps

These are best when you have a dedicated sound person capturing audio, but some models allow you to attach them to your camera. If you do not have XLR connectors on your camera (which is the case for DSLRs and some of the lower-end Blackmagic cameras), then it is recommended that you hire a sound person or get one of these devices below. They not only provide XLR inputs, but they also contain preamps and limiters that will help you to record strong audio and help prevent overmodulation (or clipping).

Name	Cost	Notes
FIGURE 7.17 Tascam DR-70D Audio Recorder and Mixer. (Courtesy of Tascam.)	~$300	I recommend this recorder/mixer for anyone shooting with a DSLR or a lower-end Blackmagic camera. This mixer and audio recorder contains four XLR inputs and is designed for DSLRs and other small cameras that don't have XLR inputs or headphone. It also has a built-in limiter so you don't accidently clip your audio. It attaches to the bottom of the camera with a tripod screw (the device has a screw receptacle on the bottom, so you can still attach a tripod to your setup). It also has a line out to feed the audio signal into the camera. Includes phantom power. It contains a 1/8" headphone jack and uses SDHC cards for recording. It uses four AA batteries for power. See: http://tascam.com/product/dr-70d/

continued . . .

TABLE 7.5

Continued

Name	Cost	Notes
FIGURE 7.18 Azden FMX-42a Field Mixer. (Courtesy of Azden.)	~$500	A four-channel field mixer (not a recorder) with limiters, 48v of phantom power. It contains a 1/8" output that you can feed into a camera that doesn't have XLR inputs (or use one of the two XLR outputs to feed into a camera with XLRs). Unless you're feeding the export directly into the camera, you'll want to record to an external recorder (the Tascam DR-40 is a good budget model). A throwback to analogue days, this device contains knobs and dial meters. It uses six AA batteries. Contains 1/4" headphone jack. See: http://www.azden.com/products/mixers/fmx-42a/
FIGURE 7.19 Sound Devices MixPre-D Field Mixer. (Courtesy of Sound Devices.)	~$930	This rugged field device contains strong preamps and will give you really nice field audio. It does not contain a recorder, so you will need to attach it to a field recorder or feed an input into your camera. It also has a built-in limiter so you don't accidently clip your audio. For an additional cost, you can get an adapter that will allow you to attach it to a camera's tripod connector. Includes phantom power. It also contains a TA3 connector dedicated to DSLR camera inputs. Contains a 1/4" headphone jack. It uses two AA batteries that will last close to four hours (if you're not using phantom power). See: http://www.sounddevices.com/products/mixers/mixpred

Microphones
There are not many alternatives to cheap microphones. You need something that's hardy, can engage in clean recordings, and provide professional sound. Below are some budget to mid-range quality mics.

Name	Cost	Notes
FIGURE 7.20 Rode NTG2 Shotgun Mic. (Courtesy of Rode.)	~$270	A quality budget microphone that can be powered by one AA battery or with phantom power. The Rode NTG-2 sounds nearly as good as a Sennheiser shotgun for half the price. You will want to get a windscreen and a shockmount that you can attach it to your camera and use as a run-and-gun mic—which is good for picking up ambient sound. You can get away with using it for interviews if you are close to your subject. See: http://www.rode.com/microphones/ntg-2
FIGURE 7.21 Audio-Technica AT8035. (Courtesy Audio-Technica.)	~$270	A strong directional shotgun mic. Uses a single AA battery or phantom power. Hypercadioid designed to minimize audio coming in from the sides and rear— strong directional mic. See: http://www.audio-technica.com/cms/wired_mics/0576da91f00c03db/

continued . . .

TABLE 7.5

Continued

Name	Cost	Notes
ETS PA911 Audio Camera Balun.	~$50	Get a professional mic and a shockmount and you can attach this to a camera that contains a 1/8" mic input. This adapter contains a built-in transformer and it will give you good sound when plugged into the mic input of a DSLR. If you want to get good audio with your DSLR and are not using a field mixer, then you'll want this device which helps make the high impedance minijack input on the DSLR much cleaner and it will give you usable audio. You can also use it on a Canon C100 (if you have don't want to use the top handle containing the XLR inputs) or Blackmagic Pocket camera. See: http://etslan.com/products.cgi
 FIGURE 7.22 Rode VideoMic Pro R. (Courtesy of Rode.)	~$225	If you're using a DSLR, Blackmagic Pocket Camera, or a Canon C100 with the top handle off—a camera without XLR inputs—and you need good audio along with portability in the field, Rode's VideoMic Pro will give you usable sound in a crunch. At the very least, if you have a separate sound person and want better backup sound than a camera's built-in mic, then get the Rode. It records out good sound for its size. This new model with the Rycote's Lyre suspension is much better than the old version which was nearly unmanageable when changing batteries and trying to set the elastic suspension. Powered by a 9v battery. For 1/8" mic inputs. Get the extra windscreen. See: http://rode.com/microphones/videomicpror
 FIGURE 7.23 Sennheiser ew 112-p G3 Wireless Lavaliere Mic. (Courtesy of Sennheiser.)	~$630	This lav mic kit is rugged and it's a power horse. When it comes to lav mics, getting a cheap one isn't worth the effort. There are better ones that are more expensive, but this is the best mid-range "budget" wireless on the market. The receiver can mount onto a camera's shoe mount, allowing you to feed the XLR wire into your camera. See: http://en-us.sennheiser.com/lavalier-clip-on-microphones-wireless-set-presentation-ew-112-p-g3

Tripods and monopods

Stability is important, so relying on handheld is not the way to go. Carbon-fiber tripods are light and strong, but tend to be more expensive.

continued . . .

TABLE 7.5

Continued

Name	Cost	Notes
FIGURE 7.24 Manfrotto MVH500A Tripod with Fluid Video Head. (Courtesy of Manfrotto.)	~$330	This is a standard video tripod. Shop around for a tripod that meets your need if this one isn't to your liking. See: http://bhphotovideo.com/c/product/944776-REG/manfrotto_mvk500am_mvh500a_plus_mvt502am_plus.html
FIGURE 7.25 Induro Carbon 8X Video Tripod. (Courtesy of Induro.)	~$330	This is the best set of tripod legs I've used. It doesn't include the head, but the Induro is an excellent carbon-fiber tripod. It's light, the legs drop when you twist the locks, and it contains a 75mm half-ball for quick leveling. This is a photo tripod, but I've used photo tripods for video work for years. See: http://www.indurogear.com/products/tripods/ Get a good video head, such as the Manfrotto MVH500AH fluid video head (for the slider): $130 FIGURE 7.26 Manfrotto fluid head. (Courtesy of Manfrotto.) See: http://manfrotto.us/product/0/MVH500A/_/Lightweight_fluid_video_head_-_60mm_half_ball_(5kg_payload)
FIGURE 7.27 Manfrotto Fluid Monopod (MVM500A). (Courtesy of Manfrotto.)	~$280	Probably the best investment for all-round use for both stability and movement. It has legs and a fluid head on the bottom of the monopod, allowing you to rotate and do push in and pull out shots. See Stillmotion's video tutorial on how to use this device to cover action: http://stillmotionblog.com/h234hs23dkw21/ See: http://www.manfrotto.us/product/0/MVM500A/_/Aluminum_Fluid_Monopod_with_500_head

continued . . .

TABLE 7.5

Continued

Name	Cost	Notes
 **FIGURE 7.28** Benro HMMA48CS4H monopod. (Courtesy of Benro.)	~$275	Similar to the Manfrotto, but you're getting it as a carbon-fiber, so it's light and strong. It doesn't have the levers of the Manfrotto, but it uses twists to hold and loosen the leg. This can hold up to 8.8lbs of weight. If you have a small camera, you can get another model for $200, which can hold up to 5.5lbs. And the aluminum models are even cheaper.

Sliders

Sliders provide cinematic motion and the Edelkrone and Cinevate are good products.

Name	Cost	Notes
 **FIGURE 7.29** Edelkrone SliderPlus (medium). (Courtesy of Edelkrone.)	~$600	There are many sliders out there, but this is one of the best since it can slide nearly twice its length when attached to a tripod. It's my favorite. It's smooth and rugged. You can attach a power module to it as well, so you can do timelapse or other types of automatic, controlled motorized movement. Put a video head on the tripod, and rotate the head, for example, and set up either a sideways tracking shot or a push-in/pull-out shot. See: https://www.edelkrone.com/p/138/slider-plus
 **FIGURE 7.30** Cinevate Inc 24" Duzi Camera Slider. (Courtesy of Cinevate.)	~$400	This is a cheaper alternative to the Edelkrone. There are add-ons, such as all terrain legs, carrying strap, and case. Includes a level bubble and the ability to lock the camera anywhere on the length of the slider. There's a 32" model for an additional ~$50 and a motion timelapse feature for ~ $175. See: http://www.cinevate.com/store2/camera-movement/camera-sliders/duzi-slider-v3.html

Cranes/jibs

The need for smooth moving shots that will allow you to get vertical as well as push-in and pull-out shots is important for many professional shoots. They also have a remote control feature for a separate operater to control them.

Name	Cost	Notes
PocketJib *TRAVELER* **FIGURE 7.31** Kessler Crane Pocket Jib Traveler. (Courtesy of Kessler Crane.)	~$500	This is a good portable jib that is designed to be attached to a tripod. It's travel size, folding up to 27", but when attached and ready to go, it'll extend to 72". Additional costs for a case and mounting plate. See: http://store.kesslercrane.com/products/cranes-jibs/pocket-jib-traveler-550.html

continued . . .

TABLE 7.5

Continued

Name	Cost	Notes

Gimbals

For full stabilization handheld mode that allows for fluid movement using a multi-axis (usually three: pan, tilt, and roll) gimbal system—meaning that the system utilizes a motorized gyro, and remains stable even when running. The camera needs to be balanced for weight, including lenses and batteries. It is recommended that you set up separate audio so it doesn't add weight and get in the way.

FIGURE 7.32
CAME-7500 Gimbal.
(Courtesy of CAME TV.)

~$900   Designed for small cameras, such as DSLRs, mirrorless cameras, Blackmagic Pocket Camera.

Supports up to 6.5lbs. Extra batteries and external monitor costs extra. Includes a joystick for pan, tilt, and mode control.

See: http://www.came-tv.com/assembled-32-bit-came7500-3-axis-gimbal-dslr-stabilizer-p-565.html

FIGURE 7.33
DJI Ronin-M Gimbal.
(Courtesy of DJI.)

~$1,600   Supports up to 8lbs.

Wireless transmitter for remote pan and tilt control. Has additional software through IOS and Windows.

See: http://www.dji.com/product/ronin-m

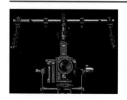

FIGURE 7.34
DJI Ronin Gimbal.
(Courtesy of DJI.)

~$2,100   This is the higher-end Ronin model that supports up to 16lbs of weight and includes a Bluetooth interface control, 15mm rods and mount points for accessories.

See: http://www.dji.com/product/ronin

Hard drives

You need a hard drive that's fast. The spin speed should be a minimum of 7200rpm and have a connector that's USB 3.0 or better, such as a thunderbolt line or eSATA connection.

RAID drives allow for backup and/or faster speeds (when multiple drives are striped—allowing multiple drives to act as one drive, provides the fastest speed).

- RAID 1 provides protection.
- RAID 0 gives you the fastest performance.

continued . . .

TABLE 7.5

Continued

Name	Cost	Notes

Below are a few models that are good to have in the field.

- Promise Pegasus (http://promise.com/Products/Pegasus/Pegasus)
- CalDigit (http://caldigit.com)
- G-Drive (http://g-technology.com/video)
- LaCie (http://lacie.com).

FIGURE 7.35
G-Drive Mini. (Courtesy of G-Technology.)

~$150

Storage: 1T

Interface connection: FireWire 800 and USB 3.0

Drive speed: 7200rpm

Power: Bus powered through interface (some computers may not be able to power it through the USB 3.0)

Note: aluminum chassis

See: http://www.g-technology.com/products/g-drive-mini-1-tb-external-desktop-hard-drive

FIGURE 7.36
G-Drive Mobile. (Courtesy of G-Technology.)

~$200

Storage: 1T

Interface connection: USB 3.0 and Thunderbolt

Drive speed: 7200rpm

Power: Bus powered through both connections

Note: aluminum chassis

See: http://www.g-technology.com/products/g-drive-mobile-thunderbolt-1-tb-portable-hard-drive

FIGURE 7.37
CalDigit VR Mini. (Courtesy of CalDigit.)

~$400

Storage: 4T RAID

Interface connection: USB 3.0 and FireWire 800

Drive speed: 7200rpm

Power: Bus powered through FireWire interface (but not through the USB 3.0)

Note: aluminum chassis

See: http://caldigit.com/vr_mini/

continued . . .

TABLE 7.5

Continued

Name	Cost	Notes
 **FIGURE 7.38** LaCie Rugged RAID. (Courtesy of LaCie.)	~$400	Storage: 4T RAID Interface connection: Thunderbolt and USB 3.0 (bus powered) Drive speed: 7200rpm Note: Shock, dust, and water resistance See: https://www.lacie.com/us/products/product.htm?id=10646

With the gear chosen, we'll now look at a couple of case studies of client-based work by Stillmotion and Zandrak in Chapters 8 and 9.

PART III
Crafting the Cinematic Style
Case Studies

CHAPTER 8
A Book Promotion Case Study
From Keywords to Storyboards in Stillmotion's "My Utopia"

159

URL of film: https://vimeo.com/112035686

FINDING THE CLIENT

Sometimes potential clients see your work and then contact you about a job because they're inspired by your work. Or perhaps you've worked with one client and through word of mouth that client recommends you to another client. More rarely a potential client is one of the subjects you're interviewing for a documentary you're producing. Patrick and Amina Moreau met Stephanie Henry during Stillmotion's shoot of their feature documentary *Stand With Me*, a story about a girl, Vivian, who makes lemonade to help fight childhood slavery. Stephanie is in the documentary, Amina Moreau tells me. "We got to know her story. When she was nine she had a very different childhood than little Vivian," Amina says. Stephanie would end up writing a book about an abusive past with her stepfather in *If Only I Could Sleep* (Emerald Book Company, 2014). "And so because of her past she felt like it was her duty, her responsibility to help her do as much good as she possibly can and so she became a big part of it."

It was during the documentary shoot that Stephanie asked Stillmotion to do a trailer for her book. Even though they decided to approach it as a narrative project, Amina says, "It's based on a true story and so we took that seriously. We really wanted to do it the justice that it deserved."

DEVELOPING THE SCRIPT AND TAKING A CREATIVE RISK

As part of his research, Patrick Moreau read Stephanie Henry's book and when he hit the section about an essay that she read to her high-school class at the age of fifteen, he called her up and said, "That essay is what will become your book promotion trailer," Patrick recalls. "We're not interviewing people, we're not doing anything else, that's too safe, that's too easy," he said. Using a narrative style for a promotional film was a risk Stillmotion took. They've done documentary-style promotions and even Emmy-Award-winning documentaries for the NFL in addition to the feature documentary, but these successes could lock them into a certain style in the minds of their audiences—and their potential clients. They've never tackled narrative storytelling before and they're not known for that style.

Patrick discusses how after doing film workshops in 30 cities in North America and across five countries in Asia, he knows that Stillmotion will be judged. "You realize that there's a lot of eyes on you, and you realize that as you venture into a new medium there's a very good chance for a lot of people to look at you and say, 'Yeah, you guys should have stuck to weddings,'" he laughs. "People are going to look at you—they're going to ask those questions. Is this the next step? Or is this a step back? Or should they be doing this? Can they do this?"

It's a risk to jump into a new project, a film that they could have shot in their compelling documentary style, a style their fan base understands, and they might say, "'You should have interviewed people, that would have been better, that's what Stillmotion does,'" Patrick confides. But at the same time, Stillmotion knows about story. "In a way we were reinventing ourselves in front of a lot of eyes and we needed to make sure that we did it in a way that stayed true to who we are, which is story first," Patrick adds. And so he felt compelled "to make sure that this is right for us, that we can do this." As he thought about the project, what went through his head was to make sure that after watching the film, "you felt like this is the right choice, that it felt strong. Because I think that has so much to say with our credibility as filmmakers and educators and storytellers, and if we do something we've never done before, and it doesn't work, then that's not good."

In essence, Stephanie's essay became the script for the book trailer (see Figure 8.1), making the trailer as personal as the book itself. Rather than just presenting the essay as a narration voice-over device or archival moment in a documentary film, they used it as the creative basis for a recreation of Stephanie's life—from the creation of an early 1980s classroom to scenes from her past.

"The essay was perfect," Patrick tells me. "It became the vehicle that would move people emotionally—it would allow them to see what Stephanie's life was like and allow the audience to come to their own conclusion and it would hopefully create intrigue into who she was," he adds. This could lead to more book sales for Stephanie. If the short film works, then, "If you want to know Stephanie better what are you going to do? You're going to read her book," Patrick explains. That's the point of a promotional book trailer.

"Her essay was short enough," Patrick adds. "It was simple enough and it was powerful enough and had enough of the story. It really touched on a lot that needed to be told while telling the story. And the irony or the magic of it—it's Stephanie at fifteen or sixteen years old standing up and reading an essay, which is the whole point of her book—the message is speak up, say something about abuse." The essay, he adds, is really the first time she actually said something about any of this abuse happening. "So it has a wonderful resonance to

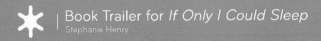

Book Trailer for *If Only I Could Sleep*
Stephanie Henry

My Utopia

Living at Grandma's house I'd get to eat fried chicken, mashed potatoes with as much ketchup as I want. Without my stepdad always making me eat the extra ketchup on my place with a spoon so I don't waste it. He's so mean and smells gross!

Grandma's house is where I can sit by the TV and don't worry about some gross guy touching me in the places that make me wanna puke! If Utopia is perfect, I guess I'd feel safe then probably. No one making fun of me because I don't have boobs or pulling my hair and laughing cause I'm stupid.

I'd be walking into our living room and my Dad reading a newspaper as he's telling me another story that makes me laugh or sometimes his stories make me cry but that's okay. He liked Dean Martin and Jerry Lewis movies for laughing and the Phantom of the Opera book for crying. But in Utopia Dad wins the hot dog eating contest at his mobile home grand opening, or was it pie eating? Or was it both?

My Utopia is where my brother and I can play office and I'm the secretary who types fast and gets to use the cool pencil sharpener that we plug into the wall.

I wouldn't have to write a thousand times "I will not talk in study hall" because Coach is mad at me again and I get in trouble even if I ain't talking. I would quit getting in trouble. Mom would be home after school and stop leaving me there with my stepdad. Why is he home anyway when it's not after work yet?

The smell of Grandma's house and fried eggs and bacon in the morning, making sure she ain't popped by the bacon grease. Listening to her sing "How Great Thou Art" at the kitchen window while she washes the breakfast dishes.

Even if Grandpa doesn't talk, it's okay because he's safe. He just sits there with his rolled up tobacco that Grandma makes him go outside to smoke and watches a stray cat he named George. Maybe I would have real clothes in Utopia and I wouldn't have to buy the polo socks, take off the polo guy, and sew it to a Hunt club brand shirt from JCPenney's to make it look like a real polo shirt like my friend has. I just want to be like my friend but my hair is really icky and she always looks good. I would live with only Nesey, Carl, and Derwin, because the four of us have fun, we laugh and no one is mean. Mom would make my stepdad go away for good. He is so gross in his boxer underwear walking around like no one can see him.

In Utopia Mom would let me sit on her bed like she used to on some Saturdays before she married him. She'd let me go through all her jewelry and see what I liked and got to have when I am old enough. Mom and I would have a special day when she would let me have two squirts of the Shalimar perfume from her bathroom.

If home looked perfect and I got to live here, it would have big trees, a bunch of flowers, and dogs. Utopia is where I look like my friend Dana, I have a huge house like my friend Joanne, tons of cool clothes like Martha, I could sing like Tracy, be beautiful like LaDonna, have Brietta's dad, Annette's eyelashes, and Tami's smart brain.

In my Utopia, Mom would listen to me when I was crying and my Dad would be alive.

www.Stillmotion.ca • 503-419-6266 • 2105 SE 7th St, Portland, OR, 97214

FIGURE 8.1
The script for "My Utopia" is the essay Stephanie Henry read in front of her high school class.
(Script courtesy of Stillmotion.)

Budget

The estimated budget for "My Utopia" is private, but the rough estimate places it between $50 and $100,000. (I've only provided estimated budget ranges for privacy purposes.) The estimated budget sheet from Stillmotion included the following:

Who we are

We're a band of filmmakers and photographers who, as a rule, always let our curiosity get the better of us.

Frankly, we believe that the process of discovery is as important as what goes on the screen.

Relentless in our process. Passionate in the chase. We dig deep because we've seen the difference a story can make.

We got our start by filming weddings, and somewhere along the way, the NFL took notice of the magic happening on our team and gave us a call. This paved the road to producing a feature-length documentary for CBS, which went on to earn us three Emmy Awards and a substantial amount of storytelling cred.

We've racked up plenty of miles and hard drive space cooking up work for Apple, Canon, Callaway and CBS. Not that unabashed name dropping tells you much about who we are, but we're pretty proud to have been trusted in some notable circles to tell some extremely powerful and diverse stories. We thrive on the uniqueness of everyone we meet and are fascinated by the impact that is made possible when people work together.

Be present. Ask questions. Share. Iterate. Connect. Dive. Dream. Repeat.

Overview

We all matter and we can make a real difference. Together we will explore your story through a narrative film that will serve as the book trailer but more importantly inspire others to stand up and do something.

Pre-production (low $10,000s)

3 days total of pre-production: 2 days with the director and DP to learn your story inside-out and then a 1 day pre-production with the whole team to do final tech prep and logistics. This includes casting, pre-interviewing, location scouting, ideation, sourcing and logistical planning.

Production (low $10,000s)

Timing: 2 days of production in the Portland area during the month of May 2014.

Resources:

1 Director

1 On-site Producer

1 Director of Photography

1 Cinematographer

1 AC

1 Field audio

1 Gaffer

4 Local Production Assistants

All camera gear & lenses required

All camera support required (including steadicam, dolly etc.)

All lighting and grip required

Post-production (high $1,000s)

Deliverables:

One edited 2–3 min film delivered in HD, web-ready

All footage downloaded, sorted, and delivered via portable hard drive

Up to two rounds of revisions included

Color graded and sound mixed for final version

Soundtrack (Cost TBD)

1 year lifespan: 1–4 songs—$750 per track

Perpetual lifespan: 1–4 songs—$1500 per track

Casting/Talent (mid $1,000s)

Stillmotion will handle all casting and talent acquisition for the film. We will screen and cast prior to production for all leading roles and extras needed.

Location Releases/Fees (mid $1,000s)

Stillmotion will take care of all location scouting and sourcing for the film. This includes location releases, fees, and set design.

Art Direction/Set Design (mid $1,000s)

Stillmotion will handle art direction, set design, and sourcing of props and wardrobe for the entire film as needed.

Travel

Stillmotion will do production for this project in Portland, minimizing the travel costs as the majority of the crew is based locally here. All travel plans for crew outside of Portland including all transportation, accommodations, meals etc. is included in this estimate.

Use/Rights

All rights owned by Stephanie Henry worldwide in perpetuity. Stillmotion also reserves the right to show the spots for promotional and/or educational purposes.

Final Project Estimate: Between $50 and $100,000.

her overall message and what she wants to encourage people to do. It doesn't feel like a book trailer, it feels like a story."

He told Stephanie about the plan. "I'm going to rebuild that day in 1981," Patrick remembers telling Stephanie, and she was "so open and trusting and she just loved the idea," Patrick says. But by taking the narrative approach (rather than shooting in a documentary style), he said, "I told her its going to cost a little bit more because we're getting into props, costumes, locations, and a cast. But that it's going to be way more effective and innovative. It's a very different approach." Stephanie agreed and they went forward into preproduction.

PLANNING THE INTENTION, KEYWORDS, AND STORYBOARDS

Despite trepidation about taking a new approach to a promotional film, Stillmotion's experience in shooting live events (weddings), as well as their promotional and documentary projects, means that the Stillmotion team are confident storytellers. "The reality is that we take something like this on with a good budget and a good team and we know we can do something good," Patrick tells me. "We have a certain level of confidence and certainly the approach and the effort and attitude that you know we're going do what it takes to make something good." But this approach—taking risks, taking on projects—only works if "it comes from within," he says. "You need to be connected to it. You need to care about it. And we did." If you're doing a project just for the flash, just to get attention, just to get the views online," he adds, "you're rarely going to get to a good piece."

As part of the preproduction planning for a narrative piece, they have more control of the set, the costumes, everything—much more so than a documentary or conventional promotional film. They could work with intention, Patrick says. "We were able to use our light, our lenses, our color, our soundtrack, every single element in a much stronger way." If we go back to the four Ps (developed in their MUSE story process—people, place, purpose, plot), Patrick explains, we see that their educational model for telling stories is based on "intention." "But that intentionality is in an event setting, and how you just think really quick." In shooting an NFL game, they have to be fast on their feet and get the shot as it happens. There is no time to stage anything. So with "My Utopia," they had more control over it. "Here's an opportunity where we can produce everything," Patrick smiles. "So it opened our eyes to how much further you can go with intention. Unlike a documentary, I can decide you're going to wear a yellow dress, because yellow represents hope," Patrick explains. "I've never been able to think about that before, but as we started having these conversations we realized how much deeper we can go."

Patrick discusses this approach in more detail and it's a lesson we can all learn when approaching production. It's about listening. "Our whole storytelling approach, MUSE, the step-by-step process, is built on the idea of listening before you construct. So knowing what it is you want to say and defining that before you actually start saying it, is important. And so we come to keywords, we come to tools that help you know what it is you are trying to say."

Keywords

Stepping back a moment, let's take a look at the keywords the Stillmotion team created for "My Utopia." The keywords they came up with are insightful, revealing the rationale behind their process in choosing and developing each:

Internalize

As she suffered several forms of abuse, Steph internalized the trauma as a feeling of no self-worth and that she was nothing more than her looks. This led to all of the trauma she then inflicted on herself—bulimia, drug addiction, selling her body. Her speaking is a way to bring all of this out to the world, and the way to heal.

Serve

She wants to share her story to help others. She is also using her story to drive her fight against sexual slavery across the world. She is using everything that has happened to her to serve others who have, or may suffer from the same realities that she did. She does frontline work across the world to help others and make sure they know they are cared about.

Hope

Despite all of the traumatic things Steph has been through (domestic abuse, failed education, rape, bulimia, drug addiction, losing custody of her daughter, life as a stripper, several marriages) she turned things around and is going back to school, treating her body right, in a great marriage, constantly growing and learning. She is a beacon of hope for others that you are valuable and can turn things around to build something better for yourself.

Speak

This book is her standing up and sharing her story. She believes that in speaking it will help her heal, and it will also let others know that they are not alone. By speaking she also believes people can deal with their demons, and only when they do that can they reach their full potential.

Emergence

The process of bringing to light after being concealed. That is what this book is. Emergence is also the idea that something is more than the sum of its parts. For Stephanie, she had the realization that she is more than just her body, the sum of her experiences, and she wanted to turn her life around.

(From internal Stillmotion document. Used with permission.)

Notice how each keyword goes back to what Stillmotion calls the "heart" of their story, the central character who expresses drives and needs, and provides the context for their mission for storytelling: to help improve the world. Other keywords they considered included truth, authenticity, numbing, worthless, potential, demons, vulnerability, looks, survivor, strength, and resilience. With the ones they chose above, we can see how the film would revolve around a sense of hope and change.

Heart of the Story

The Stillmotion MUSE process revolves around defining in a clear way who the central character is. During the listening phase of their work, they explore several viable characters, looking for levels of complexity, desire, and uniqueness. Here are their notes about what they discovered about Stephanie:

Complexity—the abused who recovers and fights to protect others.

- She grew up being taken advantage of, was made to feel worthless, and started treating herself the way others were (abusive, neglect). Not only has she found the strength to overcome this adversity, she now uses it to fight back and help other people who have suffered the same fate, and works to prevent it happening to others across the world.

Desire

- To have others feel like they are not alone.
- To really give back and serve others.
- To make sense of her story, to give it value.
- To let people know that they matter, that they have value.

Uniqueness

- Cute, blonde female who does frontline work.
- Doesn't just donate money, goes to the organizations and wants to learn about it first hand.
- Poor family now very wealthy, let the money flow through her.

As can be seen, here, a documentary-style promotional film would have been easy for Stillmotion to produce—Stephanie, as herself, would have made a compelling character. But by taking that one moment from Stephanie's life—the point where she shared her story about her abuse in high school—and making that essay the script, they took on a new type of challenge and would create a short narrative based on actual events. Although not all of this gets communicated through the film, the hope for the future—that sense of "the abused who recovers and fights to protect others"—as it ripples out through that personal essay becomes the narrative through-line for their story. But their storytelling process kept them anchored, and as they went into preproduction, they would build sets, costumes, use lighting, and develop storyboards to communicate their shots.

Storyboards

"And as you do that, as you have a set of keywords," Patrick continues, "as you know who your main character is, as you know what makes them different, and as you know your story arc, you can then look at a set of storyboards or frames or shot list and ask, 'How do I best communicate this?'" The keywords help them develop the visual story. And by extension, the storyboards shape the look and provide a way to set up a sequence and communicate that sequence to the production team. (See Figures 8.2–8.5.)

The storyboards from the opening scene of "My Utopia" reveal shots that are close to what was shot. The details on the storyboard include lens sizes and f-stops, as well as a description of the camera action and Stephanie's action. The storyboard is a tool that allows everyone to be on the same page when setting up each shot. In addition, it allowed Patrick and the cinematographer, Joyce

35mm @ F5.6 on Red Epic & Movi M10, 24fps

Open on an empty frame slowing moving down the center aisle of a classroom.

'Steph Henry, it's your turn." We hear from Ms. Connelly at the front of the room.

Steph's feet enter frame and we continue to follow her to the front. As we do, we see items lining the desks that bring us back to 1981, the year she presented the essay.

FIGURE 8.2
Storyboard of the opening sequence to "My Utopia." Notice the stock photo is set as the background, while a drawing and graphic represents the main character and action. Also take note of the lens and f-stop setting, as well as the camera used and the frame rate. A brief description of the action is presented on the storyboards—in many ways we see the storyboard embedded in the script. (Courtesy of Stillmotion.)

35mm @ F5.6 on Red Epic & Movi M10, 24fps

In one continuous shot we follow behind Steph as she turns to address the classroom.

FIGURE 8.3
Storyboard of the opening sequence to "My Utopia." Reverse angle of Stephanie. (Courtesy of Stillmotion.)

35mm @ F5.6 on Red Epic & Movi M10, 24fps

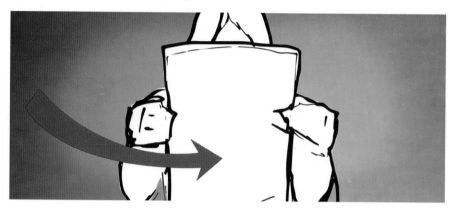

We continue around her to reveal a handwritten essay covering her face.

FIGURE 8.4
Storyboard of the opening sequence to "My Utopia." The shot pushes in from the left as Stephanie holds her essay up, with a chalkboard in the background. (Courtesy of Stillmotion.)

35mm @ F5.6 on Red Epic & Movi M10, 24fps

We pause and hold in front of Steph as she slowly lowers the paper, tilts her head up, and begins.

"My Utopia. [BEAT]

Living at Grandma's house..."

FIGURE 8.5
Storyboard of the opening sequence to "My Utopia." Stephanie reads her essay. (Courtesy of Stillmotion. Used with permission.)

Tsang, to look at potential shots on paper and ask themselves how they could go deeper into the story through the cinematography (such as choosing the right lens for a scene). The storyboard helped them previsualize the scene.

With the preproduction planning in place (their keywords, and the 4 Ps defined), they could then look at the classroom, for example, and discuss how they could light it. "How should we light the classroom that's going to show both sides," Patrick says, "that's going to show the darkness and the despair along with the hope and optimism that she has at her age? What if we split light her so that it comes right across her face? How do we highlight her? How do we empower her? Because she's standing up there and she's saying something." Notice how the shots closely reflect the storyboards (see Figures 8.6–8.8).

The Stillmotion approach didn't change because they jumped into a narrative style; it reinforced their style. By asking questions based on the four Ps (people, place, purpose, plot) and the keywords, the heart of the story, they crafted the lighting to best reflect the story and character intention that emerged from their research.

Patrick continues the discussion: "Why don't we have a slash of sunlight right across the chalkboard that frames her and comes into her and opens up as it reaches her body?" I feel like I'm in a master class with a filmmaker who approaches work in a unique way, a process that Stillmotion has shared with thousands of filmmakers and students around the world. "Because we know what we wanted to say we can keep asking those questions and we can just answer them. How do you do that with wardrobe? How do we make her feel this way? Well, it's going to be a yellow dress, it's going to look like this. We just kept asking those questions."

These questions become the foundation for making decisions that were rooted in their research—research that in many ways developed from Patrick's background in psychology. "As we worked through the lighting and the art direction and the camera movement, it was all motivation around these intentions," he explains. "When we wanted to have the abusive stepdad come up the stairs, we really knew what that scene meant—and so we shot up on him making him bigger, making her smaller. Some of the short-sided composition feels super awkward. Joyce Tsang, our cinematographer, will actually start off the shots in a very comfortable composition where Stephanie is happy, but as she get anxious I can direct her to look out of frame and Joyce would tighten up the composition, making the shot become increasingly anxious and awkward as her performance and the story gets anxious." (See Figures 8.9 and 8.10.)

In documentaries and event projects, Patrick explains, "we don't tell people what to do. I can't say as you're doing your vows, 'When you get here I want you to look up and smile.' We can try to predict this as best we can, so it was amazing to be able to direct that in the narrative piece with five takes, where you're getting a lot of these layers so that her wardrobe fits the story perfectly,

FIGURE 8.6
Claire Manning as Stephanie Henry in Stillmotion's "My Utopia." She reads an essay about her abuse in a 1981 classroom, recreated for a book promotional. Notice the lighting and the color of her dress—all of which is intentional to the story. "Why don't we have a slash of sunlight right across the chalkboard that frames her and comes into her and opens up as it reaches her body?" Patrick asked. (Courtesy of Stillmotion.)

FIGURE 8.7
Reverse-angle close-up of Claire reading Stephanie's essay in Stillmotion's "My Utopia." (Courtesy of Stillmotion.)

FIGURE 8.8
Close-up of Claire as she feels the pain from her abuse, foreshadowing a flashback in Stillmotion's "My Utopia." Notice the lighting designed to show her despair and hope. (Courtesy of Stillmotion.)

FIGURE 8.9
The lighting, the mood, is now darker: there is a loss of hope as the abusive stepfather (played by Mike Butters) climbs up the stairs to confront Stephanie in Stillmotion's "My Utopia." Notice how the lighting, focus, high angle, and framing build anxiety in the scene. (Image courtesy of Stillmotion.)

FIGURE 8.10
Over-the-shoulder shot looking down at Stephanie in Stillmotion's "My Utopia." The stepfather now looms overs Stephanie, who looks up in fear, feeling small and powerless. Notice the lighting on her face. (Image courtesy of Stillmotion.)

the lighting fit the story perfectly, and the composition is just coming in so also add that other layer. And then you've got your sound design and everything is working. We had never used MUSE with a narrative. It was awesome to see that it worked," Patrick says. "That it really helped us and our team do a much better job with the story and all this intentionality. Working through that and applying that to a narrative gave us a new way for us to tell the story."

PRODUCTION PLAN

The production plan included an overview of the scene number, time allocated for shooting that scene, a brief description for the type of shot, the storyboard number it refers to, the camera gear needed (such as tripod and lens), the frame rate for the camera (such as 24fps or 96fps), the time of day, and a detailed description of the shot. (See Figure 8.11.)

SCENE	SHOT #	DESC	DURATION	STRYBD#	GEAR	FRAMERATE	TIME OF DAY	DETAILED DESCRIPTION
1 (Tu 9:00-15:00)	1	Opening Shot	30	1-4	Movi, 35mm	24	Bright Afternoon	Continuous tracking show following and spinning around Steph as she walks (up) in Classroom
	2	Wide Read	30	12, 31, 42,	Tripod, 24mm	24	Bright Afternoon	Wide shot from back of room of Steph reading the essay from start to finish (static tripod)
	3	Medium Read	30	10, 22, 38, 44,	Tripod, 35mm	24	Bright Afternoon	Medium shot from middle of room of Steph reading the essay from start to finish (static tripod)
	4	OTS Clothes x 3	30	32	Tripod, 50mm	24	Bright Afternoon	Over a students shoulder into Steph reading. Three options, alternating foreground on L or R
	5	OTS Friends x 3	30	45	Tripod, 50mm	24	Bright Afternoon	Over a students shoulder into Steph reading. Three options, alternating foreground on L or R
Lunch (1Hr)	6	Slide Out (Right) To Essay	15	N/A	Atlas 200, 50mm	24	Bright Afternoon	Match to SHOT#20 to transition "without my stepdad always..." (slow to match mixed framerates)
	7	Hair Icky Slide Out (Right)	15	37	Atlas 200, 35mm	24	Bright Afternoon	Slide out from Steph's Hair and rack into her essay, then into the students "I just want to be like..."
	8	Tight Read	30	8, 13, 16, 46	Tripod, 85mm	24	Bright Afternoon	Tight shot of Steph reading the essay from start to finish (slight movement in tripod)
	9	Extreme Mouth Close-up	15	34	Tripod, 85mm	24	Bright Afternoon	Extreme Close-Up of Steph's Mouth as she reads the essay (slight tripod movement)
6 (Tu 15:00-16:00)	10	Tight of Steph in Study Hall	15	21	Tripod, 50mm	36	Early Evening	Short-sided composition on Steph as she endlessly writes her lines in study hall
	11	Tight Of Paper/Lines	15	20	Tripod, 50mm	36	Early Evening	Straight on shot of Steph writing 'I will not talk in study hall" (match cut to typewriter)
12 (Tu 16:00-18:00)	12	Steph Running to Utopia	90		Movi, 24mm	60	Sunset	Steph and her dog running, happily, towards this big bright house that represents Utopia
4 (Tu 18:00-20:00)	13	Jib Move In To Contest	35	14	12' Crane, 24mm	36	Sunset	Starting high and away, we lower and come into the hot dog eating contest
	14	Tight of Dad Eating Hotdog	25	15	Tripod, 35mm	96	Sunset	Straight on shot of dad eating an overflowing hotdog. Match cut to Steph Tight Read
WRAP DAY ONE								
8 (We 9:00-9:45)	15	Macro of Bacon Grease	15	26	Tripod, 180mm	96	Sunday Morning	Macro shot of bacon grease on stove to give searing cut from stepdad in bedroom
	16	Tight of Grandma singing	10	27	Tripod, 50mm	36	Sunday Morning	Grandma in the kitchen singing 'Oh Great Thou Art..' while washing dishes
	17	Wide Pull Out in Kitchen	15	28	Atlas 200, 24mm	36	Sunday Morning	We slowly leave the scene as Grandma happily washes her dishes, singing
2 (We 9:45-11:30)	18	Ketchup Macro	15	6	Tripod, 180mm	96	Bright Afternoon	Macro shot as the ketchup hits the mashed potatoes (early morning)
	19	Kitchen Push-in	20	5	Atlas 200, 24mm	36	Bright Afternoon	Slide between grandparents, into Steph, as she piles on the ketchup (early morning)
	20	Kitchen Slide Out (Right)	10	7	Atlas 200, 50mm	36	Bright Afternoon	Slide out of scene from Steph eating ketchup covered potatoes (as transition to classroom)
11 (We 11:30-12:30)	21	Steph Trying On Jewelry	15	39	Tripod, 50mm	36	Sunday Morning	Steph holding up the jewelry and looking in the mirror, playing dress-up
	22	Macro of Perfume	20	40	Tripod, 85mm	96	Sunday Morning	Macro shot of the perfume bottle erupting with particles
	23	Medium-Wide of Perfume	15	41	Tripod, 35mm	36	Sunday Morning	Medium-Wide of the perfume filling the air as Steph is happy and safe
COMPANY MOVE (90 min)								
5 (We 15:30-16:30)	24	Steph & Bro Playing Typewriter	15	17	High-Hat, 35mm	36	Daytime	Straight on shot of Steph and brother messing around at typewriter
	25	Macro of Typewriter	15	18	High-Hat, 50mm	36	Daytime	Side shot of typewriter as they both try to hit the next key
	26	Shot of Letter Coming Out	15	19	High-Hat, 50mm	36	Daytime	Straight on Shot of letter coming out of typewriter as they hit the keys (match cut to study hall)
9 (We 16:30-17:00)	27	Grandpa in Living Room	15	29	Tripod, 50mm	36	Sunday Afternoon	Through Grandpa into Steph as she is having fun, playing on the couch
	28	Tight of Grandpa	10	30	Tripod, 50mm	36	Sunday Afternoon	Straight shot into Grandpa who feels not all there, making him safe (Match tight read in classroom)
10 (We 17:30-18:30)	29	Stepdad Walking Into Kitchen	15	35	Tripod, 35mm	36	Early Evening	Stepdad, in his boxers and undershirt, emerges from the shadows and walks towards cake
	30	Swipe The Whipcream	15	36	Tripod, 85mm	36	Early Evening	Stepdad takes two fingers and swipes the whipecream off the bust of the cake topper
	31	Tasting The Whip Cream	15	37	Tripod, 50mm	36	Early Evening	Stepdad tastes the whip cream and winks at Steph (short-sided composition)
7 (We 19:15-20:15)	32	Stepdad Entering Bedroom	20	23	High-Hat, 35mm	36	Early Evening	Steph playing away and stepdad emerges from the shadows to enter her room
	33	OTS into Steph	15	24	Monopod, 50mm	36	Early Evening	Over stepdads shoulder looking down on Steph as she looks up, nervously
	34	Tight of Stepdad	10	25	Tripod, 50mm	36	Early Evening	Shooting up on Stepdad as he looks down at Steph uncomfortably
3 (We 20:15-21:00)	35	Living Room Alone Push-in	20	9	Atlas 200, 24mm	36	After Dusk	Push-In through TV as Steph stares aimlessly on the couch
	36	Tight Couch Alone	15	11	Tripod, 50mm	36	After Dusk	Short-sided composition as Steph looks lost and alone out of frame
WRAP PRODUCTION								

FIGURE 8.11
The production plan in one page for "My Utopia." This is a key communication tool and a checklist for staying on schedule and knowing what needs to be shot and when. It can be checked off as shots are completed. (Courtesy of Stillmotion.)

SHOOTING, SLOW MOTION, AND COMPOSITION IN A WIDE ASPECT RATIO

Stillmotion chose the RED Epic in order to distinguish the look from many of their other projects (mostly shot on a Canon C100 and Canon DSLRs). "Making it look and feel bigger would make the story feel bigger, and that would be part of the draw in getting people to check out her book," Patrick says in his blog about the project. The 5K and RED raw allowed them to engage in a stronger, deeper color depth (with a higher bit rate) than the 8-bit compression found in the C100 and DSLRs (see Chapter 7). With a larger bit-depth, they could also shape the look more strongly in post. (With 8-bit compression, the look tends to be burned in-camera since the image will begin to fall apart in post if you make changes to the color and exposure that are too wide. With the higher bit-rate of the RED, they were able to engage in stronger color-grading because the image contains more data to manipulate.) The RED also allowed them to shoot with dialed-in frame-rates.

Typically, a film would be shot at 24 frames per second (fps), but with the RED, they were able to dial in a frame rate of 36fps. They decided to utilize the slower frame rate in all of the flashback scenes (Stephanie's memories) in

FIGURE 8.12
The 4:3 and 16:9 aspect ratios compared to 2.4:1 chosen for the film. (Image courtesy of Stillmotion.)

order to convey a different type of feeling than the classroom (shot at the standard 24fps). Patrick felt the 36fps[1] "would give the flashbacks a bit of weight to them, a slight hesitation as the memory is being recalled, without being overly dramatic."[2] They would engage in an even higher frame rate to create moments of increased slow motion in order to accent moments of her memories in the flashbacks (such as the scene when Stephanie sprays herself with perfume).

They also made the choice to go with a super-wide frame aspect ratio for composition. A standard television frame is 4:3, while most cameras shoot in a high definition frame of 16:9. For "My Utopia," they went with a 2.4:1 aspect ratio. The 2.4:1 aspect ratio gives the short film a feature-film look. In addition, Patrick says that in some shots, it helped create anxiety in the audience, since they would frame on the short-side of the frame, leaving more space to highlight that anxiety in Stephanie (see Figure 8.12).

In other scenes, Stephanie was placed towards the center of the frame in order to show her in balance, when she was happy. (See Figures 8.13 and 8.14.)

FIGURE 8.13
Stephanie, in soft focus, squeezes out ketchup. Notice that she is centered in the frame, revealing her as balanced and happy as she's in a safe place. (Image courtesy of Stillmotion.)

FIGURE 8.14
Stephanie at her grandmother's house in "My Utopia," a place of safety—the center composition reflects that balance in her life. This shot was planned in the storyboard, as seen in Figure 8.15. (Image courtesy of Stillmotion.)

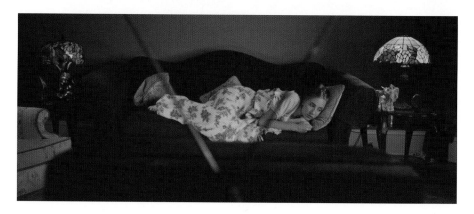

THE ART DIRECTION AND SET DESIGN

It ended up being only a two-day shoot, but three months of planning went into the project. Brody Lowe did the art direction on the film. In discussing one of their keywords—hope—Brody says they intentionally made the classroom look drab and aged. "The only things that we wanted to have pop out was her dress," Brody explains. "As a teen she's reading this story, but she was still very hopeful about the future. And so that yellow dress was the thing that popped out—she was the hope, she was the nucleus to the story itself. There was always a light shining on her face whenever she was in the shot that, too, helped convey the idea of hope." They also set up the classroom to indicate the timeframe of the film.

Here's the location before the set design (Figure 8.16).

24mm @ F2.8 on Red Epic & Atlas 200, 36fps (slow push in)

"Grandma's house is where I can sit by the TV and don't worry about..."

FIGURE 8.15
The storyboard showing the center composition that provides Stephanie a sense of balance (as she's safe) at her grandparent's house. (Image courtesy of Stillmotion.)

FIGURE 8.16
The classroom Stillmotion used for "My Utopia." (Courtesy of Stillmotion.)

After bringing in set pieces and props (and costumed extras and the lead), and setting the lighting, it became a 1981-era classroom (Figure 8.17).

Another keyword that helped set the art direction was emergence. "The idea of emergence involved a repetition and that led me to think of patterns," Brody says. "So in almost all the shots you'll see a pattern inside the shot. On the bed there will be a pattern bed spread. When grandpa's in his rocking chair, he's wearing a patterned shirt. There's a pattern behind him—everything has to have pattern in it. That represents patterns in her life that kept on going and going. Those two keywords really helped move the art along quite a bit."

In another example, when setting the look of 1981, Brody says that they avoided anything that was new in the 1980s. "So everything that was going to be in 1981 was probably purchased in the 1970s," Brody says. So the clothes would be "a little aged." They shopped in vintage stores in Portland to find the old clothing. But when it comes to hairstyles, they were definitely 1981, he adds.

Brody feels the creative process at Stillmotion—using the keywords to help inform their decisions—"really grounded where you could go with the look. In a way it created a collaborative environment where if you're going to present a look or present an idea to make sure it fits. If it doesn't fit then it shouldn't be in there," Brody adds. It helped ground the story.

FINAL THOUGHTS

In the end, Patrick feels the risk for shooting a promotional film in a narrative style was worth it. "The ultimate feeling that you want when you come out of this is that you are proud of it," Patrick says, "that you feel you did the best you could do and then it is what you wanted it to be, what you feel it deserves. And we did it as a team. We certainly felt like this is the best story we have told up to this point." They look forward to doing more narrative-style projects.

You can see Stillmotion's "My Utopia" at: http://vimeo.com/112035686

Shooting the Hook

As with any piece, the opening serves as your hook; it needs to pull you into the story and give the viewer a reason to want to watch. Present a bad hook and most people will switch off to something else, never seeing the full film.

The hook in "My Utopia" was designed to slowly bring you into the scene and the moment where Steph shares her essay. It's a seventeen-second fluid shot that slowly reveals itself to you.

1. The first few frames show you nothing but an old wooden floor along with desk and chair legs with kids' items strewn about. Everything in the scene is old. Paired with the sounds of kids' chatter and notebooks opening, we are immediately dropping you into what feels like a classroom, and one from long decades ago.

2. A few seconds in, we hear the teacher call out 'Steph, it's your turn' which introduces us to the main character as her feet enter the frame.

3. We continue to follow her up to the front of the classroom and slowly rise the camera bringing a hand-written essay into frame. This starts to reveal the plot to us. Steph is heading to the front of the classroom to share some sort of report.

4. As Steph turns around, we continue to rise up with the camera and reveal her face for the first time, full of hesitation and anxiousness as she takes the last few moments before she starts. The camera finally stops tight on her face and we live with Stephanie, feeling her hesitation and anxiousness until she begins by announcing the title of her essay, and the premise of the story "My Utopia."

From "The Making of a Scripted Short—My Utopia" by Patrick Moreau (http://stillmotionblog.com/myutopia/)

FIGURE 8.18
The sequence of shots in the opening scene from "My Utopia." (Images courtesy of Stillmotion.)

CHAPTER 9
An App Promotion Case Study

Directing with Spontaneity in Zandrak's "Our Songs"

URL of film: https://vimeo.com/106374768

Andrew Hutcheson likes to find potential stories online—but not what we might see as a conventional story or video. Instead, he looks for apps, for products. "There are certain times where you see a client or an app or product and you know that their philosophy is going to mesh well with your philosophy." What he means by his philosophy is the story-based approach to commercials, the narrative style. When David Brickel first saw Moodsnap online and read the description of the app—that "it's about emotionally driven music and decisions, and decisions driven by images and the way you feel and the mood of an environment," Andrew explains, they saw the potential. "There are images on this app and you choose an image that represents how you feel. When you press that image it'll play music that's tied to the representation of that mood." They were impressed.

"It's a really bold idea," he says, "and it's something that I felt an immediate connection to and felt like if that's how he's putting himself out into the world, I bet that he would be open to our branded story approach." Charles Frank knew that they could create a story that would be a good fit for Moodsnap, "because so much of what he's doing is centered around the narrative of an image and how music can tie into that. So of course to me that just naturally felt like a good connection."

Charles would go on to meet with David Blutenthal, the founder of Moodsnap, over a pizza, and from there create the pitch and treatment document (described in Chapter 6). This chapter will examine the creative decisions in the directing approach Charles Frank would engage for creating the scenes in this short narrative. Kyle would end up creating what they call a "docu-script." Charles explains: "It provides us with a summary of the environments and interactions we hope to capture, but doesn't pigeon-hole us in any one direction. It allows for us to translate the feeling/arc/message, but it gives us room to explore organic moments onsite, and to even make last-minute, intuition-based changes." There is no script-lock, here. The short film would be renamed from "The Travelers" to "Our Songs."

Moodsnap Script

Below is Kyler Harper's script, used as the conceptual start for the Moodsnap app story. It would evolve as they scouted the locations and worked with the actors. The characters' names would change.

THE TRAVELERS

Written by
Kyle Harper
Zandrak LLC 2014
Email: thefamily@zandrak.com

EXPOSITION—THE CHARACTERS AND THE PLAN

Our spot follows the story of two characters, CASSIE and BRENT. They are a couple, between the ages of 22–25, with a visible (but not overdone) artistic aesthetic. They are the embodiment of youth, adventure, spontaneity, sincerity, and emotion, yet still believable as characters one might sit next to on the bus or at work.

THE VOICEOVER

Throughout the piece, we will hear a conversation between the two actors about music. While this conversation is not shown in frame or overtly connected to the actions in scene, this voiceover will act as a sincere glimpse into the relationship between BRENT and CASSIE that touches on the experiences they have on their trip in thematic ways.

SCENE I: CAR. INT. DAY.

Our story opens in a car, the sort of mid-range, used sedan that every recent grad seems to drive. The perspective is first person from CASSIE'S eyes in the passenger seat as BRENT is driving. The radio is playing softly; enough that we can tell that we can make out a song but we aren't focused on it. CASSIE'S fingers come up into frame as if she were holding an imaginary camera, BRENT her subject in the center. Her finger depresses the imaginary shutter, she whispers a small "click," and the montage of their adventure begins.

SCENE II: PARKING LOT. EXT. NIGHT.

Scene opens on a deserted parking lot at night. The couple's car is on, idling but still, headlights streaming into an otherwise pitch black night. CASSIE and BRENT lay side by side in front of the headlight, their arms poking up into the air in a twisting, changing mass of fingers, palms, and elbows. We pull back to see them making finger puppets on the side of a concrete wall.

SCENE III: MINIGOLF COURSE. EXT. DAY.

The couple have reached the last hole of a mini-golf course. They're looking at the final "win-a-free-game" hole, a difficult, nearly unfair, test of golfing prowess. They turn to each other, the same idea in their eyes, and smile. They each drop their clubs, pocket their golf balls, and run out of the course as if the owner is going to chase them down for their contraband golf balls.

SCENE IV: BOWLING ALLY. INT. NIGHT.

CASSIE and BRENT are in a bowling alley. The bowlers around them are intent on their games, their form perfect, their shots either in the straight lines or smooth arcs of seasoned sportsmen. Our couple does not care about such play however. They bowl together, either dancing on their way to the line while one throws, or rolling a ball each the same time alongside one another, and other such non-regulation play. Their bumpers are up, a ward against any possibility for failure, and subtly in frame is a paper score card that has been filled all the way through with strikes.

SCENE V.1: LAKE. EXT. EVENING (SUNSET).

BRENT'S fingers are making a frame through which we see CASSIE running away from him. In the bottom of the screen we can just make out the roof of the car and CASSIE'S opened passenger side door—we get the sense she has just leapt from the car, their stop an unplanned one. CASSIE pauses to turn and beckons BRENT to follow her, only to turn right back around and leap into the lake, clothes and all.

SCENE V.2: LAKE. EXT. DAY.

The couple are wearing bathing-suits and swimming in a lake. The scene opens underwater, bubbles coming from each of their mouths as they try to speak to each other through the water. They resurface, each playfully gesturing that they can't quite hear the other. With similar gestures, they agree to go back under water, and plunge back in.

SCENE V.3: LAKE. EXT. NIGHT

The sun has fallen behind the horizon, and our lovely couple has waded into a lake under the quiet of night. CASSIE floats on her back, BRENT'S arms gently supporting her as he stands beside her. They are both gazing up at the stars in wonder. We catch a moment, however, as BRENT looks down at CASSIE'S face, his face in just as much wonder as when he looks upon the stars. He smiles, and returns to looking at the sky.

SCENE VI: SIDE OF THE ROAD. EXT. DAY.

A STATE TROOPER approaches the couple's car after pulling them over for speeding. He reaches the window, his focus still on a pad of paper in his hand. He looks up into the car and pauses. The frame changes to show BRENT and CASSIE, each holding up a picture frame with their fingers (BRENT's is landscape, CASSIE's is portrait) and looking at the officer with one eye peering through their frame.

SCENE VII: CAR. INT. DAY.

CASSIE and BRENT are back on the road, BRENT in the driver's seat. They are each looking straight ahead, their arms side-by-side on the console, but not touching. BRENT simply, gently, reaches the two inches over to place his hand on CASSIE's. CASSIE quietly, slowly, almost naturally, takes her hand out from under his and places it on her lap, out of reach. She turns ever so slightly to look out her window, and BRENT's arm returns to its original place on the console.

SCENE VIII.1: DINER. INT. MORNING.

BRENT and CASSIE sit across from each other at a small diner table. Each is working delicately on a pyramid-like structure constructed from packs of jelly, butter, and creamer. They reach the top of the structure, one last packet needing to be placed, and they look at each other perplexed: BRENT with a pack of marmalade in hand, CASSIE holding the last creamer.

SCENE VIII.2: DINER. INT. MORNING.

BRENT and CASSIE are sitting across from each other in a diner getting ready to eat breakfast. We see their table from overhead as each puts the finishing touches on a picture made from their food: a smiley face made from a pancake, maple syrup, and butter—a simple house made from bacon, eggs, toast, and hashbrowns. They put the finishing touches on each of their masterpieces, pause for a moment to look at them, and then trade plates before grabbing their silverware to eat.

SCENE IX: SIDE OF ROAD. EXT. DAY.

BRENT and CASSIE are standing in front of their car, which is parked off the road in between the two directions of

a fork. BRENT has a map spread out on the roof of the car and is insisting on going left (the direction which presumably agrees with the thick black line route he has drawn on his map), while CASSIE stands beside him, phone in hand, insisting that right is the direction they need to go. They argue for a time, until BRENT, frustrated, starts walking the direction he is sure of.

SCENE X: SIDE OF ROAD. EXT. DAY.

The couple's car is parked on the side of the road, the front end up on a jack, a spare tire leaning against the side of the car. CASSIE is sitting cross-legged in front of the bum tire, intently working on removing it from the axle. She holds out her hand. BRENT is laying on the roof of the car, a handful of tools strewn about next to him. He grabs a tool and places it into CASSIE's outstretched hand, and she continues working.

SCENE XI: BENCH/BUSTOP. EXT. DAY.

A busker sits by a bench, his case out in front of him, an assortment of drum-like objects set up around him. He is drumming haphazardly as people walk by. BRENT walks up beside him, sits on the bench, and produces a harmonica from his pocket. The drummer pauses and the two exchange some unheard words, BRENT clearly offering to play with him. Just as they're about to settle into a tune, CASSIE's fingers come into frame, making a photo frame around the pair as they play music together. She watches them with one open eye, and smiles.

SCENE XII: FARMER'S MARKET. EXT. DAY.

The couple are exploring a small farmer's market in a rural county. A crowd of people swirls around them, weaving in between wooden pallets and boxes filled with all sorts of produce. BRENT finds CASSIE inspecting a stand of fruit, comes up alongside her. She turns to show him what she's found: a citron, which she has stuffed into the end of her sleeve like a hand. BRENT nods and smiles with approval, and helps her fish out a couple coins for her citron hand, which she hands to the farmer behind the stand.

SCENE XIII: ANTIQUE SHOP. INT. DAY.

BRENT and CASSIE are in a tiny, nearly-forgotten antique/thrift shop. The walls are covered in relics and Americana from throughout history, and the couple is alone as they explore the stacks of long forgotten items. They each find a piece of art and excitedly meet in an aisle to share their discoveries—both works are horrific, tacky, kitsch in every way. And yet, they love them.

SCENE XIV: CAR. INT. MORNING (SUNRISE).

BRENT and CASSIE are sleeping in the back of their car under a mass of mismatched blankets, coats, and sweaters. They are contorted in what remains of their struggle to get comfortable in the confined space (which seems to have been futile), and their appearances are hardly magazine-cover worthy. CASSIE wakes up quietly, her eyes taking a couple moments to open fully, her hand immediately moving to rub her stiff neck. She looks over and sees BRENT, still asleep. She watches him for a moment, and then her hand moves slowly from her neck to softly move a bit of his hair behind his ear.

SCENE XV: WATERFALL. EXT. DAY.

BRENT is standing under a waterfall next to a water hole, triumphantly letting the water fall off of his back and chest. He is the ruler of this waterhole kingdom from his waterfall castle . . . right up until CASSIE sneaks up from behind and pushes him into the water below. She ignores his indignant splashes and takes in the falling water in seeming ecstasy, the usurper queen upon her rightful throne.

SCENE XVI: CAMPSITE. EXT. NIGHT.

BRENT and CASSIE are lounging around a campfire on a small campsite at the end of a day. The site is simple, just a tent and a hastily made firepit, the two of them sitting on the ground using each other for support and to cuddle. BRENT holds up a tin cup and CASSIE pours him some wine from a half-empty bottle at her side. They make eye contact and smile to each other, inches apart.

SCENE XVII.1: CAR. INT. DAY

The story ends where it began: back in the car, on the road, the moment after CASSIE has captured BRENT driving. He turns and smiles at her through her fingers, and she smiles back. Then, she pulls out her phone, opens Moodsnap, and picks out a picture that is strikingly similar to their moment. Fade in Moodsnap card. END

SCENE XVII.2: CAR. INT. DAY.

The story ends where it began: back in the car, on the road, the moment after CASSIE has captured BRENT driving. He turns and smiles at her through her fingers, and she smiles back. Both turn back to the road, our point of view moves to outside the vehicle, and we watch CASSIE and BRENT continue on their adventure, the soundtrack resolving back into the softer, quieter quality of the radio from which it started. END

DIRECTING MOODSNAP AND SETTING THE STYLE

Charles Frank, the director and editor at Zandrak, is hands-off in his directing, a style he calls bottom-up, "where I hand things off to more talented people." He trusts his cinematographer and performers to do their jobs in a creative way and the best way he feels he can do that is by not being top-down with directorial authority. For example, when working with performers, "I wanted to cover their actions but without being really distinct in calling action and cut and doing really distinct takes or anything of that nature. I wanted to set up an environment for them to exist in and almost cover them documentary style." This would give the Moodsnap film a natural style that reflects the app itself—finding the right music for a certain image, activity, or moment. He would find the right environment and have them live in it by giving them "context" for their action.

The discovery of his approach occurred during the making of "Still Life." Through this collaborative approach with Jake Oleson, Charles transitioned away from top-down control as a director to one who works "from the bottom up and trusting the team." When they build a team for a project, this collaborative approach forces them to "work really hard to find the people who are passionate with what they do. Because that allows us to trust them. That allows us to make the best work."

A graduate of the New York Film Academy's week-long summer workshops (he went before his freshman year in high school), Charles found it opened doors. He met Jake Oleson there—both were thirteen years old and he got into the DSLR cinema movement—shooting cinematic-style films on DSLRs. He had made home movies with his friends, but he did not grow up in a family that went to the movies. "My family wasn't really a movie-watching family. I hadn't really seen any films growing up and I also hadn't really been exposed to anyone else who was making them," he tells me in the Zandrak office.

He played basketball in the winter while in high school, but he convinced his teachers to allow him to drop mandatory sports in order to study film in the fall and spring. "For three hours a day I would conceptualize, shoot, edit short film." He submitted two of his films to the school's film festival, a place where a lot of the public and private schools in New England come together, he explains. "And it was during the intermission break that people had come up to me and expressed that my films had actually done something for them, which surprised me," Charles says.

By the summer leading up to his junior year, he wanted to study more film, but living in western Massachusetts, he didn't have many opportunities—he wanted to do more than just study YouTube tutorials. So he became industrious. He searched for film jobs on Google. He found Andrew Hutcheson's call for help with his Emerson College capstone film project, *April Grace*. He sent Andrew an email with a link to his film projects and Andrew invited him to come down to New Jersey over the summer to help work on the film.

> I'm sixteen years old during that shoot and I was just confused. But my time on *April Grace* is what helped me take that passion for this thing I didn't really understand, because I just knew that I liked it, but I didn't get what it was. And I think that is how it materialized, and became something real. Because I had seen a team, I had seen just more people doing it, and was like, holy shit this is an industry. This is something people do and love and I can do this.

But after the shoot, Charles had to turn back to the reality of two more years of high school, which was a challenge for him since there was no formal way for him to study film further. "I had tapped into something that was just so clear to me that this is what I need to do," Charles explains, "but I was still stuck in this community of people who didn't understand what I had found. They didn't understand that I had found a community of people that get me."

Charles would eventually request Stillmotion to come out to his high school and give a workshop (during their 36-city tour). He made a connection with them and was offered a three-month job over the summer after graduating high school. He had also applied to NYU's film school and was accepted. He deferred with NYU and took a gap year. He left Stillmotion at the end of that summer—after being enticed to work for Zandrak in Boston. "I wanted to commit myself in helping to create a brand and an identity and being part of that process. As soon as I got here we dove into the Hasbro commercial—and things starting rolling and we started seeing how this identity that we were building was actually something that could flourish and was real." At this point, Charles knew that he wanted a team-based leadership role at Zandrak. "I withdrew my application from NYU." At age nineteen, he had already directed a commercial and promotional work that many decades older would be envious of.

With his work on the Moodsnap commercial, "I wanted it to be really raw and organic and personal," Charles explains. Working with Ray Tsang, the cinematographer, he decided the best way to shoot this documentary, raw style, was with a handheld camera, because he didn't want the audience "to think they were observing in a really sterile way but I wanted them to feel part of the experiences." He feels that "different styles of camera motion and camera choices tell different things and help people buy into different experiences." In this case, the handheld camera works "because the way you see the world isn't perfectly stable. You see it in just a more raw way." It helped make the world he created with "Our Songs" something more natural.

With the actors in place doing their thing, Charles works directly with the cinematographer, "helping him decide what moments to capture and how to capture them." But they wouldn't conceptualize from the script or in a pre-imagined way. They "would visit all of our locations, all of our environments prior to shooting them," Charles says, "and we'd talk about the types of shots that we wanted to get." For example, "We know we need a wide shot. We know we need two singles and we know that we want to have a medium shot of their feet as they're walking." They would write this down in their shot list.

Once on location, Charles says, "I would talk to the actors and set them up in their environments and then I would let them off and be free to exist in them." He would let them improvise their actions, living in those spaces. Since they had already discussed what kinds of shots they needed for a scene—"the knowledge of the type of coverage we needed to get"—"we'd get the shots on the fly as the action is going on." At times he might "reposition" the performers, Charles adds, "but I wanted to as much as I could to stay hands-off to allow their performance to flow naturally. I feel that makes it authentic and real."

For example, in the scene when they're driving in the car, Charles wanted to set up the feeling of, "Let's just go for a ride and I want you to take in the environment, be happy that you are out of a city and you are in the country." He describes his intention with his prompt for the performers: "Imagine that you live in a city and you infrequently get to come out to the country with

Directing Actors

There are dozens of books on directing. Many of them focus on the role of the director in making a film—from the entire preproduction process, to onset protocols and processes, and postproduction input. Not many film books discuss how directors interact with performers. Indeed, in *Film + Music*'s interview with Lenore DeKoven, who wrote *Changing Direction*, she says, "I ended up creating the discipline of directing actors. I mean, everyone knew that was part of the job—everyone realized that it was important—but it wasn't really addressed specifically as a discipline." Film is a collaborative art, and understanding the path—the heart to working with performers—is key if you want to deliver good performances. DeKoven explains how a director needs to be observant—get their heads out of their phones, stop talking too much, and notice the details happening around them in life:

> I think that a would-be director needs to take it all in. They need to train themselves to really watch, to really listen. You can't re-create something unless you have a memory of it. Change your location. Go out into the country and think about how the air smells different.[1]

We see these types of details from Charles' film, the moments he creates with his performers in the Moodsnap piece, and perhaps that's one of the secrets to making a good short film—whether it's for a client or a personal piece—the director must be in tune with how reality, emotional reality, gets translated and communicated on film.

Just as there is no one way to shoot a camera, there is no one way to direct actors. Some of the best approaches to working with actors come out of theater. I recommend several books as a jumpstart to understanding the process for working with performers. These are from a theater perspective, but these books will give you ideas on how masters work with performers. Here are a few resources:

- Konstantin Stanislavski's *An Actor Prepares* (Routledge, 1989): The foundation of modern acting stems from this book.

- *Directors on Directing*, edited by Toby Cole and Helen Krich Chinoy (Allegro Editions, 2013).

- David Richard Jones's *Great Directors at Work: Stanislavsky, Brecht, Kazan, Brook* (University of California Press, 1987).

- Susan Letzler Cole's *Directors in Rehearsal: A Hidden World* (Routledge, 2013).

- Shomit Mitter's *Systems of Rehearsal: Stanislavsky, Brecht, Grotowski, and Brook* (Routledge, 1992).

FIGURE 9.1
Charles assists Ray in setting up a shot in the car. (Photo courtesy of Zandrak.)

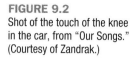

FIGURE 9.2
Shot of the touch of the knee in the car, from "Our Songs." (Courtesy of Zandrak.)

winding roads and you both are just silent, taking that in and happy to be a part of something that's away from the hectic city. And from time to time, I want you to acknowledge that with each other, non-verbally." And that was it for the prompt, for the intent of the action.

He didn't give them specific actions, but the interactions and the way they looked at each other, all became part of the organic flow of the piece. For example, Charles adds, "they would look over, touch each other's knee. It was all organic and it was all driven by the atmosphere." (See Figure 9.2.)

Charles feels that you cannot force those kinds of moments. "I don't think you can tell an actor genuinely take a little peek over at your partner," he feels. "It doesn't feel as real as when you just have them do it on their own." But he does feel that if you do provide the right context "you have to believe that those moments will happen." Being in tune with the environment helped. As for the car, the performers would sit in the car and they "just took it in and experienced it together and it was very real." That's what he means by hands off. "That's the directing approach that I like to take as much as I can," he explains.

It sounds subtle and simple, and he wants to clarify what he means. "I think that there is a little bit of a misunderstanding in the role of the director. Some people think that directors generate performances and they create the Oscar-winning actors and actresses, but to me it's more than that. As the director you create an atmosphere and you let people create for themselves." To do the job of a good director, Charles explains, is about "creating the right atmosphere to capture that atmosphere effectively." If the director steps in and directs every moment, then it falls apart, he says. "As soon as I step on their toes and tell them to look here and do this precisely they are going to feel constrained and feel rigid and it's not going to feel real." Charles doesn't want stylization. He wants to create the atmosphere of real life.

And when you're creating a piece that has minimal dialogue, "a piece like this that's largely mood and non-verbal," he feels that his approach is an effective way to go about it. But it's not all freeform. In one scene, the actress, Alexandra Chelaru, falls behind, so Charles tells her to catch up with Drew (Andrew Cashin), making it "a little more directed, obviously." And when it's naturally raw, where every moment is not rehearsed (including timing performers with the camera), the documentary style can feel a bit more rough. "Drew invites her into the space, but you can even just see the visual style, just that handheld shot, it's imperfect but it just feels real to me," Charles explains.

When Drew invites her and she rushes to catch up, Charles and Ray talked about having a steadicam shot pushing up on her as she ran up to him. "But my concern was that it would feel too epic and too grandiose and it wouldn't feel real." It would feel staged, making the audience feel, perhaps, "distant from it." By going with the handheld, the polish was lost, he says, but "even though it's imperfect it feels a little more real."

In another moment when Charles gave the performers a certain amount of creativity, he wanted Drew "to find a fabric, a ridiculous fabric to make clothes.

FIGURE 9.3
Charles tells Alexandra to catch up to Drew as Ray rushes in with the camera. (Courtesy of Zandrak.)

But I told Alexandra that I want her to be opposed to whatever fabric he chooses." He didn't tell her how to react, but to oppose whatever he chose. And she ended up doing it in a "really subtle and sweet way." Charles says, "I don't think she has the most approving eyes here. But it's sweet and it's still cute but she's not overdoing it" (see Figure 9.4). By not "pushing it on her" he brought out a "subtlety" that became "a choice that she made. She decided that that was the best way to tell him, 'bad choice,'" Charles explains. The magic came from how Charles approached that moment. "She didn't have to have me tell her how to do it. And that's what I think is pretty real. This is my favorite scene in the entire piece."

In the end, Charles feels that by "putting people in the right atmosphere does so much for direction that I've barely had to say anything. They felt it because they were there and they were on location. Just watching them interact, you can just see it. It is just natural to the performers. For example, I didn't plan the back pat and the kiss. I didn't tell them to do any of that. It just came about naturally," he says, reinforcing his hands-off perspective.

In the scene with the argument outside the car, Charles told them that there's a disagreement about which way to go. At one point he wanted Drew to "reach the tipping point where he can no longer take her input and decides to be entrenched in his decision and walk the way he thinks is right." This is an example of how he approached the scene cinematically, visually and aurally. He set the camera inside the car and recorded audio from inside the car, as well, providing the audience with a sense of distance from the scene. "Their sounds and argument is muffled. We hear that repetitious dinging of the car door being open" (see Figure 9.5).

FIGURE 9.4
Alexandra gives Drew a look of disbelief in Zandrak's "Our Songs." Charles allowed the performers a certain amount of freedom when blocking scenes. (Courtesy of Zandrak.)

FIGURE 9.5
Alexandra and Drew argue in Zandrak's "Our Songs." The camera and microphone were placed inside the car in order to create visual and aural tension. (Courtesy of Zandrak.)

By making this choice, Charles explains, he builds "an uncomfortable tension because you are far away from them and you can't quite hear what they are saying and there is this incessant sound that keeps coming over you." You, as the audience, feel the argument as an uncomfortable tension, because it's being done cinematically (the visual and aural elements) and not just from the performance. "Any way that you can cinematically express what you are trying to say through a performance," Charles says, "it just enhances it twofold. In creating the sound that makes you uncomfortable, creating a visual style that pulls the viewer away and forces them to watch this from a distance, and also through the muffled argumentative dialogue, I think all together it makes you feel tension."

In the scene occurring in the field, it was spontaneous. They had just finished the scene occurring on the side of the road when Charles noticed the magic hour light in a field and told everyone to get out of the car. "It wasn't shot listed, it wasn't planned, wasn't in the schedule, but I had a harmonica in my car and there was this beautiful field and the sun had just set and the light was gorgeous and the energy felt right." They were already pumped up from coming off a really great scene. "I told Alexandra to take the harmonica and play Drew a song and walk through the field. And so I just let them go," (see Figure 9.6 and book cover). Charles, looking at an external portable monitor, got behind Ray as they shot it documentary-style. "I was really focused just on how to capture it."

Charles feeds off this spontaneous approach, because "sometimes that stuff is the best. Especially if you capture it without interrupting it." It's key for Charles that the camera captures it without stopping or setting up another shot. "That's a really big thing for me," he explains, and that's why Ray was best for this job. "Ray comes from a documentary background," Charles says. "This is one

FIGURE 9.6
A still from Zandrak's "Our Songs" in which Alexandra plays the harmonica in an unplanned spontaneous scene. (Courtesy of Zandrak.)

FIGURE 9.7
Behind the scenes covering the action. (Courtesy of Zandrak.)

of the first narrative pieces he has done. But it benefited us so well because of his documentary sensibility for cinematography," he adds. "He was able to capture it as a documentary within the confines of a narrative structure. Which is a really cool approach that I hadn't really considered when we first conceived the piece."

Despite the improvisational nature of the performances—within the constraints of the environment and the parameters of the narrative, the story that needs to be told in each scene—Charles does see the scene unfolding in his head. When he doesn't see it, he runs into trouble. About the scene where the performers do shadow play on the wall, Charles says, "When I shot it, I was really indecisive. We would try one thing and I'd try to see that shot and then imagine the following shots but I couldn't, so I would try a different thing. We'd go in a different direction and we tried four different avenues and four different sequences." Charles says it ended up placing stress on the actors for having to do different kinds of performances and more stress on Ray for having to do more sequences than planned. "Ray talked to me afterwards and he told me, 'You got to be more direct with what you want. You were all over the place with that and it didn't work.' And I have to admit that I totally agreed with him—because I hadn't seen it play in my head. I hadn't seen the way it would cut."

In the end it worked, but Charles learned that he needs to visualize it before shooting. But as a lesson in editing and persevering in the scene and experimenting with different approaches (getting enough coverage), Charles was able to "mix and match and pull shots from two different sequences that ended up working in the end."

In another unplanned scene, they were driving to another location. Rather than waste time he decided to shoot a scene of them driving to that location. "I told them to play the radio and jam out," Charles says. "I played a song and this is them just listening to it together and jamming out. And that was it. Just a short little piece, a little sequence that could plug in at any moment in the film." But it wasn't necessarily easy for the cinematographer. "There was so much timing and focus pulling and Ray had to get the right pan at the right time so it all linked up and that was Ray just nailing it," Charles explains.

In the diner scene, Charles ended up shooting the scene in a linear way. He had Alexandra and Drew draw each other on napkins at the table. But he didn't allow them to show each other the drawings until they shot it, so the reveal of the portraits would be natural. "We just started shooting that process of them drawing each other," he says. "The looks at each other were very real and the laughs were real and then we did the reveal. The initial reaction was their real first reaction to see the images that they drew of each other. So her holding it up and laughing at it, was just what Alexandra was doing because she thought the drawing he did was funny and we were there to capture it" (see Figure 9.8).

FIGURE 9.8
Alexandra laughs at her
portrait drawn by Drew in
Zandrak's "Our Songs."
Charles had the actors reveal
the images they drew for the
first time on camera in order
to get the natural reaction
from the performers.
(Courtesy of Zandrak.)

Another aspect of the documentary approach occurred in the bowling scene. "We just walked into the environment," Charles says, "and I told them to bowl and be competitive and just have fun with it and maybe over-celebrate if anything good happened, just to shove it in each other's faces. And then we just let them bowl an entire round." He and Ray had discussed the types of shots they wanted—long takes of them bowling. "Roll one long take where you track them," Charles describes talking to Ray, "and then you cut back to a wide. And maybe you swing around and you get the profile two shot as they interact with each other as they are walking by after having bowled." He told Ray that he would "whisper in his ear if there is something different I want to be capturing." He would let the actors bowl, and then he would "tell them I want it to be a little more competitive when you get back, or I want you to condescendingly clap as he walks on his way back," he says. He mentioned how he had seen her do it earlier and wanted to use it at the point where he is "disappointed, it went poorly for him and then she claps as he comes around and it was just something she had done earlier and decided to implement when we went to shoot it" (see Figure 9.9).

In addition, there were some arcade games in the bowling alley, so he had them go and play. He told Ray to just cover it documentary style. "Ray just went in handheld." And in a moment that didn't make it in the final cut, there was sunlight coming over the mountain at the dock on a lake. "We had about five minutes before the light was about to peek above the mountain. Ray ran, he shot this one, then he got this one shot and then sprinted back and got the wide." They would wrap the shoot on this shot. "We all celebrated on the pier," Charles says. "And that was it. That was the visual style and the directorial choices I tried to make in this film."

FIGURE 9.9
Charles had Alexandra clap in a condescending way, just as he had noticed her doing earlier. (Courtesy of Zandrak.)

You can see Zandrak's "Our Songs" at: http://vimeo.com/106374768

CHAPTER 10

A Crowdfunding Case Study

Financing *Frame by Frame*

In the final chapter, we examine what it takes to put together your own personal project. Many people who freelance and/or create their own production house business got their training and start in filmmaking. There is usually a passion for telling stories—whether it's a work of fiction or a documentary. Stories—when done well—move people. In no other time in the history of cinema is it easier to make your own film project due to the low cost of gear and the ability to engage in crowdfunding to raise money for low-budget films. Crowdfunding isn't about making Hollywood blockbusters, but it does allow for the creation of personal projects that would rarely get made without it. At the same time, crowdfunding also builds a fan base for the film. Very few spec films get made in Hollywood. Harun Mehmedinovich—a graduate of the MFA program in film directing at the American Film Institute—tells me that the odds are better trying to win in a Las Vegas casino than getting your script produced in Hollywood.

Kickstarter.com, Indiegogo (https://www.indiegogo.com/explore/film), and Seed&Spark (seedandspark.com) are sites that allow filmmakers to raise money to help make their film.

SEED&SPARK CASE STUDY WITH KEEP THE CHANGE

Emily Best, the founder of Seed&Spark, argues against the idea that crowdfunding should be a way to fund a dabbler in filmmaking. She wants to fund filmmakers who need and want to make a living at doing what they love. It's a curated site, so you are expected to have your team, vision, budget, and so forth buttoned up. Emily explains to me how Seed&Spark was designed:

> To help filmmakers build meaningful businesses out of their films, giving them an infrastructure that would allow them the access and control to make a sustainable living. I want to get away from the dichotomy of "for money vs. for passion" to say that you *can* make

money in something you're passionate about. I don't view crowdfunding as the outlet for dabblers, at least not how we're framing it. We want people who consider themselves independent filmmakers to be able to pay their rent, feed their families, and grow their lives doing what they love for a living.

Seed&Spark bases its principles on the idea that most anyone can make a film with the right talent and perseverance, but to get your film watched—that's an entirely different story. Crowdfunding helps a filmmaker to build an audience. If you use Seed&Spark to crowdfund your film, they will require you to lay out such basic information as:

- Logline
- Short synopsis
- Long synopsis
- "About your team" description
- Artistic statement
- Budget information
- Production status
- Distribution plan.

They require a pitch video and remind people how the first fifteen seconds "should feel like it's in the world of your film," then shift into the personal appeal of what you need to make your film happen. They recommend that you should be sure to "make your crowd feel there is a sense of inevitability that a great project will result." Don't be a defeatist! Build incentives into the campaign, so that the funder feels like they're getting something special and unique. They recommend that the key incentives for a project are $10–25, since you'll get a larger amount of people chip in a little bit. They recommend that these incentives be "personal, visual, and sharable on social media," because if one person shares, dozens of others will see how one person shared and got something "cool," and they're be more inclined to jump on board.

One of the components that makes Seed&Spark stand out is their unique wish list—it's like a wedding registry, where your crowdfunding team can choose what they're buying for you (from batteries to a camera rental) with a brief description of why you need it.

Here's an example of some of the approaches found in a successful crowdfunded romantic comedy, *Keep the Change* by Rachel Israel, which raised over $50,000 with support from 533 people. It began as a sixteen-minute short that screened at several festivals, and helped inspire the desire to create a low-budget feature film. See: http://www.seedandspark.com/studio/keep-change.

Logline: "A young man struggling to hide his autism falls in love with a young woman who challenges his desire to appear 'normal.'"

Budget incentives of $5 and $20 (among higher end incentives), see Figure 10.1.

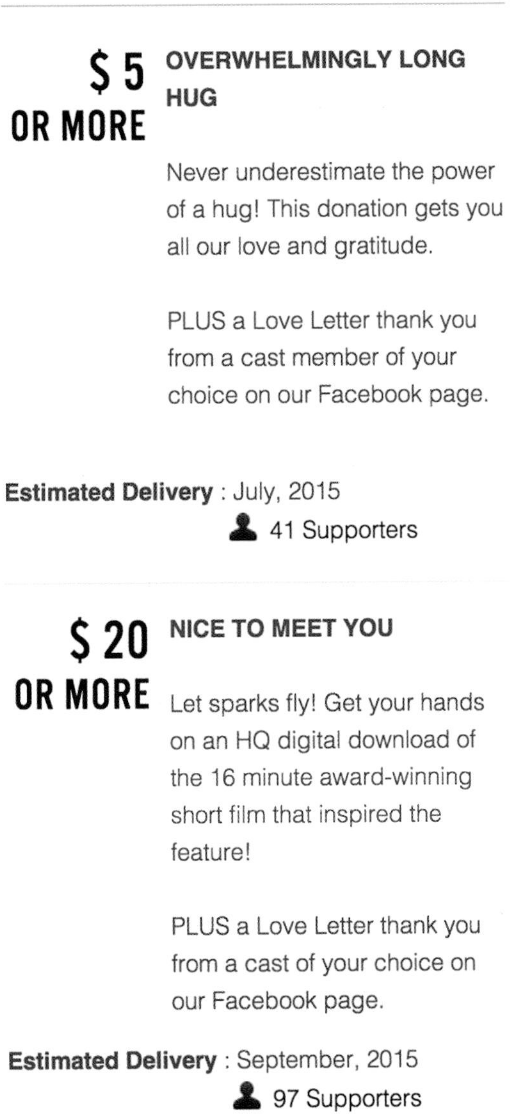

$ 5 OR MORE

OVERWHELMINGLY LONG HUG

Never underestimate the power of a hug! This donation gets you all our love and gratitude.

PLUS a Love Letter thank you from a cast member of your choice on our Facebook page.

Estimated Delivery : July, 2015

👤 41 Supporters

$ 20 OR MORE

NICE TO MEET YOU

Let sparks fly! Get your hands on an HQ digital download of the 16 minute award-winning short film that inspired the feature!

PLUS a Love Letter thank you from a cast of your choice on our Facebook page.

Estimated Delivery : September, 2015

👤 97 Supporters

FIGURE 10.1
Notice the unique incentives for this film and how they reflect the nature of the film (romantic comedy). (Courtesy of Seed&Spark.)

As you skim through their page, take note of how each incentive is unique and reflects the talents of the people they have on their team. A $1,500 or more investment, for example, would purchase a Broadway music CD "mixed by one of our main cast, music blogger – William S. Deaver"; or an Ice Box Cake by main cast member, "Nicky Gottlieb (Travis McHenry) – hand delivered by Nicky and director Rachel Israel (limited to NYC locals)"; or an "original painting by supporting cast member Amy Rosenfeld (Playing wonderful relentless Annie)." And it shows images of the five paintings (the gift is limited to five).

The wish list includes everything from hard drives, lighting, location sound, insurance, location fees, casting, vehicles, catering, legal services, among others. You can purchase units of a product or loan an item out.

OUR PRODUCTION WISHLIST

Browse the list to BUY or LOAN specific items to this production

G-TECHNOLOGY® DATA STORAGE

**G-Technology®
Hard Drive ($2000)**

G-Technology® is the gold standard for storage solutions specifically designed for content creators. We'll get a storage grant from them when we get the Green Light!

$25.00 per unit   **36** of **80** fulfilled   1 ▼   BUY   LOAN

LIGHTING

Lighting Package

You can't say "lights, camera, action!" with no lights.

$25.00 per unit   **22** of **200** fulfilled   1 ▼   BUY   LOAN

PROPS

Prop Package

Props help bring the actors into character, and help bring the scene to life.

$10.00 per unit   **24** of **50** fulfilled   1 ▼   BUY   LOAN

FIGURE 10.2
The first few items on the production wish list include a specific brand of hard drive, lighting, and props. Notice how a potential funder is not purchasing $2,000 worth of hard drives, for example, but is putting $25 towards the hard drive (or more if they purchase more than one unit of payment). (Courtesy of Seed&Spark.)

Crowdfunding campaigns allow those with a vision, to get their film made. Another approach to funding includes branding, especially if you're making a short. Andrew Hutcheson of Zandrak Productions feels that it's important that filmmakers—especially those who are working the daily grind of a production house—"stay creatively fulfilled and stimulated." He believes a good way to fund a short film is to find a brand to put into the film. "There is where your money comes in. And if you are going to raise money, use the same principles you have towards your business. Appeal to someone's emotions," he explains. At the same time, Andrew says it's important to think about your potential audience. "Is there an audience for this movie? Is someone going to want to see this? Why are they going to see it? Why am I making it? What am I making?"

Andrew, like Emily Best, believes that you're not just funding a passion project to make a film, but a business:

> If you are going to make a feature film, then you have to make it for the idea that it is a profitable venture. If you are going to make a short film probably don't try and get someone to pay for it. Maybe make a short film that's going to be part of a brand—they are just going to put this out there. And don't be dissuaded if you really want to do a short film that Bose can sponsor if you put in their headphones. But what if they say they don't want your film? Is Bose the only company that makes headphones? Call all of the headphone companies. It is a numbers game. And if you are willing to take the rejection, you will find the person that's right for you. You won't find them on your first try or your tenth. But if you keep calling and trying and keep learning what works and what doesn't and who's right for you, you might find the right person.

To help build support and a network, Andrew recommends that you "look into the film commission, all of the competitors. This will give you a list of all other filmmakers, either to collaborate or donate to your crowdfunding campaign."

KICKSTARTER CASE STUDY WITH FRAME BY FRAME

If the popularity of film schools is an indicator, a lot of people want to become a filmmaker. Alexandria Bombach graduated from Fort Lewis College[1] in Durango, Colorado in 2008—just as the Great Recession was about to begin. Her dream was to make films. She got rid of everything she had, bought a 23-foot 1970 Airstream camper, and with two friends, traveled through Colorado, Utah, Arizona, and California "to search for the stories of people who have turned their backs on the creature comforts of society to live in school buses, vans, and other small spaces." In order to live her dream as a filmmaker—to fund her passion and not look back—she's been living on the road for the past six years.

Alexandria learned the basics of filmmaking in college (she was a business major), but it was an internship at Osprey Packs that gave her the opportunity to apply her filmmaking skills to a series of creative promotional films and allowed her to hone her storytelling skills (these works can be seen at http://redreelvideo.com/gallery). "It was so many shorts in a very short amount of time," she explains, "so it was kind of just like a crash course in shooting and getting story out of a very limited budget." These projects would eventually lead to a series of beautifully shot short documentary stories sponsored by Osprey Packs (along with Horny Toad Clothing and Clif Bar) that told stories of those who engaged in creating positive change in the world (see http://www.moveshake.org/).

But it didn't begin easily. Alexandria tells me that she was glad the recession happened. It forced her to become a filmmaker. "I started a production company right in the middle of the recession," she says. "I quit my waitressing job. I was really glad the recession happened, because if I'm not going to make money anywhere I might as well do exactly what I love." She did apply for jobs, but got nothing. "I'm not getting any jobs so I'm just going to make my own thing and that was the best thing that could have happened, because just walking up to companies and asking them to give you a job doesn't work." She actually discovered that by "making your own thing, making your own style—and doing it well, then companies come to you!"

Alexandria ended up naming her company, Red Reel. "It was really super desperate times. I was not feeding myself very well, we were very worried about rent, I was living in Chattanooga, Tennessee. I just called it Red Reel and I had no idea if it would last. And I didn't really have anyone telling me that it was possible."

With these projects under her belt, among other promotional film projects she worked on, Alexandria was ready to take on a new challenge—to shoot a documentary about photographers in Afghanistan. She had helped edit a friend's short film that included footage from Afghanistan, and once she saw the footage she wanted to go and capture that beauty herself. She explains how she'd never been to Afghanistan but, she says, "as I started seeing the footage of the b-roll, of people walking down the street in normal everyday life, it made me question my own perception of what I thought I knew about Afghanistan." It made her want to go and make her own discoveries. The project began initially in the fall of 2012 as a short. Alexandria, along with Mo Scarpelli (who worked with her on several other projects), was intrigued about telling the story of local photographers.

Alexandria used all of her savings and sold her car to get plane tickets to Afghanistan, but after shooting in October 2012, Alexandria went home and started editing the film and realized the project was larger than anticipated. She explained how she had been "making shorts for a while and I believe that's a really great way to get stuff out there, but when I got back and I was looking through the interviews and the footage we had, I just really felt that this was a more compelling film than can fit into a short. I remember crying into my laptop, actually. 'Oh no, this is a feature!'" At that point, she had to make a decision, "because it's a whole other cliff to jump off of." She had to budget out the entire project and plan for what they needed to make the feature documentary happen. "This film would never have happened without Kickstarter," she explains. "As a first time filmmaker it's really hard to get grants."

In order to make a feature-length documentary film, they had to go back and spend more time there in order to capture the larger stories. It was important to Alexandria that the project remain an independent film—where they retain full control of the content and story, so they didn't ask for film funding through a traditional route. Alexandria had successfully raised just under $10,000 for her first independent short film, *23 Feet*, but this time she would need $40,000 to fund the two-month trip. The Kickstarter campaign ran for one month from July 29, 2013 to August 28, 2013. "I think we got $20,000 in the first couple of days," she explains, "and then there was kind of a lull and it was kind of scary. We made our goal and there were three days left and then Upworthy posted our trailer—then it went up like $30,000 in about three days." They ended up raising over $70,000 for *Frame by Frame*.

The story revolves around four Afghan photojournalists in post-Taliban Afghanistan. When the Taliban were in charge, it was illegal to take pictures. The four characters in the film include Najibullah Musafar, who teaches photography and feels the country's identity is at stake. Wakil Kohsar examines the heroin addicts on the streets and in recovery centers. Massoud Hossaini

Kickstarter Tip by Alexandria Bombach

It's nerve-racking asking people for money. But you just have to get past that. We had to do a lot of defining what the project was. Which was really hard because although we had been there and shot, we didn't want to define exactly what the film was going to be because we still wanted to shoot for two months. And so that was really tricky. Also just a lot of figuring out math. You know we can offer this reward at this price but it's going to have this much in shipping and how will this affect our distribution? Planning the DVD coming out before our first screen day was not a good idea, since that would impact any distribution plans.

I think the hardest part about Kickstarter with films is trying to have a lot of foresight into making the right decisions. I did one Kickstarter for *23 Feet* for the tour that I did and that was successful on a much smaller scale, but it helped me a lot. When people come and ask me for help with Kickstarter, I'm always telling them, just sign up and start backing things. You'll start learning so much. Just being a part of it at least once is really helpful.

A lot of the campaigning was behind the scenes. Emailing people, and people who are friends and influencers and asking them to be a part of the team to get the film out there. We were really lucky to have some really great people who said, "Yeah, I'm going to champion this with my connections," and they donated right away. Their priority was to share with their community. And that's a very powerful thing, since it wasn't just coming from us. So a lot of it was emails—even more than Facebook and Twitter. But it was also setting everything up on the page, such as finding the title of the film and making the trailer before the film is done.

earned a Pulitizer Prize for Breaking News Photography in 2012 for his image of a bombing during a religious procession. Hossaini's wife, Farzana Wahidy, is also a photographer who examines the women of Afghanistan—especially the lack of education among women due to the Taliban's strict policy against educating them. (See Figure 10.3.)

The film debuted at the South by Southwest (SXSW) festival. Sheri Linden, writing a review for *The Hollywood Reporter*, noted how the film is "as artful and empathetic as its subjects' work ... *Frame by Frame* is a work of profound immediacy, in sync with the photographers' commitment and hope" (March 14, 2015). It would go on to screen at film festivals in Atlanta, Cleveland, Ashland, Dallas, Nashville, Berkshire, New Zealand, and at Hot Docs, among others.

FIGURE 10.3
The four subjects of *Frame by Frame*: Najibullah Musafer, Massoud Hossaini, Wakil Kohsar, and Farzana Wahidy. (Courtesy of Alexandria Bombach.)

FIGURE 10.4
A girl smiles in the Kickstarter preview of *Frame by Frame*. Capturing the sense of hope was one of the elements Mo and Alexandria wanted to show in their documentary. (Courtesy of Alexandria Bombach.)

FIGURE 10.5
Alexandria Bombach on location in Afghanistan as she shoots with a Canon 5D Mark III. Along with Mo Scarpelli, they raised over $70,000 to fund their documentary, *Frame by Frame*. (Courtesy of Alexandria Bombach.)

Initially, they needed $40,000 to travel and shoot the project, but they ended up raising $70,000, which covered their postproduction expenses. The budget breakdown looks like this (Figure 10.6):

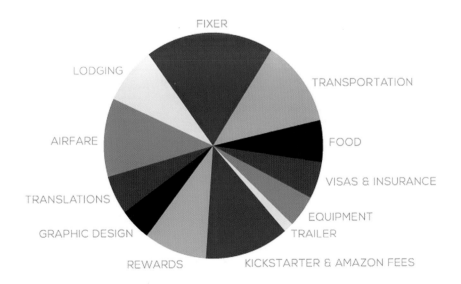

FIGURE 10.6
The budget breakdown of *Frame by Frame*'s Kickstarter campaign. The fixer is their local contact, guide, and translator in Afghanistan. Notice that the initial budget did not include postproduction work. (Courtesy of Alexandria Bombach.)

A Kickstarter campaign involves a lot of planning and vision. It's not something to be done lightly. Here's the campaign page to *Frame by Frame*. I'll break it down in sections and discuss them in more detail.

The filmmakers directly address why they're the best people for the project. They describe how they have already gone to Afghanistan and met the characters for their story: "Last year, we filmed our photographers capturing heroin addicts, the country's first boxing match, and patrons of a mosque which normally turns cameras away," they write. They also describe what the Kickstarter campaign will fund. First, they describe the importance of the story: "What it's like to help build and then stand for free press in Afghanistan while the country's future hangs in the balance." That contains a core conflict and reveals what's at stake for the characters. There's potential drama that will help make it a compelling film.

In addition, they cover the cost of making the film itself, including the costs of the rewards:

> Filming in Afghanistan is expensive, especially when it comes to being as safe as possible. Our Kickstarter goal of $40,000 will cover airfare,

FIGURE 10.7
The opening section of the campaign page contains the beginning of the rewards: $1, $10, $25. It also shows the amount of money raised and needed, a strong image from the film, and the trailer of the film, including an appeal by both Alexandria and Mo. The trailer for a film project is the most important tool you have in raising money. It shows what you can do and the potential of the story. Over $16,000 was raised from backers contributing $35 or less. Making sure a backer can get a film (whether a digital copy or DVD) is important at these lower-priced levels, Alexandria says. She's noticed that many failed campaigns don't provide a copy of the film unless backers pay $50 or more. (Courtesy of Alexandria Bombach.)

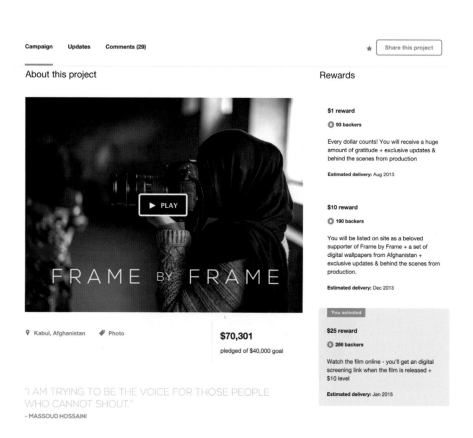

lodging, transportation, food for the production crew, hard drives, evacuation insurance, interview translations, and a team of amazing fixers and drivers that we had last year. We've also budgeted in the costs of creating the rewards, shipping them to you and the 10% fee for Kickstarter and Amazon.

They make a case for what the $40,000 budget will cover, but they also make a plea for additional funds—if they raise more than their budget, it will provide

$35 reward

🔘 202 backers

DVD of Frame by Frame with behind the scenes and extra features from production + $10 level

Estimated delivery: Jan 2015
Ships anywhere in the world

$50 reward

🔘 120 backers

An original artwork Frame by Frame t-shirt + DVD + $10 level

Estimated delivery: Jan 2015
Ships anywhere in the world

$75 reward

🔘 77 backers

An Afghan Scarf from the famous Chicken Street in Kabul + t-shirt + DVD + $10 level

Estimated delivery: Jan 2015
Ships anywhere in the world

$100 reward

🔘 123 backers

A kickstarter exclusive photo book from our friends at Artifact Uprising. This beautifully bound book will hold images from production as well as the photos from the photographers themselves + t-shirt + DVD + $10 level

Estimated delivery: Jan 2015
Ships anywhere in the world

THE POWER OF A PHOTO

In 1996, the Taliban banned photography in Afghanistan. Taking a photo was considered a crime. When the regime was removed from Kabul in 2001, their suppression of free speech and press disappeared. Since then, photography has become an outlet for Afghans determined to show the hidden stories of their country.

In this coming year, as foreign troops pull out of the country, international media will inevitably follow. The Taliban is poised to gain influence, if not fully return to power. The future of journalism in Afghanistan is unknown.

The need for local photojournalism here couldn't be more important in documenting the country's issues both now, and in the future.

Frame by Frame is a character-driven feature-length documentary that follows the story of four Afghan photographers to explore the recent revolution in local photojournalism.

These Afghan photojournalists are the storytellers, the truth-seekers, the voice of their own people. They're seizing a unique opportunity to build democracy here in a way that never existed before: through a free press. Their work is a crucial part of showing what is happening during this very uncertain time.

FIGURE 10.8
Here the filmmakers provide background on photography in Afghanistan—how it was illegal during the Taliban era. In addition, they make a plea for the need to support photojournalism in Afghanistan and how their documentary will help tell that story. Also note that about $18,000 was raised from the $50–100 reward categories—which includes a t-shirt, Afghan scarf, and photo book as the prices increase. Be clear that as you add these rewards they have to be paid for out of the money raised. Nearly $34,000— 85 percent of their goal of their $40,000—was raised from the $100 and less categories. Kickstarter—all crowdfunding sites—rely on a lot of people giving a little bit of money. Don't rely on a few giving a lot of money. (Courtesy of Alexandria Bombach.)

FIGURES 10.9 AND 10.10
The filmmakers discuss how they've already been to Afghanistan once and received open access from photojournalists—the access to their characters "opened up a very unique opportunity for us to capture subjects and issues which are usually not accessible to outside film crews," they write. This inside access assures supporters that they'll be getting a unique film and telling a story rarely—if ever—seen in the Western press. Indeed, it is such stories that attracted Alexandria to the project. (Courtesy of Alexandria Bombach.)

At the same time, they face major hurdles: threats from Taliban or other extremists, skepticism of their own people, lack of security and financial support, and for Farzana, one of the only female Afghan photographers in Kabul, gender barriers.

From left to right: Najibullah Musafer, Massoud Hossaini, Wakil Kohsar, and Farzana Wahidy

Going back to Afghanistan

Frame by Frame started production in the fall of 2012: we emptied Alexandria's bank account, sold her car, and flew to Afghanistan with the hopes of shooting a short film about local photographers. We filmed for a short period of time, then sat down with each photographer to learn about their work and their take on the future of photojournalism in Afghanistan. Each interview captivated us more and more. This was a story that needed to be told — **and we needed more time to tell it.**

So... why us?

We care about the **human stories** behind this issue, and we also have access to tell it in an incredible way. Last year, we filmed our photographers capturing heroin addicts, the country's first boxing match, and patrons of a mosque which normally turns cameras away. Our characters' access has opened up a very unique opportunity for us to capture subjects and issues which are usually not accessible to outside film crews.

A pop-up studio in Kabul with our wonderful fixer Najib and photographer Wakil Kohsar

What this Kickstarter will do

This Kickstarter will get us back to Kabul this fall to finish the production side of Frame by Frame. For five weeks, we'll follow Farzana, Massoud, Wakil and Najibullah in their day-to-day lives. We'll capture the ups and downs of their work while driving at the larger story: **what it's like to help build and then stand for free press in Afghanistan while the country's future hangs in the balance.**

Filming in Afghanistan is expensive, especially when it comes to being as safe as possible. Our Kickstarter goal of $40,000 will cover airfare, lodging, transportation, food for the production crew, hard drives, evacuation insurance, interview translations, and a team of amazing fixers and drivers that we had last year. We've also budgeted in the costs of creating the rewards, shipping them to you and the 10% fee for Kickstarter and Amazon.

$150 reward

⊙ 10 backers All gone!

$100 VSCO CREDIT!! www.vsco.co/film + a special thank you in the credits of the film + photo book from Artifact Uprising + t-shirt + DVD + $10 level

Estimated delivery: Jan 2015
Ships anywhere in the world

$200 reward

⊙ 27 backers

SEE THE FILM BEFORE ANYONE – be a part of the process. We'll send you a digital screener of the film right when we finish, PLUS a special thank you in the credits of the film + photo book + t-shirt + DVD + $10 level

Estimated delivery: Jan 2015
Ships anywhere in the world

$500 reward

⊙ 10 backers

PHOTOS FROM THE PHOTOGRAPHERS – A set of prints from the photographers themselves + see the film first + a special thank you in the credits + photo book + t-shirt + DVD + $10 level

Estimated delivery: Jan 2015
Ships anywhere in the world

$1,000 reward

⊙ 5 backers All gone!

Two tickets to a PRIVATE SCREENING in New York (transportation and lodging not included) + $500 level

Estimated delivery: Jan 2015
Ships anywhere in the world

$2,500 reward

⊙ 0 backers Limited (5 left of 5)

A 8x12 PHOTO by one of the photographers from Afghanistan on Plywerk's beautiful bamboo mounts (plywerk.com) + two tickets to the private screening in NYC + see the film first + a special thank you in the credits + photo book + t-shirt + DVD + $10 level

Estimated delivery: Jan 2015
Ships anywhere in the world

$3,000 reward

⊙ 0 backers Limited (5 left of 5)

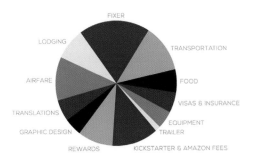

A limited edition, one-of-a-kind HARDCOVER BOOK packed with excerpts from Afghan photographers and their incredible work, including a hand-written note from the photographers + two tickets to the private screening in NYC + see the film first + a special thank you in the credits + t-shirt + DVD + $10 level

Estimated delivery: Jan 2015
Ships anywhere in the world

$5,000 reward

⊙ 1 backer   Limited (2 left of 3)

$5,000
Become a member of the PRODUCER'S CIRCLE: that means you'll receive exclusive updates from the crew during all stages of production and you'll be listed in the credits of the film as a member of the Producer's Circle + your name or logo will be listed on the Frame by Frame website as an elite Frame by Frame supporter + hard cover book + a 8x12 photo by one of the photographers from Afghanistan + two tickets to the private screening in NYC + see the film first + a special thank you in the credits + t-shirt + DVD

Estimated delivery: Jan 2015
Ships anywhere in the world

$10,000 reward

⊙ 0 backers   Limited (3 left of 3)

We will curate a GALLERY EXHIBITION of Afghan photographers' work along with a

The more funds we can raise, the better we can make this film. Right now, we have our sights set on getting back to Afghanistan to truly capture this story. But if we can raise more then $40,000, we'll have a head start in the post-production costs of completing this film.

FIGURE 10.11
The budget pie chart. They also include a still from the trailer. (Courtesy of Alexandria Bombach.)

Rewards for Backers

As a backer, you'll be with us all the way through the process of making this film. You'll receive exclusive updates and have the opportunity to meet the photographers behind this incredible revolution.

We want you to know how much you're contribution means to everyone involved with Frame by Frame, so we've included some rewards that will get you the film, but also bring you the story through the photography itself.

We couldn't be more excited and honored to have the chance to tell this story, and as a backer, you're a huge part of that. You'll be the reason their stories are brought to the world. So... what are you waiting for? Join us!

Afghan photographers' work along with a film screening at the space of your choosing. Your guests will see the film, get a Directors Q&A, and be able to purchase the work of the photographers directly + become a member of the Producer's Circle + $500 level

Estimated delivery: Jan 2015
Ships anywhere in the world

Featured

Kickstarter Films at South by Southwest
Mar 9 2015

Funding period

Jul 29 2013 - Aug 28 2013 (30 days)

FIGURE 10.12
A description of the rewards. (Courtesy of Alexandria Bombach.)

a headstart on the postproduction process. Also note the higher level rewards. There are a couple of mid-level rewards of $150 to $200, but then there are several categories from $500 to $10,000. The mid-level rewards raised nearly $7,000. Very few backers supported the high-level rewards. One backed the $5,000 reward, while five supported the $1,000 reward, and ten put in for the $500 reward—which did provide an additional $11,000. Thus the mid- to high-level categories ended up raising an additional $18,000.

The mark of a successful campaign, Alexandria says, involves hard work and treating the campaign as a full-time job. Some people just launch the campaign and hope it'll take care of itself, but it requires constant attention. Failed campaigns are a hard thing for a filmmaker to accept, but they happen. With Kickstarter, there are rewards—the incentives provide a sense that a donor will receive something tangible from the campaign. Alexandria says, "When you have a film, the first obvious thing that you're going to want as a reward is to see the film." Setting the right price for that access is key. "Sometimes I'll go on people's film campaign pages, and the first price-point to see the film is set at $45—that's ridiculous. You should never have to pay that much to see a film. It's like a preorder of a film and the most that should be is $35, but even that is pretty high." *Frame by Frame*'s Kickstarter campaign allowed donors to receive a digital copy of the film for $25.

Kickstarter campaigns also fail when filmmakers don't prepare enough before-hand, Alexandria notes. "I was working on Kickstarter for at least two months before it even started and it was just Mo and me." They also got a team together to make the trailer as strong as possible. "We had people work on the sound of the trailer and the color of the trailer on a deferred payment," she explains. "If we made money through the Kickstarter campaign, they would be placed in the budget to get paid. They were taking that risk with us, but people believed in the project so that was good. I think a lot of people who don't succeed just think that Kickstarter is going to run itself."

But to commit to that kind of business work—to plan, coordinate, decide the rewards, engage in a social media campaign—can be difficult for creatives, Alexandria explains.

> But it's also the world we're in right now. This isn't Canada providing government funds for filmmakers. We have to raise this money ourselves. I'm really glad Kickstarter is there, but it's not just the money. For us it was really crazy to have 1200 people say, 'Yes I want to see this film!' And they're not just backing it, but they're also sharing the campaign with the trailer, and more people become interested in it. It was heartening because we received a lot of great PR early on. And people are waiting for the film while you are still in the early stages of production so it's terrifying.

Risks and challenges

Well, let's talk about what you're all likely thinking: "Two women are going alone to Afghanistan?!"

We are well aware this is a war zone, and there are inherent risks in being in the country at all. We've been to Kabul before and have built trusted relationships with our contacts here. Our 'fixer' (i.e. a person devoted to getting us local access) has worked with international news crews, nonprofit organizations and other visitors for many years.

All decisions — from where to grab breakfast to how long to spend shooting in a location — are made with security as a priority.

Beyond Kabul, we both have experience filming in adverse conditions around the world. We're aware that situations can turn ugly on a dime, and we're as prepared as possible for emergency situations.

Now... on the challenges to the film itself:

One rule in documentary is that nothing ever goes according to plan; these are real stories unfolding out in the real world. Nothing is scripted, and anything can happen. This can turn out to be a really beautiful and amazing thing, but also a really trying, difficult and sometimes dangerous thing. We appreciate your patience and support through our production.

Another challenge at this point is funding for post-production. We set our Kickstarter goal to cover the bare minimum of getting us back to Kabul and finishing production of Frame by Frame. It will NOT cover the post-production costs such as music licensing, sound design, color correction, and distribution.

So -- all funds beyond our goal will help greatly! They'll go toward post-production so we can craft the film in the edit room and get it out to the world.

Thank you for believing in this project and for being a part of telling this very important story.

Learn about accountability on Kickstarter

FAQ

Have a question? If the info above doesn't help, you can ask the project creator directly.

Ask a question

FIGURE 10.13
The filmmakers confront the reality of making a film and warn that supporters are funding the actual filming of the project—not the postproduction. However, since they did raise over $70,000, they were able to get additional equipment (Canon 5D Mark IIIs with some good lenses) in addition to covering some of their postproduction costs. (Courtesy of Alexandria Bombach.)

Part of the planning was also making sure they did the story right. The most successful element of the trailer, Alexandria says, was in the importance of potential backers of the film seeing Afghans talking—"that was the biggest part of the film." She explains, "This is going to be a story about Afghans. If it was just Mo and me up there—two white women saying we're going to tell their story instead of them telling their story—I think it would have hurt us a lot. The trailer for any film needs to have some sort of visual component. It's necessary." And, she adds, "When you have a really beautiful place like Afghanistan, it helps. In our editing style we really wanted to show the beauty of the country. And we were lucky to have great access to our characters."

Providing updates to backers is important. After getting the successful campaign funded in August 2013, they planned their trip and purchased gear, traveling to Afghanistan in October and returning in early December. By January 2014, Alexandria started editing and didn't finish until a year later, then they hired a musician for the score (Patrick Jonsson). They also put together a team that included a couple of executive producers, several associate producers, a story architect, and a translator. The team of experienced documentary filmmakers would provide feedback that would get them to the final stages.

In the end, the success of their project stemmed from Alexandria and Mo's filmmaking talent honed from doing production house work in a cinematic way over several years.

APPENDIX
Sample Contracts and Film Production Forms

Forms and contracts located at: http://kurtlancaster.com/contracts-and-forms

I want to thank Andrew Hutcheson of Zandrak for providing contracts as models for this book's readers for education purposes. Stillmotion provided a call sheet, which is useful for scheduling each day's shoot with the crew and talent. Modify them as needed. It is your responsibility to hire a lawyer to make sure the contracts meet your needs. The author of this book makes no legal claim or recommendations about any of these contracts. They're provided solely for educational purposes.

1. **Location Release Form**

   In most—if not in every—case, you will want permission to shoot on location. This form provides it. It also emphasizes that the location is not liable for the production—which is why the production must have liability insurance, and the insurance will go a long way in securing permission from the property owner.

2. **Production Agreement**

   The sample production agreement contract provides a strong foundation of protection, understanding, and scope of what a project could entail with a client. If you don't have a limit on the number of edits, for example, a client could keep taking advantage by asking for too many edits. But agreeing on three edits, with new charges for additional edits, protects you from a project that never ends. In either case, you will want to put this material in a contract.

3. **Independent Contractor Agreement**

   The parameters of a person's role on a job. Use this if you're hiring someone for a particular task. You can also use it as the basis for a freelance job.

4. **Performer Agreement**

   Similar to the Standard Release Form (which covers everyone appearing in your project, including extras and other nonspeaking roles), the Performer

Agreement lays out the specifics for performers you hire for your projects, such as actors. It's tailored for their duties, expectations, and what their expectations are as to schedule, meals, travel, and so forth.

5. **Standard Release Form**

   This is key for any documentary interview or any shot that captures a recognizable person in the background of a shot. Get permission from anyone you shoot, so that there are no hassles when it comes to finishing the project. If you don't have a person's permission, you may run into legal issues, especially if you're using it for film or broadcast distribution. When Zandrak produced "Still Life" in New York City, Charles Frank and Jake Oleson shot great-looking footage. Andrew Hutcheson followed in their footsteps, going up to every person they shot and getting a release form signed.

6. **Production Quote Form**

   Zandrak's quote sheet. Use when submitting an estimated budget to a client and include it in your bid.

7. **Budget Form**

   A standard film budget. Use it to show what you need to run the budget of a particular project. Some material may not be needed, but it'll cover nearly every type of role in a production.

8. **Call Sheet**

   Provided by Stillmotion, this template allows you to set your daily shoot schedule, contact information, and location for your talent and crew.

9. **Budget Expense Worksheet**

   This will allow you to calculate your monthly expenses and so determine the cost of doing business. Amend the Excel spreadsheet as needed.

Notes

Introduction

1 Smith, Jacquelyn. "Experts and Viewers Agree: Apple's '1984' Is The Best Super Bowl Ad Of All Time," *Forbes*, January 30, 2012. http://www.forbes.com/sites/jacquelyn smith/2012/01/30/experts-and-viewers-agree-apples-1984-is-the-best-super-bowl-ad-of-all-time/

2 The department was formerly Electronic Media, then Electronic Media and Film, which focused more on broadcast work and training.

3 Due to their success, in July 2015 they moved their offices to Brooklyn, New York. They now go under the name of Voyager Studios, LLC: http://voyagercreative.co.

4 The community site has since moved their articles to and became the Film + Music site: https://www.filmandmusic.com/.

5 "Make a Dog's Day," Subaru Impreza commercial 2015: https://www.youtube.com/watch?v=v6d6C45g5NA

6 "Maddie," Chevrolet commercial 2014: https://vimeo.com/87748529

7 LeGuin, Ursula K. *The Wave in the Mind* in Brainpickings.org, October 21, 2014. http://www.brainpickings.org/2014/10/21/ursula-le-guin-dogs-cats-dancers-beauty/

Chapter 1

1 There are several different ways to engage narration—I'm specifically critiquing the omniscient voice style.

2 What I sometimes refer to generically as the broadcast style.

3 Watch "The Ascent of Alex Honnold" at http://www.cbsnews.com/news/the-ascent-of-alex-honnold-27-12-2011/

4 Watch "Shattered" at https://vimeo.com/40379197

5 It's really not a fair comparison, because *60 Minutes* didn't stage Alex shot-to-shot and if cameras got too close, it may have endangered him.

6 There's really no point to compare the content of fact versus fiction or news versus staged, since they are what they are.

7 Yes, this is a stylistic choice, but if you're trying to pull an audience into the world of the story, it becomes a mistake if you want to create stories with strong emotional impact.

8 To help simulate the rhythm of the edit, I've made the longer-duration shots larger than the short ones, which are smaller and indicate a short-duration cut. All stills from Stableford, 2012.

9 Adapted from "The Psychology of the Lens: Patrick Moreau creates filmic intimacy with DSLRs at Stillmotion" by Kurt Lancaster (from http://masteringfilm.com).

10 Dise, Justin. "Vincent Laforet and the Psychological Impact of Camera Movement." http://www.bhphotovideo.com/explora/video/features/vincent-laforet-and-psychological-impact-camera-movement

11 I've gone through the course and it is a powerful tool, so I offer this description for those who want to invest in it. If you already have storytelling down, then don't worry about it.

Chapter 2

1 Members of the Canadian company earned visa rights due to their unique contribution to the arts, Amina tells me (the Emmy Awards helped), allowing them to work in the United States.

2 Stillmotion has since moved a few blocks north in order to allow more room for the growth of Story & Heart.

3 Evnas, Jannell. "Vision and Mission—What's the difference and why does it matter?" *Psychology Today*, April 24, 2010.

4 "Simon Sinek: How great leaders inspire action." TEDxPuget Sound, September 2009. http://www.ted.com/talks/simon_sinek_how_great_leaders_inspire_action?language=en#t-251603

5 See, for example, the Chevrolet commercial, "Maddie" (https://vimeo.com/87748529), produced by The Herd Films in Vancouver, Canada or Laforet Visual's "Neighborhood" commercial for Famous Footware (http://vimeopro.com/laforet/laforetvisuals/video/17355509), to name just two.

Chapter 3

None.

Chapter 4

1 And this is a good example of where an omniscient voice narration works, because it's not telling us what we see (which is what we often get), but it instead invokes a philosophical theme in an emotional way, in a poetic essay style.

Chapter 5

1 Laforet, Vincent. "How to succeed as a creative long term: know your C.O.D.B." http://blog.vincentlaforet.com/2013/08/01/how-to-succeed-as-a-creative-long-term-know-your-c-o-d-b/

Chapter 6

1 "The Art of Articulation: A Conversation with Alex Buono." *Film + Music*, July 23, 2015. https://www.filmandmusic.com/articles/the-art-of-articulation/87

2 Llopis, Glenn. "6 Brand Strategies Most CMOs Fail To Execute," *Forbes*, March 10, 2014. http://www.forbes.com/sites/glennllopis/2014/03/10/6-brand-strategies-that-most-cmos-fail-to-execute/

Chapter 7

1 Kong, David. "Working with Less," Philipbloom.net, July 31, 2013. http://philipbloom.net/blog/working-with-less-or-get-out-there-and-shoot-part-1/

2 See Apple ProRes White Paper June 2014 for 2K and 4K bit rate and storage capabilities: https://www.apple.com/final-cut-pro/docs/Apple_ProRes_White_Paper.pdf

3 Even though the H.264 files are decompressed in post to a 4:2:2 format, the original data is lost, so the image still falls apart when pushed in post.

4 Most 4K cameras that shoot 4K are compressed, so factor that into your decision. I would rather shoot 2K uncompressed raw than 4K compressed. Also, consider that you will need more computer power and hard drive space when shooting in 4K or 2K raw.

5 Zoom the lens all the way out, then reach into the back of the lens and pull out the hard plastic flange. This gives it the space needed to fit onto the Metabones adapter.

6 Blackmagic Design have released their cameras, such as the Cinema Camera, Pocket Cinema Camera, URSA Mini, to give you the option to record in a compressed form of 12-bit raw or 10-bit Apple ProRes codecs.

Chapter 8

1 Conforming a higher frame rate back to the 24fps of the timelines, will provide slow motion.

2 Moreau, Patrick. "The Making of a Scripted Short," Stillmotion, November 17, 2014 (http://stillmotionblog.com/myutopia/)

Chapter 9

1 "Directing Actors with Lenore Dekoven," FilmandMusic.com, September 21, 2014. https://www.filmandmusic.com/articles/directing-actors-with-lenore-dekoven/

Chapter 10

1 Alexandria Bombach took a video production course from the author when he taught at this college. She and several other Fort Lewis college film students have gone on to become successful filmmakers and video production house owners, which proves the point that you do not need to go to a big-name film school to be successful in the business.

References

Apple. *Apple ProRes White Paper*. June 2014. https://www.apple.com/final-cut-pro/docs/ Apple_ProRes_White_Paper.pdf

"The Art of Articulation: A Conversation with Alex Buono." FilmandMusic.com, July 23, 2015. https://www.filmandmusic.com/articles/the-art-of-articulation/87

Carmichael Lynch Agency. "Make a Dog's Day." Subaru Impreza commercial. Carmichael Lynch, 2015. https://www.youtube.com/watch?v=v6d6C45g5NA

Choi, Lloyd Lee (dir.). "Maddie" Chevrolet commercial. The Herd Films, 2014. https:// vimeo.com/87748529

Cronin, Paul. *Werner Herzog: A Guide for the Perplexed*. Faber & Faber, 2014. ✓

"Directing Actors with Lenore Dekoven." FilmandMusic.com, September 21, 2014. https://www.filmandmusic.com/articles/directing-actors-with-lenore-dekoven/

Dise, Justin. "Vincent Laforet and the Psychological Impact of Camera Movement." http://www.bhphotovideo.com/explora/video/features/vincent-laforet-and-psycho logical-impact-camera-movement

Evnas, Jannell. "Vision and Mission—What's the difference and why does it matter?" *Psychology Today*, April 24, 2010. https://www.psychologytoday.com/blog/smartwork/ 201004/vision-and-mission-whats-the-difference-and-why-does-it-matter

Kong, David. "Working with Less." Philipbloom.net, July 31, 2013. http://philipbloom. net/blog/working-with-less-or-get-out-there-and-shoot-part-1/

Laforet, Vincent. "How to succeed as a creative long term: know your C.O.D.B." Vincent Laforet blog. http://blog.vincentlaforet.com/2013/08/01/how-to-succeed-as- a-creative-long-term-know-your-c-o-d-b/

Lancaster, Kurt. "The Psychology of the Lens: Patrick Moreau creates filmic intimacy with DSLRs at Stillmotion." MasteringFilm.com, Focal Press, ND. http://mastering film.com/the-psychology-of-the-lens-patrick-moreau-creates-filmic-intimacy-with- dslrs-at-stillmotion

LeGuin, Ursula K. The Wave in the Mind. Cited in Brainpickings.org, October 21, 2014. http://www.brainpickings.org/2014/10/21/ursula-le-guin-dogs-cats-dancers-beauty

Llopis, Glenn. "6 Brand Strategies Most CMOs Fail To Execute." *Forbes*, March 10, 2014. http://www.forbes.com/sites/glennllopis/2014/03/10/6-brand-strategies-that-most-cmos-fail-to-execute/

Logan, Lara and Jeff Newton. "The Ascent of Alex Honnold." *60 Minutes*, December 27, 2011. http://www.cbsnews.com/news/the-ascent-of-alex-honnold-27-12-2011/

Moreau, Patrick. "The Making of a Scripted Short." Stillmotion, November 17, 2014. http://stillmotionblog.com/myutopia/

Ondaatje, Michael. *The Conversations: Walter Murch and the Art of Editing Film*. Knopf, 2002.

Pearlman, Karen. *Cutting Rhythms: Shaping the Film Edit*. Focal Press, 2009.

Sinek, Simon. "Simon Sinek: How great leaders inspire action." TEDxPuget Sound, September 2009. http://www.ted.com/talks/simon_sinek_how_great_leaders_inspire_action?language=en#t-251603

Smith, Jacquelyn. "Experts and Viewers Agree: Apple's '1984' Is The Best Super Bowl Ad Of All Time." *Forbes*, January 30, 2012. http://www.forbes.com/sites/jacquelynsmith/2012/01/30/experts-and-viewers-agree-apples-1984-is-the-best-super-bowl-ad-of-all-time/

Stableford, Tyler. "Shattered." Vimeo.com, 2012. https://vimeo.com/40379197

Index

Page numbers in *italic* refer to figures. Page numbers in **bold** refer to tables.